International Arbitration

A Practical Guide, Second Edition

Stuart Dutson, Andy Moody and **Neil Newing**

Consulting editors
Stuart Dutson (Simmons & Simmons LLP), Andy Moody (Baker McKenzie),
Neil Newing (Signature Litigation LLP)

Managing director
Sian O'Neill

International Arbitration: A Practical Guide, Second Edition
is published by

Globe Law and Business Ltd
3 Mylor Close
Horsell
Woking
Surrey GU21 4DD
United Kingdom
Tel: +44 20 3745 4770
www.globelawandbusiness.com

Printed and bound by CPI Group (UK) Ltd, Croydon CR0 4YY

International Arbitration: A Practical Guide, Second Edition

ISBN 9781787421608
EPUB ISBN 9781787421615
Adobe PDF ISBN 9781787421622
Mobi ISBN 9781787421639

Table of contents

Preface 5

1. What is international arbitration? 7
1. The difference between arbitration and other methods of dispute resolution 8
2. Why use international arbitration? 15
3. Types of international arbitration 20
4. Diversity in international arbitration 23

2. The legal framework 25
1. The New York Convention 25
2. National arbitration laws 27
3. Major institutional arbitration rules 30
4. Internationally accepted rules and guidelines 40

3. The legal effect of agreeing to arbitrate 45
1. The arbitration agreement 45
2. The legal effect of agreeing to arbitration 48
3. Jurisdiction and an arbitrator's powers 49
4. Arbitrability 53

4. Drafting arbitration clauses 55
1. Essential matters to include in an arbitration clause 55
2. Optional matters to include in an arbitration clause 64
3. Pathological arbitration agreements 72
4. Model arbitration clauses 73
5. Expedited arbitration 73

5. Pre-commencement of arbitral proceedings 83
1. Introduction 83
2. When to commence arbitration 83
3. Gathering evidence 91
4. Other pre-commencement steps 99

6. Commencing an arbitration 111
1. Whether to be claimant or respondent 111
2. How to start an arbitration proceeding 112
3. Jurisdictional challenges 119
4. Urgent interlocutory relief: emergency measures and emergency arbitrators 124

7. Selecting the tribunal or arbitrator 131
1. Criteria required from arbitrators 131
2. How to choose an arbitrator 135
3. Number of arbitrators 137
4. Methods of selection 138
5. Frustration, delay and default 141
6. Confirmation of appointment and constitution of the tribunal 141

8. Dealing with the tribunal 143
1. Contacting the tribunal 143
2. Administrative secretaries 145
3. Keeping the tribunal informed 145
4. Unresponsive tribunals 147
5. Suspicions of bribery, corruption or money laundering 147

9. Establishing procedure 151
1. Establishing the procedural timetable and conduct of the arbitration 151
2. ICC Terms of Reference 152
3. Agreeing the procedural timetable 159
4. Amendments to the procedural timetable 172

10. Interlocutory applications and provisional measures 179
1. Interim, conservatory or provisional measures 179
2. Court or tribunal? 180
3. Types of application 181
4. Making the application 183
5. Default and summary procedures 188

11. Developing the case 189
1. Written submissions 189
2. Evidence 200

12. The hearing 217
1. Practical arrangements for the hearing 217
2. Procedure at the hearing 221
3. Closing oral submissions versus written post-hearing submissions 227

13. Costs 237
1. Overview 237
2. Costs of arbitration 238
3. Applications for costs 240

14. After the hearing 251
1. The award 251
2. Enforcing the award 253
3. Challenging enforcement at the place where it is sought 257
4. Challenging the award at the seat of arbitration 262
5. Correcting an award 268

15. Table comparing key provisions of arbitration rules 271

About the authors 287

Index 289

Preface

Ultimately, international arbitration is merely a form of dispute resolution. The substantive dispute remains to be resolved pursuant to the *lex causae*. However, as is detailed in this book, the determination of the *lex causae*, its application and the impact of laws other than the *lex causae* can be addressed differently within international arbitration as compared to the determination of a dispute in a national court. Similarly, the procedures and practices applied within international arbitration have, quite rightly, resulted in the addressing of arbitration law, and international arbitration law in particular, as a separate discipline within law. The practice and procedure of international arbitration are not prescribed in the way that court rules and their subsequent interpretation and application by the courts are carefully delineated. For example, while the arbitral rules of most leading institutions will run only to a few pages, the court rules of the High Court in England and Wales are contained in two 10 centimetre thick volumes known as 'The White Book'. The fact that these practices and procedures of international arbitration are, when compared to court proceedings, in many respects still at large and subject to the determination of the parties and the tribunal means that the practice of international arbitration brings with it a much greater role (and responsibility) for arbitration counsel, for their clients and for the arbitral tribunal.

This book, therefore, in addition to dealing with the underlying arbitration law and rules, examines the opportunities and challenges that arbitration counsel face as a result of the nature of arbitration law, practice and procedure. As is discussed in detail, at many junctures in an arbitration – from when counsel first discuss a dispute with their clients, right up to the execution of an award – opportunities arise for sophisticated international arbitration counsel to have a huge impact and influence on their client's position and the position of the other side. This second edition provides an update to take into account the rule changes that have been adopted by arbitral institutions in the six years since the first edition was published, and to include up-to-date guidance on topical issues such as: third-party funding in international arbitration; the increase in the number of multi-party arbitrations; procedural trends including the adoption of expedited timetables and guidance around the use of tribunal secretaries; and issues of ethics applicable to counsel and tribunals in cross-border disputes. All content is correct as at September 2018.

We would like to take this opportunity to thank most sincerely all of our colleagues for their assistance in putting the second edition of this book together, in particular, David Bridge, Basil Woodd-Walker, Alexander Sussman, Ryan Cable, Leo Meredith, Lucy Alexander, Judith Mulholland and Katherine Harper. We are also most grateful for the invaluable secretarial support provided by Claire Clark and Stefanie Krause.

1. What is international arbitration?

International arbitration is a method of dispute resolution that parties may select as an alternative to the courts. They may choose this option once the dispute has arisen, but more commonly, they will have made that choice in an agreement or arrangement prior to the dispute arising, often in the form of a dispute resolution clause in a contract.

Arbitration is therefore the product of an agreement between the parties. In accordance with their agreement, the parties appoint an arbitrator or set of arbitrators (an arbitral tribunal) to decide the dispute. The final decision of an arbitrator or arbitral tribunal is known as an award. This is final and binding on the parties.

International arbitration is increasingly the preferred method for resolving international disputes. As international trade and commerce increase, so too does the need to resort to international arbitration to enforce agreements and uphold rights internationally.[1] Disputes related to international trade, finance, infrastructure and projects, and oil and gas are all increasingly resolved in this way. This positive correlation between increasing international business and international arbitration is no coincidence. It comes as a result primarily of the combination of one major multilateral international development with one very human concern: the creation of, and the worldwide subscription to, the Convention on the Recognition and Enforcement of Foreign Arbitral Awards 1958 (the 'New York Convention'), and a reluctance on the part of many parties to litigate their disputes in the courts of less developed countries.

The international enforceability of arbitral awards is a key factor in the increasing popularity of arbitration as a method of commercial dispute resolution, at least at the international level. The New York Convention, which commits party states to recognising and enforcing arbitral awards made in other party states throughout the world, has been signed by over 140 countries. The New York Convention effectively provides for the worldwide enforcement of

1 For example, in the past few years the number of new arbitrations being referred to the International Chamber of Commerce (ICC) each year has averaged around 800 (with a bumper year of 966 new cases in 2016), compared to only around 300 in 1992.

arbitral awards. It thereby builds the foundation for international arbitration as a universally recognised method for dispute resolution, particularly given the limited grounds under the Convention that can be invoked to resist recognition and enforcement. Arbitration would not enjoy the increased use that it does today without it.

In contrast, the lack in most of the world's jurisdictions of an equivalent multilateral international regime for enforcing a foreign court judgment means that this is still problematic. Although foreign court judgments may be recognised and enforced under regional regimes[2] and between states that have entered into reciprocal enforcement treaties, the coverage of regional or mutual regimes is very small in comparison to that of the New York Convention.

At the national level, arbitrations and awards are given legal efficacy by national legislation which governs arbitrations held within that state. Each state has legislation governing the interaction of arbitrations and awards with the courts. This legislation varies between states, although it is increasingly based upon a model or template law – the United Nations Commission on International Trade Law (UNCITRAL) Model Law (the 'Model Law').

In general, states have increasingly treated arbitration more favourably, and have become less likely (or willing) to interfere with awards. In theory, an award made anywhere in the world should be enforceable anywhere else, without a court looking into the decision of the arbitrator(s). There are, naturally, qualifications to this. Yet the independence of awards from court scrutiny is another important factor in the rising number of parties agreeing to submit their disputes to arbitration.

International arbitration can therefore be understood, in general, as an agreement:

- between parties to submit a dispute to an arbitrator (or arbitrators) whose decision is final and binding;
- that is not subject to court review; and
- that is enforceable throughout the world.

1. The difference between arbitration and other methods of dispute resolution

Arbitration is in some senses a unique form of dispute resolution. This book looks at each stage in the process of a typical international arbitration, but before doing so, it is useful to examine how arbitration differs from other common forms of dispute resolution.

There are essentially two forms of dispute resolution: 'soft' dispute resolution, which involves parties resolving disputes themselves; and 'hard'

2 Such as the Brussels Regulation and Lugano Convention within the EU and European Free Trade Area (EFTA).

dispute resolution, which involves some external person or body imposing a decision on the disputing parties. Arbitration is a form of hard dispute resolution, and is closer to litigation (at least in the form in which it is practised in the commercial world) than any other form of dispute resolution.

1.1 'Soft' dispute resolution

(a) Negotiation

'Negotiation' refers to the simple method of the parties themselves trying to find a resolution to their dispute. It can be conducted directly between the parties and/or their counsel on a less formal basis, either through an exchange of correspondence or in a face-to-face meeting. Arbitration differs from negotiation in several ways:

- Arbitration is an external process. Parties present their arguments to the arbitrator(s), who then makes a decision. Although the parties may negotiate between themselves about the arbitration procedure, and an arbitrator (like a judge) may encourage the parties to negotiate certain topics, in arbitration, decisions on the substance of the dispute are made external to the disputing parties.
- Arbitration is a binding process which the parties choose instead of going to court (it is not an interim stage before court). One party cannot, if it decides that an arbitration is proceeding poorly, decide to bring court proceedings instead (at least, not if it is party to a valid arbitration agreement, and it does not want to breach that agreement). The result of the arbitration is also binding.
- Arbitration is an enforceable process. Disputing parties that negotiate a compromise can reach a settlement agreement, which will be contractually binding on those parties.[3] An award, on the other hand, is an enforceable decision in and of itself – although, like a court judgment, further steps may be required to enforce that decision.

Of course, arbitration, like litigation, does not exclude negotiation. Parties will invariably make at least some attempt to negotiate a dispute prior to commencing proceedings in arbitration. Once an arbitration has commenced, the disputing parties are still able (and often encouraged) to continue negotiating outside the arbitration, including by making 'without prejudice' offers to settle the dispute. These cannot be disclosed within the arbitration. Arbitration is therefore not so much an alternative to negotiation as a more formal method of dispute resolution that is available in addition to it.

3 The parties may attempt to have that settlement agreement entered as a consent judgment or award of the court or arbitral tribunal.

(b) Mediation

Mediation is a flexible, voluntary and confidential process in which a neutral third-party mediator seeks to facilitate an agreement between the parties. However, unlike a tribunal, the mediator does not rule on the merits of the dispute. The parties therefore retain control of the decision to settle and on what terms. Once the parties have resolved to mediate and agreed upon the identity of a mediator, they will enter into a mediation agreement which will deal with, among other things, the procedure for the mediation, the mediator's fees, the documents to be produced by each party and confidentiality/privilege in those documents. This agreement will usually be provided in standard form by an alternative dispute resolution organisation, such as the Centre for Effective Dispute Resolution (CEDR), which will administer the process and provide a pool of potential mediators. However, for an *ad hoc* mediation, this may be negotiated separately.

Usually, the parties prepare and exchange concise case summaries supported by key documents in advance of the mediation. This is so as to identify the main issues and provide the mediator with a focus. The parties will agree that documents disclosed in the mediation cannot be produced in subsequent court/arbitration proceedings. However, this may not prevent their examination in certain circumstances. For instance, if a dispute arises as to whether a settlement was agreed during the course of the mediation. In terms of costs, a common approach is for the parties to agree to split the mediator's fees and any expenses related to the mediation itself, and to bear their own legal expenses. However, mediation agreements often provide for such costs to be recoverable as costs in the case should the mediation fail. The parties then resort to litigation or arbitration, where the court or arbitral tribunal has the power to assess or make orders as to costs.

While mediation also involves the appointment of a third-party mediator, the key difference between it and arbitration is that the latter involves a legally binding decision by the arbitrator, whereas a mediator is appointed only to assist the parties in negotiating an outcome between themselves. A mediator may be very forceful in doing so; might suggest the sort of offers which a party might consider making; and might even give his or her view as to the merits of a disputing party's case, the need for that party to reconsider urgently its view on the merits of the case and accordingly perhaps consider a corresponding increase in its offer of settlement. Nevertheless, any agreement struck in a mediation derives from the consent of the parties and is not imposed on them by the mediator. For this reason, parties in a mediation can agree any remedy that they wish.

In an arbitration, on the other hand, the decision of an arbitrator is not an agreement. The parties have agreed that the arbitrator will make a decision that will bind them. The decisions contained within the award will be confined to those matters which the parties have agreed are subject to arbitration. However, the decision itself is made externally – and may or may not be one with which both, either or indeed any of the parties are happy.

Furthermore, an arbitration, unlike a mediation, cannot fail to reach an outcome. Parties to an arbitration cannot walk away. Unless the parties reach a settlement, once an arbitration is commenced it will continue through to a decision by the arbitrator(s), which will bind the parties in their dispute, whether they agree with it or not.

(c) Other methods of 'soft' dispute resolution

There are, of course, a range of other dispute resolution services that may assist parties in resolving their dispute: conciliation, appraisal, expert evaluation and so on. The key element in these forms of 'soft' dispute resolution is that any recommendation or finding is not binding upon the parties. In that sense, any appraisal which is adopted by the parties has force not because of the appraisal, but because of the parties' agreement to adopt it.

1.2 'Hard' dispute resolution

Unlike 'soft' dispute resolution, 'hard' dispute resolution involves imposing a decision on the parties. Arbitration, like litigation, is an example of 'hard' dispute resolution.

(a) Expert determination

Expert determination is the referral of a dispute to a third-party agent who is an expert in a particular area. This may happen because the parties wish for an expert to use his or her own experience and expertise to determine the dispute, although it should be noted that he or she cannot use such expertise to provide new evidence for a party. An expert determination may or may not be final and binding: it depends upon the nature of the referral to the expert by the parties.

An expert decision is, in practical terms, a rewriting of the contract. The parties agree that they will abide by the decision of the expert in the same way as if it were a new term of the contract. This means that an expert decision is not self-executing in the same way as a court judgment or an arbitrator's award. A court judgment or an arbitration award can be self-executed (albeit in the case of an arbitration award with a largely administrative process from a court). In contrast, an expert determination, if not complied with, must be enforced through bringing court or arbitration proceedings. There is no international enforcement regime like the New York Convention for expert determination.

Expert determinations are common in cases where there are very specific disputes, such as accounting disputes, completion accounts or valuations in mergers and acquisitions (M&A) contracts, and construction aspects in specific parts of construction matters. They are also common in cases where the decision to be reached is really one that is commercial rather than legal – for example, a deadlock-breaking mechanism in a joint venture agreement.

Agreements to refer to expert determination in international contracts increasingly provide that they are to be enforced by way of arbitration – that is, the expert determination agreement is itself subject to an arbitration agreement. Whether in court proceedings or as part of an arbitration award, any expert determination will be enforced essentially in the manner of a summary judgment, unless the party refusing to comply is attempting to challenge an expert's determination.

(b) *The difference between litigation and arbitration*

Arbitral proceedings are, on their face, different from formal court proceedings. The styles of advocacy and the sorts of argument that are considered 'likely' to prove persuasive can be very different. As discussed in the preface to this book, the procedures of court litigation are heavily circumscribed, whereas arbitral procedures are at large and thereby demand the greater involvement of counsel and tribunals. The advantages and disadvantages of arbitration against litigation are discussed below. However, despite their differences, both arbitration and litigation are, at their core, dispute resolution processes in which a decision maker analyses the facts and law presented to him or her, and issues a binding decision.

Conceptually, however, there are three important differences between arbitration and litigation:

- The decision of an arbitrator or arbitral tribunal on the substantive dispute is final. There is no court of appeal that will consider an award. As discussed in Chapter 14, there are certain limited ways to challenge an award before the courts, and a party that is successful in an arbitration may find it necessary to re-argue certain matters about the award or the arbitration agreement if it hopes to enforce that award in another state. However, none of those procedures amounts to an appeal on the law, in the sense of an appeal that is available as of right from a first instance court proceeding.
- The basis for an arbitrator's jurisdiction is the agreement of the parties. Although an arbitration will have a particular place or 'seat' which provides for certain elements of the arbitration to be governed by the law of the seat. For example, a Paris-seat international arbitration will be governed in certain aspects by French international arbitration law (as laid down in Book IV, Title II, Articles 1504 to 1527 of the French Code of Civil Procedure). The fundamental basis for the arbitral tribunal's jurisdiction is not the law of the seat (eg, France), but the arbitration agreement. The basis for a judge's jurisdiction, on the other hand, is the inherent power of the court and, ultimately, the coercive power of the

state. Once a tribunal has been constituted, the most significant consequence of this is that arbitrators have jurisdiction only over the parties before the tribunal. They have no inherent power to summon witnesses or compel third parties to join the dispute.

- The procedure is significantly more flexible. An arbitral tribunal will not be bound by strict rules of evidence or disclosure, or the application of court litigation civil procedure rules. Although many arbitral institutions have produced rules and procedural guidance for parties, this guidance is very different (and significantly shorter) from the rules which apply to court proceedings. The London Court of International Arbitration (LCIA) Arbitration Rules 2014, for example, have only 32 simple articles, whereas the Civil Procedure Rules 1998 (The White Book) governing English court procedures are comprised of 89 parts, of which the longest itself contains about 50 rules. Court proceedings in most jurisdictions have, of course, evolved and modernised. Most significant commercial jurisdictions have adopted commercial lists, use case management conferences to allow a judge to tailor the applicable procedural rules to fit the circumstances of a case and no longer impose evidential rules, especially in commercial proceedings, as strictly as they once did. However, the most responsive commercial court still does not offer the flexibility of arbitration.

Depending on how it affects you and your client's case, this flexibility may be an advantage or a disadvantage. For instance, it can accommodate very complex applications such as jurisdiction applications where, essentially, the finding in relation to jurisdiction will determine disputes about whether an arbitration agreement does or does not apply, and in turn, whether the governing law is the law of country A or country B. In many cases this will be the single most important decision that the tribunal has to make and will directly affect the case's substantive outcome. Arbitrators are able to take account of this and provide a procedure that accommodates it. However, counsel will always try to do their best for their client, and there will no doubt be cases where a dilatory or recalcitrant party may use the flexibility that arbitration provides in order to advance its cause, for example, by challenging the arbitrator(s), and ultimately raising the spectre of a challenge based on procedural impropriety. Such a delay may give a strategic advantage to one party and arbitration, with its greater flexibility, could be more malleable in this sense.

Arbitration has undoubtedly become more procedurally complicated. More can be done, and is done, within arbitrations and in related court proceedings. Those present at the British Institute of International and Comparative Law's 11th Annual Arbitration Review in 2008 will recall Lord Mustill lamenting whatever had happened to arbitration simply being about two parties having their dispute determined efficiently and effectively by someone they trusted. Perhaps in an effort to address concerns such as these (as well as issues around the time and costs of arbitration more generally) a number of arbitral institutions have addressed summary procedures in their rules[4] and the Financial Sector Branch of the London Arbitration Club developed the Financial Services Expedited Arbitration Procedure, which provides for detailed provisions to be added to institutions' standard clause for the swift resolution of disputes in that sector.[5]

(c) *The differences between litigation and arbitration – particular international dimensions*

There are two important international distinctions between arbitration and litigation. The first relates to jurisdiction. The second relates to enforcement.

As discussed above, the fundamental basis for an arbitrator's jurisdiction, and for the binding nature of an eventual award, is the agreement of the parties. Accordingly, a contract between an English company and a Japanese company about an investment in India might contain an arbitration agreement providing for a Singapore-seat arbitration. Such an agreement is not unusual, and provides the underlying basis for a Singapore-seat arbitral tribunal – whose members may themselves be from yet further countries – to exercise jurisdiction over the dispute.

A court, on the other hand, will be governed by legislation and supplementary rules that indicate the circumstances in which it is able to exercise jurisdiction over foreign nationals. It is, of course, true that a Singapore court might also be willing to exercise jurisdiction if the hypothetical contract above contained an agreement to submit to the jurisdiction of the courts of Singapore, rather than an agreement to arbitrate. However, that is because the parties have, through their agreement, agreed to bring themselves within the jurisdiction of that court. The principle – that a court requires a connection with the dispute to exercise jurisdiction over it – remains the same.

Second, an arbitration award is international in relation to its enforcement. The enforcement in one state of an award made in another is governed by several international treaties between states, of which the most important is the New York Convention. In essence, the New York Convention provides that an award will be enforced in a party state, subject to certain limited, and in theory uniform, exceptions.

In contrast, a court judgment – at least outside specific regimes such as the Brussels Regulation within the EU – is a foreign court judgment. The steps to

4 See Chapter 10.
5 See further details at: www.elexica.com/financial-services-expedited-arbitration-procedure.

enforce such a judgment may vary and, because such a judgment is not the product of the parties' agreement, may involve different considerations for enforcement. As a general proposition it is significantly more complicated and, as is discussed below, this is a major reason why parties in an international transaction may elect to use international arbitration.

2. Why use international arbitration?

There are a number of reasons why parties to a commercial agreement may choose international arbitration instead of litigation before a national court. The flexibility of arbitration and the enhanced international enforceability of arbitral awards are key among these. This section explains the major pros and cons of international arbitration that the parties to a dispute should consider when deciding whether it is appropriate to refer it to arbitration.

2.1 Advantages

(a) International enforceability

Beyond the Brussels Regulation and Lugano Convention, there are relatively few multilateral conventions for the enforcement of court judgments. It is notable that the Hague Convention on Civil Procedure 1954, which was a multilateral attempt to establish an international regime for the enforcement of court judgments, has failed to bring this about. As a result, the enforceability of a foreign court judgment largely depends on a reciprocal enforcement treaty between the two countries. Depending on the jurisdiction, such an enforcement may be subject to a costly and time-consuming procedure. If the enforcement of a court judgment is challenged, this may even lead to the entire case being reheard in the courts of the jurisdiction where enforcement is being sought.

By contrast, as discussed above, the New York Convention effectively established a universal regime for recognising and enforcing arbitral awards throughout the world. If clients want to obtain an ultimately enforceable decision and remedy for their disputes, then in many cases international arbitration may be the only option available.

The recognition and enforcement of the arbitral award under the New York Convention is subject to only limited exceptions set out in the New York Convention itself. Some states that are party to the New York Convention have been known to interpret these limited grounds rather broadly. However, this tends to be the exception, rather than the rule.

(b) Party autonomy and procedural flexibility

A significant advantage of arbitration is that the procedure can be tailored to the particular dispute. The established principle of procedural autonomy in international arbitration is distinct from the formalities of national court proceedings. For example, specialised procedures can be adopted to deal with technically complex disputes that involve much expert evidence. In simpler cases, or if time is of the essence, the parties may also avoid the time and expense of a disclosure phase or other trial procedures, and may even adopt a documents-only arbitration with no oral hearing.

(c) *Neutrality of forum*

International transactions typically involve parties from more than one country. Many parties have greater confidence in a dispute resolution process if it avoids referring disputes to the 'home' courts of one of the contracting parties. Arbitration can provide a neutral forum in terms of the composition of the tribunal, the seat of arbitration and the location of the oral hearing. In addition, arbitration can be used in cases where it is desirable to avoid local courts, which may be inefficient, inadequately developed or otherwise inappropriate to the dispute. Furthermore, if one of the parties to the dispute is a state or state entity, it may object to submitting to the jurisdiction of any foreign court, again making arbitration a more suitable and neutral forum.

(d) *Expertise of tribunal members*

In local courts, judges are often selected from a large list and assigned to a particular dispute. Parties usually have no say in who will be assigned to their case. The judge assigned may not have sufficient training or experience in resolving disputes arising out of international transactions; for example, if he or she is a recently appointed lawyer whose career to date has focused on domestic transactions or a niche area of law. The judge's ability to appreciate fully the business context of the parties' transaction and disputes will inevitably affect the efficiency and quality of decisions.

Arbitration offers parties the flexibility to choose who they want to determine their dispute and how such individuals are to be appointed. It gives them the ability to choose an arbitrator who is most appropriate to the nature of the dispute: for example, quantity surveyors, project managers, an IT expert or a lawyer with a number of years' experience or expertise in a particular area. The opportunity for parties to select arbitrators with different skills and experience is normally considered one of the most substantial benefits of the arbitral process. This, combined with the limited ability to challenge an arbitral award, makes selecting the right arbitrator vitally important.

Cross-reference For more information on arbitrator selection, see Chapter 7.

(e) *Finality of decision*

As mentioned above, there are very limited grounds on which arbitrators' awards can be appealed to the courts. There is generally no appeal on the merits of the case, and grounds for appeal on points of procedure are more limited than those for court proceedings. Therefore, a party's ability to challenge or appeal a decision is more limited in arbitration than in court proceedings. Whether parties view this feature of arbitration as an advantage or disadvantage depends on whether they win or lose.

The general lack of appellate review for arbitral awards can reduce cost and delay. Business users often prefer the finality and efficiency of arbitral procedures, although forgoing appellate rights may mean that wrong arbitral decisions cannot be corrected.

(f) *Privacy and confidentiality*

Litigation in national courts is a public affair. Judgments are publicly available, and non-parties (including the press) are generally able to attend hearings and obtain copies of documents filed at court. The opposite is the case for international commercial arbitration. Arbitrations tend to be private and confidential: the award is private, the hearings are not open to the public and the evidence is not available to anyone outside the arbitration. Indeed, it is not uncommon for no one outside the dispute to know there has been an arbitration at all.

In some jurisdictions (eg, England and Wales, Singapore and Hong Kong) a duty of confidentiality is implied into international arbitration agreements as a matter of law. Some institutional rules (eg, LCIA, the Singapore International Arbitration Centre (SIAC) and Swiss Rules) also provide for confidentiality. This means that neither documents produced or disclosed during an arbitration (including statements of case, witness statements and expert reports) nor the award itself can subsequently be made public. This can be important if there is an ongoing commercial relationship or if the subject matter is such that at least one of the parties would prefer for any dispute in relation to it to remain confidential.

Confidentiality can be important, in relation not only to a dispute, but also to any underlying deal. Parties may wish to keep the fact of any dispute between them confidential; but often, more importantly, they also may want to keep details of the underlying deal confidential (eg, the price an asset was sold at or what the asset was). In these circumstances it is important to consider choosing arbitration because any documents can be kept confidential. This contrasts with the public and searchable nature of the records in court cases, which may make these important details public.

TIP If confidentiality is of a particular concern (eg, in an intellectual property (IP) context), the parties can include a confidentiality provision in the arbitration agreement from the outset in order to ensure confidentiality of the entire arbitral proceedings.

> **Cross-reference** For more information on drafting arbitration agreements, see Chapter 4.

(g) ***Cost and speed***

Both international arbitration and litigation can involve significant expense and delay. Contrary to popular perception, international arbitration is not always quicker and cheaper (unless it is deliberately designed to be so, in which case its flexibility offers a major advantage over court litigation). Parties to an arbitration may even incur greater expenses than litigants, as arbitration involves the additional costs of the parties paying for the arbitrators and arbitral institution. Parties may also need to pay logistical expenses, including costs of accommodation for the hearings; the use of courtrooms in litigation is normally free of charge. In addition, international commercial arbitration is not always speedy. Complex disputes may take between 18 and 36 months to reach a final award.

The flexibility of arbitration enables parties to construct a process which is less costly and takes less time than court litigation. Parties that want a quick and cheap arbitration can take steps to achieve this, while parties that are less concerned with time and expense, and more concerned with the quality of proceedings can provide for more extensive proceedings. Parties can agree, at the outset or after disputes have arisen, to limit or eliminate time-consuming and costly processes such as disclosure and cross-examination. The lack of appellate review may also keep delays and costs down in the long run, in comparison with litigation.

> **TIP** Arbitration may be appropriate where the nature of the case means that a more efficient timetable can be put together or where the alternative is litigation in a national court which is known to be slow and less efficient.

2.2 Disadvantages

(a) ***Limited powers of arbitrators***

Generally, powers accorded to arbitrators are limited, compared with those conferred upon judges in a court of law. For instance, an arbitral tribunal has no power to summon witnesses under criminal penalty. Also, unlike a court, an arbitral tribunal generally has no power to join third parties to an arbitration or to consolidate related disputes, even if this is desirable in the interests of justice, unless all of the parties (and potential parties) agree. This is because of the consent-based nature of arbitration.

(b) *Multi-party arbitration can be unwieldy*

Complex commercial transactions may often involve extensive subcontracting, particularly in the construction sector. Parties to the various contracts may want all disputes in connection with the transaction to be resolved, as far as practically possible, under one arbitration. Therefore, it may be necessary to consider including 'umbrella' arbitration agreements or bespoke consolidation clauses in the transaction documents. These can provide for related parties to be joined and related arbitrations to be consolidated.

Most of the main arbitral institutions' rules now allow for the joinder of related parties and the consolidation of related arbitrations on the basis of the agreements between all of the parties. To give one example, specific provisions on joinder and consolidation were a significant part of the International Chamber of Commerce's (ICC) reform of its procedural rules (culminating in its 2012 Rules on Arbitration).

However, many arbitral rules, such as the UNCITRAL Rules, still do not provide detailed and sophisticated mechanisms for issues connected with related arbitrations, such as the timing of joinder. In these cases, one party to the arbitration cannot join a further party unless the rules permit joinder or the other party agrees to it. Even if the other party does consent, there may still be delays if the parties cannot agree on the joint appointment of an arbitrator, the timing of joinder or pleadings.

(c) *Lack of expedited default or summary procedures*

Historically, parties could not seek expedited relief in arbitration because of the need to constitute a tribunal from which to seek relief. Most arbitral institutions have recognised this and introduced expedited procedures which provide for the appointment of an emergency arbitrator within a few days to deal with requests for urgent relief.[6]

Likewise, until recently, arbitral tribunals did not have the power (unless the parties expressly confer it) to order default awards in the absence of a defence – the claimant is normally still required to prove its case in full. The landscape is changing and rules from certain arbitral institutions now expressly provide for summary procedures to dismiss unmeritorious claims or defences.[7] However, even if they are granted summary powers to determine a matter, arbitrators are often hesitant to exercise these, because the principle of due process requires

---

6 The ICC Rules 2017, the Stockholm Chamber of Commerce (SCC) Expedited Arbitration Rules 2017, the International Centre for Dispute Resolution (ICDR) Rules 2014, the Hong Kong International Arbitration Centre (HKIAC) Administered Arbitration Rules 2013 and the SIAC Rules 2016 specifically provide for an expedited procedure. The LCIA Rules 2014 provide for the emergency formation of a tribunal in cases of "exceptional urgency". See Chapter 10 for further detail.

7 The SCC Arbitration Rules 2017, the International Centre for Settlement of Investment Disputes (ICSID) Arbitration Rules and the SIAC Rules 2016 specifically provide for a summary procedure. See Chapter 10 for further detail.

that both parties have an equal opportunity to present their case. It is thought that an arbitral award rendered by default or summarily might be open to challenge in enforcement proceedings including under the New York Convention, which allows states to refuse recognition and enforcement of an award if one party was not given the opportunity to present its case.

(d) No system of precedent

There is no system of precedent in international arbitration, as an arbitral award will, in theory, be binding only on the parties to the arbitration (and, as mentioned above, it tends to remain confidential between the parties). A precedent binding on third parties, such as on the interpretation of a standard form contract, can be achieved only through court litigation.

(e) Cannot be stopped once started

Again, agreement to arbitrate is a mutual contract between the parties. Terminating an arbitration therefore needs the agreement of all parties. By contrast, claimants are normally free to drop a claim in court litigation, provided that the related costs of the other parties are paid.

3. Types of international arbitration

A fundamental choice that parties must make in an arbitration agreement is whether to refer their dispute to an arbitration institution or to choose an *ad hoc* arbitration. An *ad hoc* arbitration is one in which the arbitral process is established independently of all arbitral institutions and without the benefit of their administration, supervision and institutional rules. An *ad hoc* arbitration is conducted pursuant to rules agreed by the parties (although in practice they will often agree to adopt published rules, such as the UNCITRAL Rules, or the rules of an institution). An institutional arbitration is one that is administered and supervised by an arbitral institution in accordance with its own institutional rules of arbitration.

Arbitral institutions do not themselves arbitrate the merits of the parties' disputes. Institutional rules normally contain provisions that set out a basic procedural framework and timetable for the arbitral proceedings, authorise the arbitral institution to select arbitrators, resolve challenges to arbitrators, designate the place of arbitration, fix or influence the fees payable to the arbitrators, and (sometimes) review the arbitrators' award to reduce the risk of unenforceability on formal grounds. There are a number of different arbitration institutions across the world, ranging from general commercial arbitration organisations such as the ICC, the LCIA or the American Arbitration Association (AAA) to more specialist arbitration institutions, such as the London Maritime Arbitration Association (LMAA) or the Grain and Feed Trade Association (GAFTA). However, the latter do not generally serve as full-function institutions, and may offer parties only limited administrative services (apart from providing their rules or terms of arbitration).

In the past few years, there has been a proliferation of regional arbitration institutions, including, for example, the Lagos Chambers of Commerce International Arbitration Centre (LACIAC), the Mumbai Centre for International Arbitration (MCIA), the Saudi Centre for Commercial Arbitration (SCCA) and the British Virgin Islands (BVI) International Arbitration Centre. This reflects the increasing globalisation of international arbitration, even if the leading internatinoal institutions remain dominant for the time being.

TIP Although *ad hoc* arbitrations do not necessarily involve an institution or a set of published rules, many institutions are willing either to act as an appointing authority (in order to prevent or resolve any disagreement on the appointment of arbitrators) or even fully to administer *ad hoc* arbitrations.

Cross-reference For more detail on choosing between *ad hoc* and institutional arbitration, see Chapter 4.

3.1 Institutional arbitrations

(a) *Detailed procedural rules available*

Having been tested in practice, institutional rules effectively take care of the fundamentals, and ensure a reliable and expeditious arbitral process. This helps to minimise uncertainty, avoid unnecessary delays and reduce the risks of procedural breakdowns and other technical defects in the arbitration proceedings and awards. Well-drafted procedural rules will also help to avoid any uncertainties arising from having to resort to national courts and non-mandatory arbitration laws for guidance. Relying on national courts and applicable arbitration procedural laws to resolve every procedural issue that the parties may encounter will be very costly and time consuming. Furthermore, adopting the rules of an institution can save negotiation time which parties would otherwise need to spend on agreeing the procedural rules of arbitration.

(b) *Panel of arbitrators and professional administration staff*

Another advantage of arbitration institutions is that they provide ready access to qualified arbitrators and experienced professional staff. Arbitral institutions retain a list of qualified arbitrators who are familiar with the rules and have a certain level of experience. Protecting the reputation of the institutions provides a great incentive to ensure that they appoint competent arbitrators who enter good awards. Specialised staff can provide a better administrative service than the national courts, which have little specific arbitration experience and few resources. It is generally easier to obtain timely support from an arbitral institution in difficult situations than from national courts, to which parties in an *ad hoc* arbitration will have to resort from time to time. In *ad hoc* arbitrations, administrative tasks may often be assigned to a member of the arbitrator's own staff or to the parties themselves. The administration carried out by the dedicated staff at leading institutions is therefore generally perceived to be more efficient and expedient.

(c) Greater likelihood of award enforcement

An arbitral institution may lend its prestige to awards that a tribunal has rendered, and this may enhance the likelihood of judicial enforcement. Some institutions, such as the ICC, may review an arbitral tribunal's award before it is formally issued. This internal review process provides a further level of assurance as to the credibility of such awards.

(d) Dealing with sensitive matters

An institution may be able to bridge the culture divide between parties that come from different jurisdictions and cultures. Institutions can also provide key administrative support mechanisms, such as having rates for arbitrators' remuneration and taking deposits from the parties to cover the costs of the arbitrators. Declarations of impartiality and independence can be difficult in an *ad hoc* arbitration. Arbitral institutions can ensure that the arbitrators understand precisely what is required from them and then deal with the sensitive matter of asking them whether they are independent and impartial.

(e) Cost

The advantages of institutional arbitration come at a price. Institutions charge fees for their services, and these vary depending on the institution and/or the size of the case or the amount in dispute. However, it is often considered worth paying these fees in order to obtain the efficient service and involvement of an institution rather than having an *ad hoc* arbitration.

Many institutions have also actively sought to moderate their costs and the fees charged by the tribunals they appoint. It can therefore be argued that the costs of arbitration costs might be better controlled under the supervision of an established institution than in an *ad hoc* arbitration.

3.2 *Ad hoc* arbitrations

(a) Harder to determine procedural rules

Negotiating the rules of procedure by the parties can be time consuming and costly. UNCITRAL has developed a set of off-the-shelf arbitration rules to be used in an *ad hoc* arbitration. If parties do choose *ad hoc* arbitration, they often choose to use these rules so as to avoid the extra costs and delays that may arise in agreeing the rules of procedure.

(b) More reliance on the national legal system

Greater reliance may be placed on the national legal system in the place of arbitration, which may also bring uncertainty, extra costs and delay.

4. Diversity in international arbitration

As arbitration continues to develop as a forum for international dispute resolution, there is increasing recognition of the need for arbitral tribunals to overcome their reputation as "pale, male and stale" and reflect the diversity of parties.

In May 2016, members of the arbitration community launched the Equal Representation in Arbitration Pledge to take action in relation to the under-representation of women on international arbitration tribunals. In May 2018, the Pledge for Africa was launched, which seeks to increase the number of Africans appointed as arbitrators, especially in arbitrations connected with Africa. Aside from principled concerns about diversity in arbitration, there are compelling, practical reasons to take under-representation seriously: diversity among arbitrators should promote greater competition and expanded choice, it will assist in establishing the legitimacy of the process in all countries, and contribute to a fairer process and outcome.

2. The legal framework

1. The New York Convention

1.1 What is the New York Convention?

The Convention on the Recognition and Enforcement of Foreign Arbitral Awards 1958 (the 'New York Convention') is the cornerstone of international arbitration. In broad terms, it requires the courts of signatory states to give effect to agreements to arbitrate and to recognise and enforce arbitration awards made in other states.

At the time of writing, 159 states have ratified the New York Convention. These encompass all major international commercial centres and trading states, including all member states of the EU, the US, China and many other Asian, Middle Eastern, Latin American and African states.

> **TIP** A list of the signatories to the New York Convention is available at www.uncitral.org/uncitral/en/uncitral_texts/arbitration/NYConvention_status.html.

Signatories to the New York Convention are allowed to enter certain reservations to the general obligations of recognition and enforcement. These permitted reservations include the 'reciprocity' reservation. This is the most common reservation and allows signatory states to limit the application of the New York Convention to awards made in other signatory states.

> **TIP** It is therefore logical for parties to select a seat or legal place for the arbitration in a state that is a signatory to the New York Convention, as this will be the place that the award is 'made' for the purposes of recognition and enforcement.

The general requirements of recognition and enforcement are subject only to specific limited exceptions. For example, courts are permitted to refuse to recognise and enforce an award where there has been a major procedural injustice – such as the party against which the award is being enforced not being given proper notice of the appointment of the arbitrator or of the arbitration proceedings – or where the award contravenes fundamental public policies. In pro-arbitration locations, the courts will follow the letter and spirit of the exceptions so that they are construed very narrowly; this is not always (or even often) the case in other places.

Cross-reference | Chapter 14 examines the grounds for challenging the enforcement of an award in more detail.

1.2 Why is the New York Convention important?

(a) *Jurisdiction of national courts*

The New York Convention's requirement to give effect to arbitration agreements means that where a contract includes an arbitration clause, national courts should refer parties to arbitration rather than allow a dispute to proceed before the court. (Again, this is subject to narrow exceptions where the agreement can be shown to be null and void, inoperative or incapable of being performed.) National courts will enforce arbitration obligations either positively, by requiring the parties to arbitrate – as in the United States, where an injunction can be obtained compelling a party to arbitrate the dispute that it has attempted to refer to court – or negatively, by staying court proceedings brought in breach of an arbitration agreement, as in the United Kingdom.

The principle of '*compétence-compétence*' – a feature of most pro-arbitration jurisdictions – permits arbitrators to hear detailed submissions on a challenge to the jurisdiction of the tribunal on the basis that, among others, there is no valid arbitration agreement. If necessary, this can be heard as a preliminary matter, with the possibility of a subsequent party challenge to the arbitrators' decision before the local courts.

Cross-reference | The principle of *compétence-compétence* is discussed further in Chapter 3.

(b) *Enforcing arbitral awards*

The problem of cross-border enforcement is highlighted when trying to enforce a national court judgment before foreign courts. It is not always possible to enforce a judgment from a national court in another state. This may be because there is no reciprocity between the state where the judgment is based and the state where the party wants that judgment to be enforced. Alternatively, recognition of the judgment may be subject to domestic rules that allow significantly more intrusive review, and so increase the chance of recognition and/or enforcement being refused.

As noted above, one of the main reasons for preferring arbitration as a method for resolving international disputes is that the New York Convention enables cross-border enforcement of arbitration awards in signatory states. This is a critical consideration when parties want to ensure that they are committed to a process which will result in a binding determination "with teeth" – that is, one that is enforceable before the courts of a state in which the award debtor has assets. There is no equivalent multilateral convention that deals with the recognition and enforcement of foreign court judgments.

TIP Before signing up to a contract containing an arbitration agreement, check whether at least one of the countries in which the counterparty has significant assets is a signatory to the New York Convention.

2. National arbitration laws

While the New York Convention provides a uniform framework for the recognition and enforcement of arbitration awards, national laws may continue to play a significant role in arbitration proceedings. This is because the procedural aspects of the arbitration are governed by the laws of the state in which the arbitration has its seat (also known as the curial law). The curial law is, in effect, part of the system of law governing the arbitration itself – as distinct from the proper law applicable to the underlying contract. This system of law is commonly referred to using the Latin phrase '*lex arbitri*'.

The curial law or *lex arbitri* may, and frequently does, differ from the law applicable to the parties' underlying contract. For example, a London arbitration relating to a contract governed by New York law will be subject to the English Arbitration Act 1996 and any related procedural rules that may apply under English law.

Sometimes the parties may select a specific procedural law other than that of the arbitral seat. However, this is rare and can give rise to difficulties where the mandatory procedural laws of the seat, which cannot generally be overridden, are inconsistent with those of the system chosen by the parties (see below).

The scope of the national procedural laws imported into the arbitration process varies between states. As a general principle, the laws tend to be directed towards supporting, rather than disrupting, the conduct of the arbitration. In particular, it is common for the curial law or *lex arbitri* to control the extent of court intervention, including addressing matters such as the grant of interim measures, the appointment of arbitrators and the attendance of witnesses. For example, in England and Wales, the Arbitration Act 1996 (Section 9) permits a party to an arbitration agreement to apply to the court for a stay of legal proceedings brought in breach of that agreement. It also provides a general presumption that a stay will be granted in such circumstances, even where the arbitral seat is outside of England and Wales.

In common with many other countries' procedural laws applicable to arbitration, certain provisions of the Arbitration Act are mandatory and so override any other agreement between the parties. These are listed in Schedule 1 to the Arbitration Act. Most of these mandatory provisions apply only where the arbitral seat is within the jurisdiction; however, a number apply irrespective of the location of the seat (including Section 9, which deals with stays of legal proceedings). Broadly speaking, the trend in most national arbitration laws is for relatively few mandatory provisions. This reflects the position in the UNCITRAL Model Law on International Commercial Arbitration, produced in 1985 by the United Nations Commission on International Trade Law (UNCITRAL) with the aim of helping states to reform and harmonise their national arbitration laws. The UNCITRAL Model Law aims to facilitate and ensure the proper functioning of international commercial arbitration, for instance by including provisions regarding the presumed validity and enforceability of arbitration agreements, the conduct and procedure of arbitration proceedings, and the recognition and enforcement of arbitral awards (under the New York Convention). The UNCITRAL Model Law affirms the principle of party autonomy with regard to arbitral procedures, and prescribes only limited areas in which national courts can intervene.

In 2006, UNCITRAL made limited amendments to the Model Law. By 2018, legislation based on the UNCITRAL Model Law has been adopted in 80 states, with the 'newer' states including Qatar, South Africa and Republic of Korea. The widespread adoption of the Model Law provides parties with a predictable and pro-arbitration legislative framework in which to conduct arbitrations or enforce arbitral awards across a significant number of jurisdictions. National courts in countries which have adopted the UNCITRAL Model Law are beginning to produce a reasonably consistent body of precedent concerning its interpretation and application. This helps to provide even greater certainty.

The English Arbitration Act 1996 contains a number of provisions based upon the UNCITRAL Model Law, but does not adopt the Model Law in its entirety. The recommendations for the basis on which this legislation should be adopted and the extent to which provisions of the Model Law should be incorporated have been set out in a series of reports by the Departmental Advisory Committee (DAC) on arbitration law. These can be very helpful as a tool when analysing the English Arbitration Act.

It is notable that one of the grounds upon which an award may be refused recognition and enforcement under the New York Convention is where the award has been annulled or suspended under the applicable procedural law (see Article V(e)). However, in practice this may not result in non-enforcement in the courts of other states. For instance, in France the courts will in certain circumstances still permit enforcement of an award that has been set aside under the *lex arbitri*. This approach has since been followed in the Netherlands, where the Supreme Court held in 2017 that an enforcement judge does have the discretion to ignore an earlier annulment of the award made in the seat of arbitration, provided certain conditions are met, such as the annulment decision being irreconcilable with Dutch private international law.

TIP The question of whether the courts of the seat or legal place chosen by the parties are pro-arbitration is important. Being a signatory to the New York Convention is the logical starting point for such an assessment, but there are also other important points to keep in mind, relating to the courts' approach to the recognition and enforcement of arbitration awards. Preferred locations will usually be those with modern national arbitration laws that support the arbitral process. Broader practical factors such as convenience for the parties, judicial independence, judicial sophistication and efficiency, and the availability of specialist arbitrators/counsel and relevant experts should also be taken into account. The issue of a jurisdiction's attitude to third-party funding may also be of importance to the parties to an arbitration. Seats where third-party funding is not expressly allowed or is illegal, presents risks to the funded party. On the one hand, an impecunious party may not be able to bring a good claim. However, on the other hand, if there is not express allowance of third-party funding or it is illegal, the opposing party may seek to have the proceedings terminated on grounds of abuse of process, or they may also seek to set aside any award on the basis of conflicting public policy grounds. This may also be a risk if a funded party's award needed to be enforced in a jurisdiction in which third-party funding is illegal.

The International Chamber of Commerce (ICC) publishes statistics showing the most common venues for ICC arbitrations. For 2016, these were France, Switzerland, the United Kingdom, Germany, the United States, Singapore and Belize. These countries are all generally considered to be pro-arbitration.

TIP To avoid any confusion where different regions within a country may apply different rules to international arbitration (as is the case for Hong Kong as compared to mainland China), it is normal practice to specify the city. Examples include stating the seat or legal place in the arbitration agreement as 'London, England', 'Paris, France' or 'Geneva, Switzerland'.

Although there have been attempts to create transnational or non-national arbitrations that are not subject to any national laws, these have in large part failed in the sphere of international commercial arbitration. The vast majority of arbitrations are conducted pursuant to one set of national laws or another – that is, the curial law or *lex arbitri*. Perhaps the example that comes closest to being transnational as an arbitral process are investment treaty disputes at the International Centre for the Settlement of Investment Disputes (ICSID) arbitrations. These arbitrations are largely brought pursuant to an investment protection treaty between states as opposed to being a contractual agreement between two or more commercial parties.

3. Major institutional arbitration rules

International arbitrations are referred to as either 'institutional' or '*ad hoc*'. As noted in Chapter 1, an institutional arbitration is one in which the parties have chosen the arbitration rules of an institution to complement the *lex arbitri* and to have the overall supervision and assistance that institutions can provide to the arbitral process. Chapter 15 sets out a comparison of the major institutional rules.

The sections below provide a brief overview of the different institutions and their rules.

3.1 International Chamber of Commerce

The International Court of Arbitration of the ICC is one of the pre-eminent arbitration institutions. It is headquartered in Paris, France and accepts over 900 cases each year.

The ICC Court is the body responsible for administering arbitrations conducted under the ICC Rules and is at the time of writing comprised of 176 members from 116 states appointed on three-year terms, many of whom are leading international arbitration practitioners. It is supported by the secretariat, which consists of teams of lawyers from different parts of the world, acting in a case management role and serving as the link between the parties, the arbitral tribunal and the ICC Court. This includes making recommendations to the court on issues that may arise in the course of proceedings.

Neither the court nor the secretariat plays any direct role in determining the merits of a dispute or in conducting the arbitration proceedings (they do not, for instance, attend the arbitration hearing). Their function is purely administrative, dealing with such matters as the selection and appointment of arbitrators (in the absence of party agreement), reviewing draft awards before issue to the parties and fixing the arbitrators' compensation at the close of the proceedings.

The ICC Rules have undergone a recent review, with new rules coming into effect on 1 March 2017. These apply to all ICC arbitrations begun on or after that date, unless the parties have agreed otherwise.

> **TIP** The 2017 ICC Rules are available at https://cdn.iccwbo.org/content/uploads/sites/3/2017/01/ICC-2017-Arbitration-and-2014-Mediation-Rules-english-version.pdf.pdf.

A peculiarity of ICC arbitration, preserved in the 2017 Rules, is the requirement that 'Terms of Reference' setting out the issues and summarising the parties' positions be prepared at the outset of the process. This can help to focus minds early on; however, it can also be a cause of delay and additional costs if not carefully managed.

As with the 2012 Rules, the 2017 Rules reinforce the role of the ICC Court by providing that it, rather than any other institution (or *ad hoc* body), is the only body authorised to administer arbitrations. This has been implemented in light of a recent decision of the Singapore Court of Appeal which permitted a Singapore International Arbitration Centre (SIAC) administered arbitration to proceed under the ICC Rules.

In common with several other institutions, the 2017 Rules also include provisions first adopted in the ICC's 2012 Rules that allow for the appointment of an emergency arbitrator to deal with any requests from the parties for urgent interim or conservatory relief. This is, in practice, one of the most significant amendments, and it is subject to a separate set of Emergency Arbitrator Rules contained in Appendix V to the 2017 Rules. The procedure will not apply where the arbitration agreement was concluded before the new Rules came into force or where the parties have agreed to opt out of the procedure, whether expressly or by agreeing to another pre-arbitral procedure that enables interim urgent relief to be granted (eg, the ICC Pre-Arbitral Referee Procedure).

In addition, the 2017 Rules strengthen the tools available to a tribunal to undertake and enforce efficient case management. These include a mandatory case management conference, the fixing of time limits for arbitrator appointments, notification from the arbitrator of when the award will be submitted and a requirement for the conduct of the parties to be taken into account when determining any costs award.

A filing fee (currently US$5,000) is payable on submission of the Request for Arbitration as an advance of the administrative costs. The full amount of the administrative costs payable to the ICC, as well as the arbitrator's fees, are calculated by reference to a scale based on the amount in dispute, including any counterclaims, or, where the amount in dispute is not stated, at its discretion. By way of example (under the 2017 scale, currently in force), the estimated fees per arbitrator for a US$5 million dispute with three arbitrators are indicated at between US$32,767 and US$141,900, plus an average ICC administrative charge of US$45,015. For a US$50 million dispute with three arbitrators, these rise to between US$63,767 and US$281,200 per arbitrator, plus average ICC administrative expenses of US$95,515.

In exceptional circumstances, the court has the power, under the ICC Rules, to fix the arbitrators' compensation at higher or lower levels than those specified by the scales.

TIP A costs estimation tool is available on the ICC website at www.iccwbo.org/products-and-services/arbitration-and-adr/arbitration/cost-and-payment/cost-calculator/. A schedule of the current fee rates can be found at Appendix III of the ICC Rules.

3.2 London Court of International Arbitration

The London Court of International Arbitration (LCIA) is headquartered in London and typically deals with between 100 and 200 new international arbitrations each year involving parties from around the world. In 2017, approximately 19.3% of its cases involved UK parties, 11% involved North American parties and 6.5% involved Russian parties, with the remainder split across a wide spectrum of countries and regions, from Cyprus to Singapore to Africa. Regional arbitration centres – founded upon a strategic partnership with, or closely modelled upon, the LCIA – exist in Dubai and Mauritius.

In many respects, the service provided by the LCIA is similar to that of the ICC. It has a secretariat housed at the International Dispute Resolution Centre in London which undertakes the administration of arbitrations referred to it. It also has a court made up of leading arbitration practitioners. The LCIA court is responsible for managing its caseload in much the same way as the ICC Court – for example, by dealing with challenges to and the replacement of arbitrators.

The LCIA administers arbitrations under its own Arbitration Rules (the current rules being in force since 2014, which can be found at www.lcia.org). It will also act as appointing authority/administrator in *ad hoc* proceedings such as under the UNCITRAL Rules. In the absence of party choice, the default seat for the arbitration will be London. However, the LCIA frequently administers arbitrations in other seats across the world.

TIP A particular feature of the LCIA Arbitration Rules is the ability for the arbitral tribunal to be formed on an expedited basis, possibly within days. This can be a major advantage when one party is seeking urgent injunctive or interim/conservatory relief, and may avoid the need to resort to separate court litigation (especially where local courts cannot offer the same relief on an expedited basis).

In contrast to the ICC, administrative charges and arbitrators' fees are calculated on an agreed hourly rate, regardless of the amount in dispute. A portion of the LCIA's charges is based on the arbitral tribunal's fees. A filing fee is also payable on filing of the Request for Arbitration; this is currently £1,750.

TIP The LCIA schedule of costs is available at www.lcia.org/Dispute_Resolution_Services/schedule-of-costs.aspx.

3.3 American Arbitration Association/International Centre for Dispute Resolution

The American Arbitration Association's (AAA) international disputes arm is called the International Centre for Dispute Resolution (ICDR). It manages its caseloads principally from New York. The latest available data shows that it administered over 1,000 international disputes and it also maintains regional offices in South Korea, Mexico and Singapore.

The AAA is the largest US arbitration institution by some margin, administering thousands of domestic cases every year. As a result of the AAA's strong US focus, the ICDR is viewed by some as being less international in outlook and arbitrations managed under its International Arbitration Rules – which are modelled on the UNCITRAL Rules – can sometimes be infused with features of US domestic litigation.

The ICDR case managers undertake a more limited role than the courts and secretariats of the ICC and LCIA, though the general case management and support functions are still well covered. Where necessary, they will assist in the selection of arbitrators – from a database of over 650 international arbitrators – based on input provided from the parties (or party-appointed arbitrators) about any required attributes, such as sector specialism and nationality. A shortlist is prepared, from which the parties (or party-appointed arbitrators) must agree the identity of the arbitrator (or chair). Failing agreement, the ICDR will make the appointment.

In the absence of party agreement on the number of arbitrators, the International Arbitration Rules provide a default preference for a sole arbitrator (Article 11), subject to circumstances in which the Administrator may decide that a three-member tribunal is more appropriate because of the size, complexity or other circumstances of the case.

The administrative charges levied by the ICDR are determined according to the value of the claim or counterclaim. There are standard and flexible fee schedule options, with the latter involving lower initial filing fees, but potentially higher total administrative fees if the case proceeds all the way to a final hearing. The arbitrator's fees are calculated on an hourly rate that takes into account the size and complexity of the case. They will typically be agreed with the parties at the start of proceedings, before the ICDR confirms the appointment.

TIP The ICDR publishes its Administrative Fee Schedule at www.icdr.org/sites/default/files/document_repository/International_Dispute_Resolution_Procedures_Fee_Schedule.pdf.

Similarly to those of the ICC, the ICDR International Arbitration Rules (Article 37) provide for the appointment of an emergency arbitrator where a party seeks urgent relief from the tribunal in place of an application to the local courts.

3.4 International Institute for Conflict Prevention and Resolution

The International Institute for Conflict Prevention and Resolution (CPR) describes itself as an independent non-profit organization that helps global businesses and their counsel prevent and resolve commercial disputes more effectively.

Historically, CPR's arbitration rules were tailored to non-administered arbitration. However, since this book was first published, CPR have launched two sets of rules for administered arbitration: the CPR Rules for Administered Arbitration (July 1, 2013); and the CPR Rules for Administered Arbitration of International Disputes (December 1, 2014).

CPR have stated that their rules on administered arbitration are designed to address complaints with arbitration as to costs, time and partisanship. Concerns as to an arbitrator's independence or impartiality are dealt with by a "Challenge Review Committee", comprised of three individuals from CPR's "Challenge Review Board". All of the Challenge Review Board undertake the year long appointment on a *pro bono* basis

As to costs, the administration fees are capped for disputes at US$34,000 for claims above US$500 million. CPR's fee structure for administered arbitrations is based on delivery of the final award by the Tribunal to CPR for review within 12 months after the pre-hearing conference. While CPR has the ability to charge an additional administrative fee after that period, the rules seek to keep some control over timing in that CPR must approve any scheduling order or extensions that would cause a final award to be delivered to CPR for review more than 12 months after the pre-hearing conference. In this respect, CPR consider that there is time frame accountability.

Both sets of CPR's administered arbitration rules provide that, in the absence of agreement, the tribunal consists of three arbitrators.

Interim measures of protection before the tribunal has been constituted are possible under both sets of rules.

3.5 Singapore International Arbitration Centre

SIAC is the leading arbitration institution in Singapore and, alongside the Hong Kong International Arbitration Centre (HKIAC) (see below), one of the dominant Asian regional institutions. SIAC's active caseload as of 31 March 2017 was approximately 650 disputes.

SIAC operates through a board of directors (led by a chairman), a council of advisers and a secretariat. The last of these, headed by a registrar, is the body responsible for general case administration and management, including the approval of arbitrator appointments and fees. The chairman also plays a key role in arbitrator appointments when the parties cannot agree.

The fourth edition of the SIAC Arbitration Rules came into effect on 1 July 2010 and apply to all arbitrations begun on or after that date. (The previous rules were issued in 2007.) The SIAC Rules are supplemented by a Practice Note that addresses the appointment of arbitrators and fees/expenses (including advance deposits payable by the parties).

TIP The SIAC Arbitration Rules can be found at www.siac.org.sg.

Subject to other agreements between the parties, the SIAC Rules set a presumption in favour of Singapore as the arbitral seat and the appointment of a sole arbitrator. The registrar can vary this where it is justified by the complexity, financial value or other particular features of the case.

TIP In common with the rules of other major arbitral institutions, the 2016 SIAC Rules allow a party to apply for urgent relief from an emergency arbitrator; the procedure for doing so is set out in Schedule 1 to the rules.

The 2016 Rules also provide for an expedited procedure for disputes below S$5 million, where the parties agree or in cases of "exceptional urgency" and the amount in dispute does not exceed the equivalent amount of S$6 million representing the aggregate of the claim, counterclaim and any defence of set-off. If applied, the expedited process requires a sole arbitrator to hear the dispute (unless the chairman of the SIAC board of directors decides that a larger tribunal is appropriate) and to render an award within six months, providing only summary reasons.

The 2016 Rules removed the requirement (introduced in 2007) for a Memorandum of Issues. This was broadly similar to the ICC Terms of Reference, albeit prepared at a later stage in the proceedings. Many users and commentators did not see this requirement as a positive development, potentially increasing delays and costs, and its removal has generally been welcomed.

The SIAC Schedule of Fees provides for a charging structure based on the value of the dispute similar to that of the ICC. A filing fee of S$2,140 for Singaporean Parties, and S$2,000 for overseas parties is payable by the claimant at the time of submitting its Notice of Arbitration (and in respect of any counterclaim made by the respondent). Thereafter, administration fees are levied according to the amount in dispute, from S$3,800 for disputes valued up to S$50,000, to a maximum of S$95,000 for claims valued above S$100 million, with various gradations in between. For arbitrators' fees, the maximum fees payable for a sole arbitrator are specified at S$6,250 for a dispute valued at up to S$50,000, up to S$605,000 and more for claims exceeding S$500 million. Again, there is a stepped charging structure for claims at other intermediate values.

These fees are significantly lower than those referred to above in relation to ICC arbitrations.

3.6 Hong Kong International Arbitration Centre

HKIAC is a well-regarded regional institution. In 2017, it handled 297 arbitration cases, and 73.1% of these were international disputes.

HKIAC exhibits a less 'hands-on' approach to the day-to-day administration of arbitrations than the ICC or LCIA, while still providing general support with case management. It has its own set of rules, the Administered Arbitration Rules, which are modelled on the UNCITRAL Rules.

TIP The HKIAC Administered Arbitration Rules can be viewed at www.hkiac.org/sites/default/files/ck_filebrowser/PDF/arbitration/2013_hkiac_rules.pdf.

HKIAC is governed by a council, comprising members from various different countries and professional backgrounds. The secretariat is responsible for the general case management of proceedings until the arbitrator is appointed. If necessary, the council can assist with arbitrator appointments and challenges.

3.7 The Swiss Rules

The Swiss Rules of International Arbitration (the most recent edition of which was introduced with effect from 1 June 2012) are a unified set of arbitration rules developed from the separate rules of a number of regional Swiss Chambers of Commerce and Industry. They are based on the UNCITRAL Rules. The various chambers appoint representatives to an Arbitration Committee, which is responsible for exercising the case management powers under the rules.

The parties can agree between them the number and identities of the arbitrators. However, in the absence of agreement the chamber will make the appointment; the default position under the rules is for a single arbitrator. The rules require that party-appointed arbitrators be confirmed by the chambers. The 2012 Rules aim to improve the efficiency of arbitration proceedings by, for instance, obliging all parties to avoid unnecessary costs and delays, seeking to speed up proceedings by placing more emphasis on the first round of submissions and requiring the nomination of arbitrators at an earlier stage.

TIP The Swiss Rules are available at www.swissarbitration.org/Arbitration/Arbitration-Rules-and-Laws.

3.8 Stockholm Chamber of Commerce Institute

The Stockholm Chamber of Commerce Institute (SCC), headquartered in Stockholm, Sweden, administers the 2017 SCC Rules. In 2017, 200 new cases were filed with the SCC, 96 of which were international in nature. The caseload is made up predominantly of disputes between parties from Sweden and countries such as Russia, Germany, the United Kingdom, the United States and Norway. A number of cases also come from China, Turkey and Norway.

The SCC is made up of a board and a secretariat, with the former being responsible for matters such as the appointment of arbitrators in the absence of party agreement. The default position under the SCC Rules is that, in the absence of agreement between the parties, the board will determine whether to appoint a sole or a three-member tribunal having regard to the complexity of the case, the amount in dispute and any other relevant circumstances.

The SCC sets the arbitrators' fees and the administrative fees based on the amount in dispute.

TIP The SCC Rules can be accessed at www.sccinstitute.com. A separate set of rules can be used for expedited arbitration proceedings, and there are also provisions for appointing an emergency arbitrator.

3.9 China International Economic and Trade Arbitration Commission

The China International Economic and Trade Arbitration Commission (CIETAC) is the leading player in international arbitrations between Chinese and foreign businesses. In 2016, CIETAC accepted over 2,183 cases between its head office in Beijing and sub-commissions across China. The CIETAC secretariat handles day-to-day case administration work under the guidance of the secretary general.

The current CIETAC Arbitration Rules came into effect in 2015. These rules are more closely aligned to users' expectations of international arbitration from other major institutions. They include a number of new provisions that allow for more flexibility and transparency in CIETAC arbitration, and grant further powers to arbitral tribunals.

TIP The CIETAC Arbitration Rules can be found at www.cietac.org/Uploads/201703/58c0fe0c7337a.pdf.

Parties are allowed to appoint arbitrators who are not on the CIETAC approved panel, so long as this is agreed by all parties. Such appointments are subject to confirmation from the chairman of CIETAC. The tribunal can be comprised of one or three arbitrators, with three being the default position under the 2015 Rules.

Challenges to arbitrators are determined by CIETAC's chairman. The chairman also reserves the power to appoint the presiding arbitrator for three-member tribunals in circumstances where this is not agreed by the parties, based on a common candidate in each party's shortlist. Foreign parties in an arbitration against a Chinese party might find this mechanism unappealing if it results in the appointment of a Chinese national. In response to this concern, Article 30 of the 2015 Rules expressly sets out the factors that the chairman must consider when appointing arbitrators. Those include the applicable law, the seat and language of arbitration, the nationalities of the parties and any other factors that the chairman thinks appropriate.

> **TIP** Parties must include the right to appoint foreign arbitrators (especially those not on the CIETAC panel) in their arbitration agreement if they do not want to be restricted in their choice of arbitrators to those on the CIETAC panel.

CIETAC publishes a fee schedule, which sets the fixed arbitration fee to be paid by the parties based on the value of the claim. A separate registration fee is also payable when the claim is lodged with CIETAC. A different charging system applies to purely domestic disputes.

> **TIP** In principle, the arbitration fee is intended to cover both CIETAC's administrative expenses and the arbitrators' fees and expenses. In practice, the fee is unlikely to be appropriate for arbitrations involving foreign arbitrators; the rules therefore permit CIETAC to charge the parties any other extra and reasonable costs, including but not limited to arbitrators' special remuneration, their travel and accommodation expenses incurred in dealing with the case (Article 82).

The tribunal has a general authority under the rules to assess costs according to factors such as the complexity of the case, expenses incurred and the financial value of the claims.

3.10 United Nations Commission on International Trade Law

UNCITRAL first published its Arbitration Rules in 1976. These are designed for use in *ad hoc* arbitrations: unlike the other arbitration bodies referred to above, UNCITRAL is not an arbitral institution and does not administer or oversee arbitrations. As such, any arbitration under the UNCITRAL Rules is carried out on an *ad hoc* basis, with the parties and the arbitrators solely responsible for case management issues. In practice, however, parties often agree for arbitrations conducted under the UNCITRAL Rules to be administered by an institution such as the LCIA.

A revised set of UNCITRAL Arbitration Rules came into effect from 15 August 2010 ('2010 Rules'). The 2010 Rules were later amended with effect from 1 April 2014 ('2013 Rules'). The purpose of the amendment was to include a new paragraph to Article 1 (*Scope of application*) which provides that the 2013 Rules incorporate the UNCITRAL Rules on Transparency in Treaty-based Investor-State Arbitration ('Transparency Rules'). Article 1 (*Scope of application*) of the Transparency Rules sets out that it shall apply to Investor-State arbitration initiated under the UNCITRAL Arbitration Rules pursuant to a treaty providing for the protection of investments or investors concluded on or after 1 April 2014 unless the parties to the treaty have agreed otherwise. In all other respects, however, the 2010 and 2013 Rules remain the same.

Parties to an arbitration agreement concluded after 15 August 2010 will be presumed to have referred to the Rules in effect on the date of the commencement of the arbitration, unless the parties have agreed to apply to a particular version of the Rules. The 1976, 2010 and 2013 Rules expressly allow for modified in any way by agreement of the parties.

TIP All versions of the UNCITRAL Arbitration Rules can be found at www.uncitral.org/uncitral/en/uncitral_texts/arbitration.html.

Under the UNCITRAL Rules, if the parties are unable to reach agreement on the appointment of the arbitrator(s), the appointment will be managed by an 'appointing authority' chosen by the parties. If the parties cannot agree on the appointing authority within 30 days (or 60 days under the 1976 Rules), the Permanent Court of Arbitration in the Hague will designate the appointing authority.

TIP As this two-stage process of appointing the tribunal can take a considerable length of time, the parties should try to agree upon an appointing authority in the arbitration agreement. It is also wise to provide here for the seat and language of the arbitration, as the tribunal will determine these issues if they are not agreed by the parties.

The 2010 Rules introduce a number of changes designed to promote active case management. These include a specific obligation on the tribunal to avoid unnecessary delay and expense, and a requirement that the tribunal formulate a provisional timetable as soon as practicable after it has been constituted. The 2010 Rules also expand upon the powers of the tribunal to award interim measures. However, unlike a number of institutional rules, because UNCITRAL does not itself act as an appointing body, there is no mechanism for appointing an emergency arbitrator to deal with any requests from the parties for urgent interim or conservatory relief.

The arbitration fees are dealt with entirely by the tribunal itself, which can require deposits (and supplementary deposits) for these to be paid equally by both parties. The rules do, however, require that the tribunal set its fees at a reasonable level, taking into account such factors as the amount in dispute, the complexity of the proceedings and the amount of time required to deal with the matter. One advantage of the parties agreeing to an institution to administer the rules is that the institution will handle issues such as arbitrator's fees and deposits.

4. Internationally accepted rules and guidelines

4.1 IBA Rules on the Taking of Evidence in International Arbitration

Most institutional rules do not deal in detail with evidential issues; in general, they leave these to the parties and/or the tribunal. For this reason, in many international arbitrations the parties agree to apply the International Bar Association (IBA) Rules on the Taking of Evidence in International Arbitration. IBA updated these rules in 2010, and they currently seek to strike a balance between common law and civil law approaches to evidence gathering that can vary widely across different jurisdictions. As such, they can be particularly helpful in cases where the parties are used to different legal codes.

TIP The IBA Rules can be found at www.ibanet.org/Publications/publications_IBA_guides_and_free_materials.aspx.

The IBA Rules provide guidance on dealing with the production of contemporaneous documents, factual witness evidence and expert evidence. They have a number of advantages, including providing certainty over the procedure to be used for gathering evidence (often the costliest part of any dispute), as well as a degree of flexibility to the parties. Although not binding, parties and arbitrators can agree that the IBA Rules will apply in part or in their entirety. Most often they tend to be used in relation to document production and requests made by parties for the disclosure of specific documents. This is dealt with in more detail in Chapter 11.

The IBA Rules operate in conjunction with those of the relevant institution, and the parties or arbitrators can agree to alter them in any way to make them more applicable to the particular issue or issues in dispute.

TIP The IBA Rules can be adopted by or incorporated into the arbitration agreement. The parties should therefore consider whether to do this in order to give clarity on evidential issues at the outset of the arbitration and avoid the potentially lengthy delays that can be incurred in debating the approach to be taken to evidence gathering.

4.2 IBA Guidelines on Conflicts of Interest in International Arbitration

One of the cornerstones of international arbitration is that each arbitrator must be impartial and independent of the parties. If a party is concerned that one of the arbitrators is not independent or impartial, it may seek to challenge the appointment of the arbitrator.

Most arbitral rules provide a procedure for challenging the appointment of an arbitrator, but do not give detailed guidance on when an arbitrator may not be considered to be independent or impartial. The IBA Guidelines on Conflicts of Interest in International Arbitration (revised in 2014) provide guidance on the disclosures expected of arbitrators in consideration of their impartiality and independence, and thus what circumstances may leave an arbitrator open to challenge.

The IBA Guidelines are not rules or law, but they do broadly reflect standard practice in the international arbitration community. They are increasingly used by institutional bodies and courts when hearing challenges to the appointment of an arbitrator.

TIP If considering whether to challenge the independence or impartiality of an arbitrator, it is often useful to engage with the IBA Guidelines at an early stage to help assess the merits of the challenge. Close consideration of the national law of the arbitral seat will also be necessary.

The IBA Guidelines begin by setting out a number of general standards regarding impartiality, independence, independence and disclosure that arbitrators should observe, including (unsurprisingly) that each arbitrator should be impartial and independent of the parties at the time he or she accepts an appointment and must remain so throughout the entire course of the proceedings. They also advise that arbitrators should decline an appointment if he or she has any doubts as to his or her ability to be impartial or independent. Further, an arbitrator should refuse to continue to act if facts or circumstances exist, or have arisen since the appointment which, from the point of view of a reasonable third person having knowledge of the relevant facts and circumstances, would give rise to justifiable doubts as to the arbitrator's independence or impartiality. Doubts are justifiable if a reasonable third person, having knowledge of the relevant facts and circumstances, would reach the conclusion that there is a likelihood that the arbitrator may be influenced by factors other than the merits of the case as presented by the parties in reaching his or her decision. Justifiable doubts exist in situations such as when the arbitrator is a legal representative of one of the parties or has a significant financial or personal interest in the dispute. The guidelines also set out that where there are factors that might make a party question the independence or impartiality of the arbitrator, the arbitrator should disclose these to the parties.

The guidelines categorise such disclosures on a traffic light system according to their severity:

- Non-waivable red list – this consists of the most obvious conflicts, such as the arbitrator having a significant financial interest in the matter. These conflicts must be disclosed and cannot be cured by waiver of the parties.
- Waivable red list – these examples must be disclosed as they do (rather than may) give rise to a justifiable doubt about the arbitrator's

independence or impartiality. However, they can be expressly waived by the parties. They include issues such as the arbitrator being a lawyer in the same firm as one of the parties' legal team, or the arbitrator's close family having a financial interest in the dispute.

- Orange list – these are issues that should be disclosed by the arbitrator as they may raise doubts as to the arbitrator's impartiality or independence in the eyes of the parties. Disclosure allows either party to object if it so wishes. However, unlike the waivable red list, which requires an express waiver, if neither party has objected within 30 days of disclosure by the arbitrator, they will be presumed to have no objections. Issues on the orange list include the arbitrator having been appointed as an arbitrator by one of the parties on two or more occasions within the last three years, and the arbitrator having acted against one of the parties on an unrelated matter.
- Green list – this consists of circumstances which do not give rise to an objective justifiable doubt, such as the arbitrator having previously expressed a legal opinion (such as in an article or in a public lecture) on an issue that also arises in the arbitration, or a firm in association or in alliance with the arbitrator's law firm (but that does not share significant fees or other revenues with the arbitrator's firm) rendering services to one of the parties (or an affiliate of one of the parties) in an unrelated matter. These matters need not be disclosed by the arbitrator.

TIP Other helpful guidance publications include the UNCITRAL Notes on Organising Arbitral Proceedings (which can be found online at www.uncitral.org/uncitral/en/uncitral_texts/arbitration.html), and the Chartered Institute of Arbitrators' Guidance on Interviewing Witnesses (which can be found, along with a number of useful guidance publications, at www.ciarb.org/information-and-resources/practice-guidelines-and-protocols/list-of guidelines-and-protocols/).

4.3 International Court of Arbitration: Note to Parties and Arbitral Tribunals on the Conduct of the Arbitration under the ICC Rules of Arbitration (October 2017).

The ICC Note to Parties and Arbitral Tribunals on the Conduct of the Arbitration under the ICC Rules of Arbitration includes a section on acceptance, availability, impartiality and independence of arbitrators. The Note makes clear that an arbitrator or prospective arbitrator must disclose in his or her Statement, at the time of his or her appointment and as the arbitration is ongoing, any circumstance that might be of such nature as to call into question his or her independence in the eyes of any of the parties or give rise to reasonable doubts as to his or her impartiality, with any doubt being resolved in favour of disclosure. The Note lists out the sorts of circumstances which an arbitrator should take into account when making an assessment as to what circumstances may call into question their independence in the eyes of the parties or give rise to reasonable doubts as to his or her impartiality. The circumstances (which the ICC makes clear are not limited to that which are listed) includes where the arbitrator or the prospective arbitrator or his or her law firm represents or advises, or has represented or advised, one of the parties or one of its affiliates.

3. The legal effect of agreeing to arbitrate

1. The arbitration agreement

1.1 What is an arbitration agreement?

As defined in Chapter 1, arbitration is a means of dispute resolution which depends upon the parties' agreement. As the name suggests, an arbitration agreement is a contractual agreement between parties to resolve their disputes by arbitration. While arbitration agreements come in many forms, care must be taken with their drafting to ensure their validity and enforceability.

Cross-reference Further information on the drafting of arbitration agreements can be found in Chapter 4.

Definitions for 'arbitration agreement' in the various institutional rules, international conventions and domestic legislation are broadly similar.

By way of example, Article II of The Convention on the Recognition and Enforcement of Foreign Arbitral Awards 1958 (the 'New York Convention') defines an 'arbitration agreement' as an:

...agreement in writing under which the parties undertake to submit to arbitration all or any differences which have arisen or which may arise between them.

Article 7 of the United Nations Commission on International Trade Law (UNCITRAL) Model Law (the 'Model Law') defines it as:

...an agreement by the parties to submit to arbitration all or certain disputes which have arisen or which may arise between them in respect of a defined legal relationship, whether contractual or not.

And Section 6(1) of the English Arbitration Act 1996 defines it as:

...an agreement to submit to arbitration present or future disputes (whether they are contractual or not).

As these definitions indicate, both present and/or future disputes can be referred to arbitration. Traditionally, there are two types of arbitration agreement: the submission agreement ('*acte de compromis*'), by which an existing dispute is referred to arbitration; and the arbitration clause ('*clause compromissoire*'), by which a possible future dispute will be submitted to arbitration. Submission agreements take the form of a separate contract entered into between parties after the dispute has arisen, while arbitration clauses are generally contained within the parties' commercial contracts at the outset.

While the definitions above do not distinguish between the submission agreement and the arbitration clause, Article 1442 of the French Code of Civil Procedure provides a helpful explanation of the two forms of arbitration agreement (albeit in the context of domestic arbitration as there are no requirements as to form under French law for international arbitration agreements):

> *An arbitration agreement may be in the form of an arbitration clause or a submission agreement. An arbitration clause is an agreement by which the parties to one or more contracts undertake to submit to arbitration disputes which may arise in relation to such contract(s). A submission agreement is an agreement by which the parties to a dispute submit such dispute to arbitration.*

1.2 Getting it right

To avoid compromising your position should a dispute later arise, it is essential to get agreements right at the outset. Poorly drafted agreements can lead to costly and time-consuming litigation to determine their applicability and scope, before the merits of any dispute are even considered. Unless the most suitable seat and governing law are chosen, they may also prejudice the enforceability of any arbitral award eventually rendered. On a practical level, an effectively drafted arbitration agreement will ensure that the procedural rules and costs applicable to a given dispute are those most appropriate to the circumstances.

Cross-reference Further guidance on the effective drafting of arbitration agreements is set out in Chapter 4.

1.3 Written and oral arbitration agreements

While oral agreements to arbitrate may be valid and binding in certain jurisdictions,[1] it is advisable to commit such agreements to writing as a matter of course. On a practical level, this will reduce the scope for disagreement between the parties as to what they have agreed. More importantly, it will also ensure that the agreement does not fall foul of the requirement found in various jurisdictions that arbitration agreements be written.

English law affords a very broad definition of what constitutes a written arbitration agreement. This broad-brush approach to the requirement for writing is also found in the Model Law (see Option 1 of Article 7). The relevant provisions of the English Arbitration Act 1996 (primarily Section 5) are wide

---

1 French law, for example, does not require an international arbitration agreement to be in writing (see Article 1507 of the Code of Civil Procedure). Article 1504 states that "[a]n arbitration is international when international trade interests are at stake".

ranging in scope and state that 'in writing' means 'recorded by any means'; this will include agreements recorded electronically, those contained in exchanges of communications and those contained in exchanges of written legal submissions. Thus, for example, the signature by the parties of the Terms of Reference in an International Chamber of Commerce (ICC) arbitration agreeing which disputes the tribunal is to determine can constitute an agreement to refer those disputes to arbitration (unless there is a clear reservation or objection to jurisdiction). Similarly, participating in an arbitration and making written submissions to the tribunal without challenging or objecting to jurisdiction can be sufficient. The English Arbitration Act 1996 will also apply to arbitration agreements which are not themselves recorded in writing, but for which there is evidence contained in some other written documentation. An example of a written arbitration agreement of this sort would be one in which parties refer in a contract to another document which contains an arbitration clause (although it should be noted that in some jurisdictions a specific reference to the arbitration clause and not just the document in which it is contained is required). The inclusion of this provision in the English Arbitration Act 1996 allows the English courts a large degree of flexibility in determining whether an arbitration agreement exists.

As a general rule, parties will be bound by written arbitration agreements whether or not they have signed them; the Model Law does not require the signature of a written agreement for validity, and while the New York Convention's definition of 'agreement in writing' refers to it being 'signed by the parties', it recognises that arbitration agreements may also be contained in an exchange of letters or telegrams. In English law, a written arbitration agreement will be binding on the parties, whether or not it has been signed, provided that an intention to be bound can be ascertained from the surrounding circumstances.

TIP While an arbitration agreement does not generally require a signature in order for it to be valid and binding, problems may arise when a party seeks to enforce an arbitral award based on an unsigned arbitration agreement. In order to avoid any such problems arising at a later stage, it is advisable to ensure that all parties sign the Terms of Reference at the outset of the arbitral proceedings. This is explained in more detail in Chapter 9.

1.4 Separability

Given that the majority of arbitration clauses are contained within commercial contracts, it is not difficult to envisage a situation whereby the validity of the arbitration agreement is called into question on the basis of the invalidity of the underlying contract. Importantly, however, it is a recognised principle of international arbitration law that an arbitration agreement which is contained within a contract or other agreement will not be regarded as invalid, non-existent or ineffective simply because the agreement in which it is contained is found to be invalid, non-existent or ineffective. In this context, the arbitration agreement is treated as a distinct agreement; in other words, an agreement within an agreement. This doctrine is known as the principle of separability.

The practical significance of the doctrine is that the arbitration agreement will survive the 'death' (frustration, repudiation, termination) of the agreement in which it is contained. It will continue to exist so that any disputes arising out of the main contract can be resolved through arbitration.

The doctrine of separability is well established in many jurisdictions and is, by way of example, provided for in the following:

- Section 7 of the English Arbitration Act 1996;
- Section 3 of the Swedish Arbitration Act 1999;
- Article 1447 of the French Code of Civil Procedure;
- Article 357(2) of the Swiss Code of Civil Procedure;
- Section 34 of the Hong Kong Arbitration Ordinance (Cap 609); and
- the Singapore International Arbitration Act, which adopts the Model Law, Article 16 of which enshrines separability.

French law recognises a broader concept of separability within the principle of *autonomie juridique ou de rattachement*. While many jurisdictions recognise that an arbitration agreement can exist independently of the agreement in which it is contained, French law develops this theory further by recognising that the arbitration agreement may also exist independently of any national legal system. This principle is premised on the crucial concept of party autonomy and the belief that the validity of an arbitration agreement in international contracts results solely from the will of the parties (and is independent of any reference to the law of the main contract).

Separability is discussed further below in the context of the tribunal's power to rule on its own jurisdiction.

2. The legal effect of agreeing to arbitration

The concept of party autonomy, which derives from the Model Law,[2] is one of the fundamental principles of international arbitration. It means, essentially, that parties should be free to choose how their disputes are resolved. As such, parties that have agreed to submit their disputes to arbitration are free to do so, and thereby to exclude the jurisdiction of relevant national courts over those disputes. Excluding the jurisdiction of national courts is the principal legal

---

2 See Article 19 of the Model Law: "the parties are free to agree on the procedure to be followed by the arbitral tribunal...". See also Section 1(b) of the English Arbitration Act 1996: "the parties should be free to agree how their disputes are resolved, subject only to such safeguards as are necessary in the public interest". Finally, Article 21 of the ICC Rules 2017: "the parties shall be free to agree upon the rules of law to be applied by the arbitral tribunal to the merits of the dispute."

effect of agreeing to arbitrate and is a natural corollary of party autonomy. Where parties have agreed to arbitrate, the ability of national courts to intervene should be extremely limited.

Article 5 of the Model Law provides that no court (defined as a body or organ of the judicial system of a state) shall intervene in respect of arbitration except as provided for under the Model Law. Similarly, Article 1(c) of the English Arbitration Act 1996 provides that "the court should not intervene except as provided by this Part".

Where a dispute which is subject to an effective arbitration agreement is brought before a national court, that court is therefore required (except in specific circumstances) to uphold the arbitration agreement and decline jurisdiction. The Model Law and various domestic statutes address what the court should do in such circumstances. Article 8(1) of the Model Law provides that:

> *A court before which an action is brought in a matter which is the subject of an arbitration agreement shall…refer the parties to arbitration unless it finds that the agreement is null and void, inoperative or incapable of being performed.*

Article 1448 of the French Code of Civil Procedure provides that:

> *…when a dispute subject to an arbitration agreement is brought before a court, such court shall decline jurisdiction, except if an arbitral tribunal has not yet been seized of the dispute and if the arbitration agreement is manifestly void or manifestly not applicable.*

In English law, Section 9 of the English Arbitration Act 1996 allows a party to an arbitration agreement against which legal proceedings are brought to apply to the court for a stay of those proceedings. The English court will grant this unless it is satisfied that the arbitration agreement in question is null and void, inoperative or incapable of being performed. In order to determine whether a stay is appropriate, the English court must thus determine whether the arbitration agreement is valid. This is different from the approach taken in some other jurisdictions (eg, France and Switzerland) where, provided that there is a *prima facie* case for the existence of an arbitration agreement, the domestic courts will not consider the validity of the arbitration agreement. The issue is then left to be determined by the arbitral tribunal. This approach is founded on the principle of *compétence-compétence,* discussed in the next section, and the belief that an arbitral tribunal should rule on its own jurisdiction.

3. Jurisdiction and an arbitrator's powers

3.1 *Compétence-compétence* and the separability of arbitration agreements

The doctrine of *compétence-compétence* has been developed to ensure the efficiency of arbitral proceedings. It is a recognition of the importance of party autonomy. Its practical effect, as noted above, is that an arbitral tribunal is able itself to determine whether it has jurisdiction to hear the dispute before it, ie, it has the competence to rule on its own competence. Questions as to the validity of arbitration proceedings need not, therefore, generally be referred to domestic courts for consideration, although in most jurisdictions the parties will retain the ultimate ability to challenge any decision on jurisdiction before the courts of the seat.

Cross-reference For more on challenges to awards before national courts, see Chapter 14.

Although not publicly recorded by arbitral institutions, it is generally accepted that challenges to the jurisdiction of arbitral tribunals are relatively common, particularly on the basis that there is no valid arbitration agreement. Such challenges are often brought as a tactical measure to delay proceedings; the fact that the tribunal can consider these challenges itself helps to speed up what might otherwise be a lengthy process.

Article 16(1) of the Model Law provides that:

...[t]he arbitral tribunal may rule on its own jurisdiction, including any objections with respect to the existence or validity of the arbitration agreement. For that purpose, an arbitration clause which forms part of a contract shall be treated as an agreement independent of the other terms of the contract. A decision by the arbitral tribunal that the contract is null and void shall not entail ipso jure the invalidity of the arbitration clause.

It is notable that the power conferred on the tribunal to rule on its own jurisdiction in the Model Law is not subject to the parties' agreement. It is therefore bestowed upon the tribunal in all cases. This approach is mirrored in some of the most commonly used arbitration rules. For example, Rule 28(2) of the Singapore International Arbitration Centre (SIAC) Rules 2016 provides:

...[t]he Tribunal shall have the power to rule on its own jurisdiction, including any objections with respect to the existence, validity or scope of the arbitration agreement. An arbitration agreement which forms part of a contract shall be treated as an agreement independent of the other terms of the contract. A decision by the Tribunal that the contract is null and void shall not entail ipso jure the invalidity of the arbitration agreement, and the Tribunal shall not cease to have jurisdiction by reason of any allegation that the contract is non-existent or null and void.

The ICC Rules 2017 provide for a similar approach (Article 6) as do the 2014 London Court of International Arbitration (LCIA) Rules (Article 23).

In English law, the position is slightly different. The competence of the tribunal to rule on its own jurisdiction is enshrined in Section 30 of the English Arbitration Act 1996. In a departure from the Model Law, Section 30(1) of the Arbitration Act begins with the phrase "[u]nless otherwise agreed by the parties...". It is clear from this that the parties may agree to vary and/or exclude the tribunal's powers in this regard. This is, however, extremely rare in practice.

The remainder of Section 30(1) sets out what specifically the tribunal can rule on, namely:

- whether there is a valid arbitration agreement;
- whether the tribunal is properly constituted; and
- what matters have been submitted to arbitration in accordance with the arbitration agreement.

The above are examples of provisions that can be found in varying forms in many jurisdictions' arbitration laws (both legislation and case law) and in institutional rules. It can also be seen from these examples that the concepts of separability and *compétence-compétence* go hand in hand: not only can an arbitral tribunal rule on any issue relating to its substantial jurisdiction, including a dispute as to whether the contract which contains the arbitration clause is valid, but in addition a finding that the contract is null and void will not ordinarily invalidate the arbitration agreement or the tribunal's jurisdiction.

Cross-reference For a detailed discussion on the structure of jurisdiction hearings and bifurcation of jurisdiction and merits, see Chapter 6.

3.2 Sources of arbitrators' powers

An arbitral tribunal's powers come from three main sources:

- the arbitration agreement between the parties;
- the arbitration rules applicable to the arbitration; and
- any applicable national laws.

These establish the basis of the tribunal's jurisdiction and also determine the scope of its procedural powers.

The parties to an arbitration are generally free to agree what procedural powers they want to confer upon the tribunal. This is another key aspect of international arbitration that upholds the important principle of party autonomy. It is important to note, however, that the parties' freedom to agree the procedural framework for their arbitration may be limited by any mandatory rules contained in the procedural law of the seat of the arbitration. An example of one such mandatory provision can be found in Section 33(1) of the English Arbitration Act 1996. This imposes a duty on the tribunal first to:

...act fairly and impartially between the parties, giving each party a reasonable opportunity of putting his case and dealing with that of his opponent.

Second to:

...adopt procedures suitable to the circumstances of a particular case, avoiding unnecessary delay or expense, so as to provide a fair means for the resolution of the matters falling to be determined.

While most jurisdictions recognise that arbitrators should afford parties equal treatment and a fair opportunity to put their case, not all include a requirement for expediency. Examples of rules which do require expediency and efficiency include:

- Stockholm Chamber of Commerce (SCC) Rules 2017: the institution, tribunal and parties are to act in an efficient and expeditious manner throughout the proceedings (Article 2(1)).
- Vienna International Arbitral Centre (VIAC) Rules 2018: both the tribunal and the parties are under an express obligation to conduct proceedings in an efficient and cost-effective manner, with tribunals expressly permitted to take the contribution by the parties in this regard into consideration in their decisions on costs (Articles 16.6, 28.1 and 38).
- German Arbitration Institute (DIS) Rules 2018: at every stage, the tribunal is to seek to encourage an amicable settlement (Article 26) and in a time- and cost-efficient manner (Article 27.1). Efficiency is also promoted through a requirement to discuss certain issues during the case management conference following the constitution of the tribunal.
- ICC Rules 2017: the tribunal and parties are to make every effort to conduct the arbitration "in an expeditious and cost-effective manner, having regard to the complexity and value of the dispute."

The first place to look to establish what powers the tribunal possesses is the arbitration agreement. Without an agreement to arbitrate, there will be no jurisdiction and the tribunal will lack any power to hear the dispute before it. In some instances, the arbitration agreement itself will prescribe specific provisions regarding which procedures are to be adopted in the arbitral proceedings. This is particularly common in cases where the agreement has been entered into after a dispute has arisen. The parties will then tailor the procedure accordingly. More usually, however, the parties will agree the procedural framework after the arbitration agreement has been concluded – often in the course of proceedings.

The tribunal may also derive powers from any arbitral rules which the parties have agreed will apply to their dispute. Where parties have agreed to adopt a set of rules, they are effectively treated as being read into the arbitration agreement, and thus constitute an agreement between the parties as to content of those rules. They can also operate to vary any default provisions of the relevant national law (to the extent possible), such as in English law excluding the right to appeal an award on a point of English law under Section 69 of the English Arbitration Act 1996. It is therefore important, when reviewing the arbitration agreement, to note which (if any) institutional rules apply, and to review those rules in order to assess what the tribunal can and cannot do. Most arbitration rules bestow broad procedural powers on the arbitrators. A good example of the types of procedural powers which a tribunal possesses can be found in the detailed procedural provisions of the LCIA Rules 2014 which deal with hearings (Article 19), witnesses (Article 20), experts (Article 21) and so on.

Cross-reference A brief analysis of the major institutional rules can be found in Chapter 2; more information on the procedure of arbitral proceedings can be found in Chapter 9.

When the arbitration agreement and applicable rules are silent on a particular issue, it will be necessary to consider the applicable law of the seat of arbitration (or '*lex arbitri*') to determine whether a certain act is within the tribunal's powers. This is the case particularly in *ad hoc* arbitrations. As noted above, it is important to take account of any national mandatory rules which cannot be contracted out of and which will limit the parties' freedom to control the procedure of the arbitration.

TIP The mandatory provisions of the English Arbitration Act 1996 are listed in Schedule 1 to the English Arbitration Act 1996. Any provision which states that it applies "unless otherwise agreed by the parties" is non-mandatory.

4. Arbitrability

There is no internationally recognised standard as to which disputes are, and are not, capable of being referred to arbitration. Generally speaking, disputes that are of a commercial nature can be referred to arbitration. It is not, however, correct to say that all matters can be arbitrated, and there is significant academic debate on the question of arbitrability. For the purposes of this practical guide to arbitration, however, it is necessary only to appreciate that there are some disputes which it will not be appropriate to arbitrate, and to note that certain jurisdictions prescribe what may and may not be referred to arbitration. By way of example, Article 2059 of the French Civil Code provides that "[a]ny person may submit to arbitration the rights of which he has full disposition" (emphasis added). Article 2060 gives examples of rights of which a party does not have full disposition, including, for example, disputes relating to the civil status or capacity of a person, or disputes relative to divorce or legal separation.

In 2016, the Russian Federation sought to address some uncertainties with regard to what types of dispute may be arbitrated in that jurisdiction. Whilst the Russian Courts had previously held that corporate disputes are not arbitrable, the 2016 updates to Russia's law on arbitration partially removed the non-arbitrable status of corporate disputes in Russia on the condition that the arbitration is seated in Russia and the arbitration agreement is unanimously approved in the company's articles of association. The 2016 updates also provided a list of certain types of corporate disputes which remained non-arbitrable, including those concerning "strategic" Russian companies, bankruptcy, class actions and disputes relating to public issues such as employment and taxation.

In contrast, in the United States, the US Federal Arbitration Act does not place any limits on what disputes may be resolved through arbitration. The English law definition of an 'arbitration agreement' covers references to arbitration of disputes, whether contractual or not. However, it does not go any further in setting out what matters are and are not arbitrable. Yet it is generally accepted that, as a matter of English law, issues which give rise to public (rather than private) rights are incapable of arbitration. This is seemingly on the basis that the public interest in the subject matter of the dispute warrants examination in public by the national courts and renders resolution in the private (and confidential) forum of arbitration inappropriate. It is also not possible to arbitrate disputes relating to rights which have been granted by statute and affect the rights of third parties – for example, the Employment Rights Act 1996 and the Equality Act 2010.

The parameters of arbitrability in England and Wales have been developed in case law. It has been held, for example, that bankruptcy proceedings and petitions for the winding up of insolvent corporations are not arbitrable. Criminal prosecutions, divorce and the grant or validity of a patent and trademark (but not necessarily disputes concerning the licence of a patent or trademark) have also been determined as being inappropriate for resolution by arbitration.

It is important to recognise that while most commercial disputes are arbitrable, some are better suited to other dispute resolution mechanisms. If the parties to a dispute are essentially seeking a commercial, rather than legal, decision, for example, it may be more appropriate to specify a form of expert determination rather than arbitration. An example of such a situation would be where a deadlock provision is sought in a corporate joint venture agreement: expert determination by experienced businessmen might be a more efficient way to resolve the issue than commercial arbitration. In particular, if the dispute related to particular accounting matters, such as the correct preparation of completion accounts or the valuation of assets in a sale and purchase agreement, it may be more appropriate to provide for expert determination by a qualified accountant.

Cross-reference

For more on other types of dispute resolution methods, see Chapter 1.

4. Drafting arbitration clauses

1. Essential matters to include in an arbitration clause

In an arbitration clause, the parties should always:

- select a seat;
- consider whether they wish to select the rules of an arbitral institution or have an *ad hoc* arbitration;
- consider the number of arbitrators (and their appointment method);
- choose the language of the arbitration; and
- choose a law to govern the arbitration clause.

Although it is technically separate from the arbitration clause itself, the parties should always include provisions on governing law for the substantive contract.

1.1 Governing law

(a) The law governing the substantive contract

All contracts should include a governing law clause. This determines the rights and obligations of the parties under that contract. If it is omitted, any subsequent contractual dispute may well begin with a lengthy and expensive argument over the appropriate applicable law.

Parties are generally free to choose which law should apply to a contract, subject to certain limitations. For instance, under the Rome I Regulation (EC) No 593/2008 on the law applicable to contractual obligations (the 'Rome I Regulation') – which applies in all EU member states (except Denmark) to all contracts concluded after 17 December 2009 – the court must (in addition to the chosen governing law) apply any rules which cannot be derogated from by agreement under the laws of the country in which all elements relevant to the contract are located. Any overriding mandatory provisions of the forum must also be applied. Parties' freedom to choose which law should apply to a contract is also often restricted in relation to insurance, employment, consumer and passenger contracts.

It is also recommended that parties agree in advance on the governing law for non-contractual obligations. The Rome II Regulation (EC) No 864/2007 on the law applicable to non-contractual obligations (the 'Rome II Regulation') – which applies in all EU member states (except Denmark) since 11 January 2009 – allows parties to agree the law governing certain non-contractual obligations subject to certain overriding rules. This agreement can be reached after a dispute arises, or beforehand if the agreement is 'freely negotiated' and the parties are engaged in 'commercial activity'. Non-contractual obligations are widely defined and include tort and restitutionary claims, but not personal-type claims such as defamation.

TIP The following suggested clause sets out the parties' choice of law in respect of both contractual and non-contractual obligations: "This Agreement [and any non-contractual obligations arising out of or in connection with it] will be governed by [ ] law."

Choosing the governing law can be difficult. For contracts involving parties based in the same country and/or where the subject matter of the contract relates to a specific country, it is usual to start on the basis that the law of that country should apply. However, the parties may choose a law unrelated to any or all of the contracting parties. Laws that are frequently chosen include those of England and Wales, New York and Switzerland, since they are well developed and generally considered suitable for commercial transactions.

In addition, where arbitration is to be the chosen dispute resolution form, the parties can specify a non-state law, for example Shariah law, Jewish law or the law of a particular country supplemented by principles of international law, *lex mercatoria* and so on. They may also allow the arbitrator/tribunal to assume the powers of an '*amicable compositeur*' or to determine the dispute on an '*ex aequo et bono*' basis – both of these mean that the dispute is to be determined based on principles of fairness and equity, rather than any particular law. It should be borne in mind that specifying a non-state law or allowing the arbitral tribunal to assume the powers of an *amicable compositeur* remains controversial and in certain countries might not be enforceable. However, this practice is not uncommon in certain insurance-related arbitrations.

(b) The law governing the arbitration agreement

The law governing the arbitration agreement plays an important role in determining how the arbitration agreement should be interpreted. In many jurisdictions the arbitration clause is deemed to be a separate agreement from the contract in which it is found. This means that the arbitration clause can be governed by one law (such as the law applicable at the legal seat) while the rest of the contract is governed by a different law.

In order to avoid any ambiguity about which law applies to the arbitration agreement, the parties should make an express choice of law to govern their arbitration clause.

1.2 Legal seat

(a) *What is the legal seat of the arbitration?*

The 'seat' is where the arbitration is considered to be legally based. However, hearings may take place elsewhere if the parties agree. It is entirely separate and may well differ from the substantive governing law of the underlying contract. Parties often select a seat in a 'neutral' location where neither party is based.

As set out in Chapter 2, the Convention on the Recognition and Enforcement of Foreign Arbitral Awards 1958 (the 'New York Convention') commits signatory states to enforcing arbitral awards made elsewhere. However, there are limited exceptions. One of these is that many signatory states have agreed that an award will be enforceable in their jurisdiction only if the seat of the arbitration is also in a New York Convention signatory state. It is therefore usually essential to choose a seat in a New York Convention contracting state.

TIP Popular choices of seat in New York Convention countries include London, Paris, Stockholm, New York, Geneva, Zurich, Brussels, The Hague, Dublin, the Dubai International Financial Centre, Singapore, Vienna and Hong Kong. These seats are popular because they are in arbitration-friendly jurisdictions; that is, they have adopted arbitration legislation that supports the arbitration process and restricts judicial interference as far as possible.

(b) *Matters to consider when selecting the seat of the arbitration*

The choice of seat is important, as it decides:

- Which country's law governs the procedural aspects of the arbitration. This includes questions of day-to-day procedure in the absence of agreement between the parties (eg, where the arbitration rules that may have been selected by the parties are silent on specific issues – see below).
- The extent to which an award may be challenged or appealed (again, determined by the legislative framework of the seat of the arbitration). For instance, if the seat is in England and Wales, a limited right of appeal to the court on a point of substantive English law is available, but is usually excluded. Such right of appeal does not exist, however, in countries such as France or Switzerland. Indeed, if the seat of the arbitration is located in these countries it is, in certain circumstances, possible for the parties to fully waive the right to challenge arbitral awards.
- How far the local courts can assist or intervene in the arbitral proceedings. Some jurisdictions, such as England and Wales, are more prepared to

intervene on issues such as allowing the parties to obtain interim relief from the local courts or determining questions of jurisdiction. Others, such as France or Switzerland, ordinarily require such issues to be determined by the tribunal (at least in the first instance).

- The enforceability of any award. As mentioned above, an award will, in many cases, be enforceable under the New York Convention only if the seat of the arbitration is in a New York Convention contracting state.

The Chartered Institute of Arbitrators has developed a series of ten elements, called the 'London Principles', to help parties evaluate potential legal seats. They incorporate factors which are both legal and practical, including:

- an arbitration law providing a good framework for the process, limiting court intervention and striking the right balance between confidentiality and transparency;
- an independent, competent and efficient judiciary with expertise in international arbitration;
- an independent competent legal profession with expertise in international arbitration;
- an implemented commitment to the education of counsel, arbitrators, judiciary, experts, users and students of the character and autonomy of international arbitration, and to its future development;
- a clear right for parties to be represented by representatives of their choice, whether from inside or outside the legal seat;
- accessibility to the seat for parties, witnesses and counsel, and adequate safety and protection of the participants, their documentation and information;
- functional facilities for the provision of services to international arbitration (including transcription services, hearing rooms and translation services);
- professional norms which embrace a diversity of legal and cultural traditions, and the developing norms of international ethical principles governing the behaviour of arbitrators and counsel;
- adherence to treaties for the recognition and enforcement of foreign awards and arbitration agreements; and
- a clear right to arbitrator immunity from civil liability for anything done or omitted to be done by the arbitrator in good faith in their capacity as an arbitrator.

1.3 Choosing institutional or *ad hoc* arbitration

(a) What is institutional arbitration?

Institutional arbitration does not mean choosing an institution to determine the dispute. It typically means choosing the rules of arbitration of an institution which will administer and support the arbitral process in accordance with those rules, regardless of the seat.

Many arbitral institutions (eg, the International Chamber of Commerce (ICC), the London Court of International Arbitration (LCIA)) are well respected and their rules have been derived by arbitrators and users following many years of experience in handling arbitrations.

Cross-reference A *précis* of each of the major arbitral institutions is set out in Chapter 2.

It should also be noted that choosing institutional arbitration (and subscribing to any set of rules) does not displace the legislative framework of the seat. Often, they supplement it. Some rules may replace those in the legislation (to the extent that they can be excluded or varied) – for example, the LCIA Rules automatically exclude the right to appeal on a question of law under the English Arbitration Act 1996 and set out a default timetable for written pleadings.

In some countries, such as China, *ad hoc* arbitration is not recognised, and so it is essential to choose institutional arbitration.

Advantages: The main advantage of institutional arbitration is the support provided by the institution if things go wrong. For instance, if the tribunal is not being responsive, the institution will be able to contact and put pressure on the arbitral tribunal.

Choosing institutional rules will, to a degree, prevent parties from engaging in certain delaying tactics. Examples include where a party refuses to appoint or seeks to challenge an arbitrator. In the former case, most institutional rules provide that the arbitrator will be appointed by the institution (eg, the ICC or the LCIA Court). Likewise, institutions usually deal promptly with challenges to arbitrators. Without institutional support, parties may have to refer to the local courts to deal with appointments or challenges, which may be time consuming and costly.

Most arbitral institutions will have a list of experienced arbitrators from which they will be able to draw if parties fail to agree on the identity of any of the arbitrators themselves.

Some institutions review awards before publishing them, ensuring award writing that is of a high standard and procedurally compliant. An award from an institution will also benefit from the reputation and standing of that institution, which may help with its enforcement.

In an attempt to speed up the enforcement process, many institutional rules exclude appeals as much as possible.

Finally, the costs of institutional arbitration might be easier to predict than in *ad hoc* arbitration (see Chapter 13).

Disadvantages: There are few disadvantages to institutional arbitration. The main criticism is cost. Institutional arbitration is sometimes considered more expensive than *ad hoc* arbitration because the parties have to pay for the institution's administrative expenses. However, these are usually modest compared to the fees and expenses of the arbitrators and the parties' legal expenses (mainly lawyers' fees). The advantages of choosing institutional arbitration are generally considered to far outweigh the downside of this additional cost.

Cross-reference More on how fees and expenses are dealt with in institutional arbitrations can be found in Chapter 13.

(b) *What is* ad hoc *arbitration?*

Ad hoc arbitration does not subscribe to any institution. It may subscribe to a set of rules, for example, the United Nations Commission on International Trade Law (UNCITRAL), or it may rely on the legislative framework of the seat of the arbitration, enabling the parties to determine their own rules, usually together with the arbitral tribunal. This does not mean, however, that parties cannot later choose to apply a set of rules, or that an institutional arbitration is inflexible. If the parties to an *ad hoc* arbitration require support during the proceedings, they will need to apply to the tribunal and/or the local courts.

Some sectors – such as shipping (London Maritime Arbitrators Association (LMAA)), construction (Construction Industry Model Arbitration (CIMAR)) and commodities (Federation of Oils, Seeds and Fats Association (FOSFA) and London Metal Exchange (LME)) – have adapted *ad hoc* procedures that are commonly used and are preferable in those areas to institutional rules. These are not institutional but are backed by trade association bodies.

Advantages: The main perceived advantage of *ad hoc* arbitration is cost. Because the parties are not appointing an institution to administer the arbitration, they can save the cost of paying its administrative charges.

Ad hoc arbitration can be a very efficient way to resolve disputes, provided that:

- the arbitration agreement is well drafted – for example, it states where the seat will be located, includes an appointing authority (see below), and sets out the arbitration procedure or refers to a set of rules designed for *ad hoc* arbitration, the most famous being the UNCITRAL Rules;
- the parties cooperate during the arbitration and do not use delaying tactics (see below); and
- an experienced arbitral tribunal is appointed, whose members are used to dealing with arbitration proceedings.

However, there are a number of potential disadvantages to *ad hoc* arbitration.

Disadvantages: The main disadvantage is the lack of institutional support. If the parties are unable to agree on the appointment of the arbitral tribunal, they will have to rely on the local courts to do this. This can be costly and time consuming. Local courts will also not have the same knowledge and experience in the selection of arbitrators as an arbitral institution, meaning that the individual(s) selected might not be suitable to the dispute (eg, due to a lack of relevant skills or experience). To avoid this problem, parties often nominate an 'appointing authority' in their arbitration agreement. If the arbitration is governed by the UNCITRAL Rules, for example, the appointing authority will be the Secretary-General of the Permanent Court of Arbitration at The Hague, unless the parties select otherwise.

TIP Including an appointing authority in an *ad hoc* arbitration clause can help to reduce the time and costs involved in the event of a disagreement between the parties on the appointment of the tribunal, because the appointing authority will resolve such disputes and thus avoid the need for the parties to apply to the local courts.

In an *ad hoc* arbitration a recalcitrant party may use delaying tactics such as challenging one or more members of the arbitral tribunal. As stated above, such challenges are usually dealt with quickly by an arbitral institution. Bringing the challenge before the local courts wastes more time and money than if the challenge had been dealt with by an efficient and experienced arbitration institution. Again, choosing an appointing authority can help to avoid these problems.

While *ad hoc* arbitration is sometimes considered cheaper than institutional arbitration, it may in fact end up more expensive. As detailed above, a recalcitrant party is more likely to be able to use delaying tactics such as challenging the arbitral tribunal or refusing to appoint or agree to an arbitrator. Furthermore, an institutional arbitration usually fixes the fees and expenses of the arbitral tribunal according to the rules of the institution. In *ad hoc* arbitration, the tribunal fixes its own costs, making them less predictable.

Finally, awards made in *ad hoc* arbitration will not be scrutinised by an institution, thereby increasing the risk of them being poorly drafted and thus susceptible to being set aside.

1.4 Choosing arbitral rules

As stated above, the major arbitral institutions that are generally recommended include the ICC, the LCIA, Swiss Rules, the Singapore International Arbitration

Centre (SIAC), the Hong Kong International Arbitration Centre (HKIAC) Administered Rules, the Stockholm Chamber of Commerce (SCC) and the Dubai International Financial Centre (DIFC). Their rules are frequently revised to take into account developments in international arbitration practice. The HKIAC, for example, revised its administered arbitration rules in 2013, the LCIA revised its rules in 2014, the SIAC revised its rules in 2016, and the ICC's new arbitration rules came into force on 1 March 2017. Institutional rules are modified to reflect current arbitral practices, to respond to developments in international arbitration and to adapt to the changing needs of the international business community.

For *ad hoc* arbitration, the most famous rules are those designed by UNCITRAL. Like the institutional rules mentioned above, the UNCITRAL Rules have been revised to respond to developments in international arbitration. They were last amended in 2013, following more wide-ranging revisions in 2010, and are under constant review.

1.5 How many arbitrators?

An arbitral tribunal will usually consist of one or three arbitrators, depending on what the parties have agreed.

Most arbitration rules and legislation provide for a default position in case the parties have not made a choice in this respect. Thus, under Article 12(2) of the 2017 ICC Rules, where the parties have not agreed upon the number of arbitrators, the ICC Court of Arbitration will appoint a sole arbitrator "save where it appears to the [ICC] Court that the dispute is such as to warrant the appointment of three arbitrators". Likewise, under Article 5(8) of the LCIA Rules, a sole arbitrator will be appointed unless the LCIA Court determines that a three-member tribunal is appropriate. In contrast, Article 7.1 of the UNCITRAL Rules provides that if the parties have not agreed that there will be only one arbitrator, three will be appointed.

TIP The current practice in the ICC is that one arbitrator will generally be appointed for any dispute worth US$20 million or less, and three for disputes over US$20 million or other complex disputes. This is worth bearing in mind if you are making submissions to argue for the appointment of either one or three arbitrators based on the complexity of the issue at hand.

Appointing a sole arbitrator minimises the costs of the arbitration, as only one arbitrator's fees must be paid. It also tends to reduce the length of an arbitration as it does not require three people all to be available at the same time and come to a decision between them. Where a short timetable may be needed, the amount at stake is unlikely to be large or the issues not complex, it may be advisable to provide for the appointment of a sole arbitrator.

However, the general trend in international arbitration is to appoint three arbitrators, except where the sum in issue does not justify it. Generally, each party appoints one arbitrator and either those two arbitrators choose the presiding arbitrator or an institution may do so, depending on the parties' decision set out in the arbitration agreement or any particular institutional rules to which the parties have chosen to subscribe. If each party has appointed an arbitrator, this will contribute to a feeling of confidence in the tribunal. Where there are more than two parties, they will be divided into two sides – claimant and respondent – for the purpose of nominating one arbitrator for each side. Where this fails (eg, because two different sides cannot be identified or the members of the different sides are unable to agree upon a common choice of arbitrators), the arbitral institution will usually nominate all three arbitrators. In an international arbitration, each of the parties and the members of the tribunal may come from different legal backgrounds and cultures, and even speak different languages. A party-appointed arbitrator, while remaining impartial, should be able to ensure that his or her appointing party's position is properly understood by the other members of the tribunal.

Cross-reference

More on how to choose an appropriate arbitrator is set out in Chapter 7.

1.6 Language of the arbitration

Unless the parties are based in the same country or come from countries where the same language is spoken, choosing the language of the arbitration in the arbitration clause can be crucial. This will often be the same as the language of the contract. The language of the arbitration will be essential in determining who can or cannot be selected as an arbitrator, as it is highly desirable for him or her to be fluent in that language. The choice of language(s) will normally apply to the various statements of case, written submissions and written statements filed during the proceedings, as well as any oral hearings that may take place.

Most arbitral institutions include a provision regarding the language of the arbitration in their recommended clauses. Where the language of the arbitration has not previously been selected, most arbitration rules allow the tribunal to choose it.

If during the proceedings a document is submitted which is expressed in a language other than that of the arbitration, the arbitral tribunal will usually have the power to order for a translation to be provided. Some arbitration rules expressly provide for this, including the LCIA Rules (Article 17.5), the AAA International Arbitration Rules (Article 18) and the UNCITRAL Rules (Article 19.2).

2. Optional matters to include in an arbitration clause

Parties often use the model arbitration clauses recommended by well-known arbitration institutions such as the ICC or the LCIA. These clauses have been drafted carefully by arbitration specialists with considerable experience in international arbitration matters. They may even have been tried and tested before national courts. This means that they are likely to be valid in most countries. However, this 'one size fits all' approach does not necessarily suit all parties, who may wish to adapt the recommended clauses to their needs.

2.1 Hybrid or optional dispute resolution clauses

If the contract includes an arbitration clause, it should not ordinarily contain a court jurisdiction clause too. Hybrid or optional dispute resolution clauses, however, give one or both parties (respectively 'sole' and 'mutual' option clauses) the right to choose between arbitration and litigation. The rationale behind this type of clause is that it gives parties the ability to choose the most appropriate forum for resolving a dispute after it has arisen. However, these clauses have been subject to greater scrutiny in recent years as the courts in several jurisdictions have held them to be unenforceable.

(a) Sole option clauses

A sole option clause gives only one of the parties the option to choose between arbitration or litigation. Occasionally, certain parties (in particular, banks and financial institutions) insist upon retaining the option to litigate so that if the dispute relates to a simple debt claim they will be able to turn to a speedier or summary judgment procedure that may be available in the local courts, and so obtain a quick resolution.

Most sole option clauses provide that the default mechanism is litigation, but give one party (eg, a bank) the option to choose arbitration. A clause providing for arbitration with an option for one party to litigate is less common.

Under English law, a sole option clause is valid as long as it is clear and unequivocal, and the party with the right to exercise the option does not lead the other party to believe that the option will not be exercised. The option can be exercised by the party to which it was granted both as claimant and as defendant. This type of clause does not, however, appear to be valid in some jurisdictions. For instance, whilst some US Courts have upheld sole option clauses, others have found that such one-sided agreements may be unconscionable, oppressive and thereby unenforceable. The Russian and Chinese courts may refuse to recognise any arbitration clause which contains an option to litigate and refuse to enforce any foreign arbitration award made pursuant to such a clause. Courts and lawyers in other jurisdictions (such as Poland, Saudi Arabia and Turkey) have also questioned the enforceability of these clauses.

The variation in treatment of sole option clauses by national courts has received wide-spread attention. If the counterparty is in a jurisdiction where the enforceability of these clauses may be challenged, or if the counterparty does not have sufficient assets outside such a jurisdiction, sole option clauses should normally be avoided.

Unilateral arbitration clause – litigation as default, arbitration as an option: The following sets out an example of a unilateral arbitration clause:

> *[Subject to [ADR],] all the parties irrevocably agree that any dispute arising out of or connected with this Agreement, including a dispute as to the validity or existence of this Agreement and/or this clause [number], shall be resolved:*
>
> *(a) by proceedings brought in the courts of [England], which courts are to have exclusive jurisdiction; or*
>
> *(b) at the sole option of [contracting party having the benefit] by arbitration in [seat] conducted in [language] by a [single] arbitrator [see Number of Arbitrators].*
>
> *For the avoidance of doubt, clause [[number](b)] is for the benefit of [the contracting party having the benefit] alone.*
>
> *In the event that court proceedings have been brought by [contracting party not having the benefit] prior to or at the time when [contracting party having the benefit] elects to submit the dispute to arbitration in accordance with clause [[number](b)] above, then [contracting party not having the benefit] shall immediately take all necessary steps to discontinue such court proceedings.*

Unilateral litigation clause – arbitration as default, litigation as an option: It should be noted that if a party with a sole option to litigate starts arbitration proceedings, or participates sufficiently in an arbitration brought by the other side, it will normally be considered to have waived its right to litigation. The dispute will then be determined by arbitration.

The following sets out an example of an arbitration clause with an option to litigate:

> *[Subject to [ADR],] all the parties irrevocably agree that any dispute arising out of or connected with this Agreement, including a dispute as to the validity or existence of this Agreement and/or this clause [number], shall be resolved:*
>
> *(a) by arbitration in [seat] conducted in [language] by a [single arbitrator] [see Number of Arbitrators]; or*
>
> *(b) at the sole option of [contracting party having the benefit] by proceedings brought in the courts of [England], which courts are to have exclusive jurisdiction.*
>
> *For the avoidance of doubt, clause [[number](b)] is for the benefit of [the contracting party having the benefit] alone.*

(b) *Mutual option clauses*

A mutual option clause usually allows both parties to agree to submit their disputes to arbitration but each retain the option, in certain circumstances, to bring proceedings in the courts of a specified jurisdiction. It may also allow all disputes to be litigated, with an option for either party to commence arbitration proceedings. Mutual option clauses can trigger forum races in instances where it may be advantageous for one party to have the dispute heard in court, or in a particular jurisdiction. They are, as such, quite unpredictable in nature and run the risk of parallel proceedings. The general view is that this type of clause should be avoided.

2.2 Consolidation of related proceedings and joinder of third parties

Due to its consensual nature, one of the downsides of arbitration is that arbitral tribunals, unlike the courts, often have limited powers to consolidate arbitration proceedings or join third parties to them. In most cases, the arbitral tribunal will be unable to do either without the consent of all the parties involved (including the third parties).

By selecting certain arbitration rules, the parties agree in advance that the arbitral tribunal will be authorised to consolidate related arbitration proceedings in certain circumstances, such as where the arbitration proceedings to be consolidated are between the same parties and/or are being conducted pursuant to the same arbitration agreement.[1] Likewise, some arbitration rules give the arbitral tribunal the power to order, or the arbitral institution to decide, that third parties be joined in limited cases – for example, provided that the party making an application to join the third party and the third party have both consented in writing;[2] or provided that the third party is *prima facie* bound by the arbitration agreement.[3]

Rather than relying on the limited provisions set out in arbitration rules, the parties sometimes prefer to include specific provisions on joinder or consolidation in their contracts. This is the case where, for instance, a number of separate but related/associated contracts are negotiated and the parties would like to be able to consolidate disputes arising under both the 'main' and associated contract(s). In this case, a key consideration will be that all parties have agreed in advance to the proceedings being consolidated. Consolidation will, however, not always be appropriate, such as when the first arbitration is too far advanced.

A suggested provision is as follows:

[Insert standard e.g. ICC or LCIA arbitration clause here]

Where disputes arise under this Contract and under any of the [Associated

---

1 See, for example, Article 15 of the SCC Rules, Article 10 of the ICC Rules and Article 4.1 of the Swiss Rules.

2 See, for example, Article 22.1(viii) of the LCIA Rules.

3 See, for example, Article 7.1(a) of the SIAC Rules and Articles 6.4(i) and 7 of the ICC Rules.

Contracts] which, in the [reasonable opinion/absolute discretion] of the first [arbitrator/arbitral tribunal] to be appointed in any of the disputes, are so closely connected that it is expedient for them to be resolved in the same proceedings, that [arbitrator/arbitral tribunal] shall have the power to order that the proceedings to resolve that dispute shall be consolidated with those to resolve any of the other disputes (whether or not proceedings to resolve those other disputes have yet been instituted), provided that no date for [exchange of witness statements/the final hearing of the first arbitration] has been fixed. If so ordered, the parties to each dispute which is a subject of such order shall be treated as having consented to that dispute being finally decided:

(i) by the [arbitrator/arbitral tribunal] who ordered the consolidation unless the [LCIA/ICC etc] decides that [he/they] would not be suitable or impartial; and

(ii) in accordance with the procedure, at the seat and in the language specified in the arbitration agreement in the contract under which the arbitrator who ordered the consolidation was appointed, save as otherwise agreed by all parties to the consolidated proceedings or, in the absence of such agreement, ordered by the [arbitrator/arbitral tribunal] in the consolidated proceedings.[4]

Alternatively, one party only (with strong bargaining power) might be given the option to consolidate, as follows:

Where a dispute arises under this Contract and a dispute arises out of, in connection with or relating to any [Associated Contract(s)] and [party A] by written notice to [party B] and to the [party/ies to Associated Contract(s)] elects that the proceedings to resolve all of these dispute(s) shall be consolidated (whether or not proceedings to resolve those disputes have yet been instituted), the parties to each dispute which is a subject of [party A]'s written notice (including for the avoidance of doubt [party B]) shall be treated as having consented to that dispute being finally decided:

(i) by the Arbitral Tribunal appointed under this Contract; and

(ii) in accordance with the procedure, at the seat and in the language specified in the arbitration agreement in this Contract, save as otherwise agreed by all parties to the consolidated proceedings or, in the absence of such agreement, ordered by the Arbitral Tribunal in the consolidated proceedings.[5]

2.3 Escalation clauses

Escalation clauses can incorporate several different combinations or tiers of dispute resolution options. These may include, for instance, a meeting of senior representatives of each party followed by mediation and then arbitration. They

---

4 This clause needs to be repeated mutatis mutandis in any associated contract so that the parties to the other contract(s) also consent to this arrangement; that is, they consent to the dispute under the associated contract being resolved by the tribunal that is appointed under the main contract.

5 As above, this clause needs to be repeated *mutatis mutandis* in any associated contract so that the parties to the other contract(s) also consent to this arrangement.

are increasingly popular in commercial contracts as a way of controlling disputes and costs. However, in the absence of agreement and/or good faith, they may simply delay the start of a conclusive formal procedure.

A binding escalation procedure can often help to resolve disputes without any party needing to resort to arbitration. However, it is potentially risky to use mandatory or binding escalation provisions in contracts in which arbitration is the ultimate dispute resolution mechanism. This is because there is a concern, at least if English law applies to the arbitration agreement, that a mandatory or binding escalation provision (eg, mediation) could be construed as a condition precedent to arbitration. If this is the case, failure to comply fully with a mandatory or binding escalation provision may lead to the validity of the referral to arbitration being challenged at a later stage.

The parties should therefore ensure that the route to accessing arbitration does not require the various steps in the escalation provision to be undertaken or completed before arbitration can start. This can be achieved by using one of the following suggested clauses:

> *The commencement of a [mediation] shall not prevent the parties commencing or continuing arbitration proceedings.*
>
> Or:
>
> *Without prejudice to clause [reference to ADR/escalation clauses above], any dispute shall be finally resolved by arbitration in accordance with the following procedure [...].*

Cross-reference More on escalation clauses is set out in Chapter 5.

2.4 Arbitrators' qualifications

One advantage of arbitration is that the parties can select arbitrators who are expert in the field in dispute. While parties often choose legally trained individuals who are experienced in dealing with international arbitration disputes, it is not unusual, for example, for engineers or accountants to be selected.

Arbitration rules do not generally require arbitrators to have specific qualifications. For instance, Article 13.1 of the ICC Rules requires only that the ICC Court consider the prospective arbitrators' ability to conduct the arbitration in accordance with the ICC Rules. Article 12.4 of the AAA Rules refers only to 'suitable arbitrators', while Article 13.2 of the SIAC Rules requires the chair, when making an appointment, to pay due regard to any qualifications required of the arbitrator by the agreement of the parties.

TIP Some specialist arbitration rules such as the LME Arbitration Rules and Regulations require that only members of its panel (who, in the context of the LME panel, are all required to demonstrate substantial experience within the metals trade) may be selected as arbitrators.

Two suggestions for a clause specifying the qualification(s) of arbitrator(s) are as follows:

[Each arbitrator][The presiding arbitrator] shall be [a lawyer/an accountant, etc].

Or:

[Each arbitrator][The presiding arbitrator] shall have experience in [specific industry].

2.5 Nationality of arbitrators appointed

In international arbitration where three arbitrators are to be appointed and the parties are of different nationalities, it is common for each to select an arbitrator who is a national of its own country. In this case, it is desirable to appoint a 'neutral' chair who should not have the same nationality as any party. Likewise, where a sole arbitrator is to be appointed it is also usually preferable that he or she does not have the same nationality as any party.

A number of arbitration rules already provide for this, including Article 6.1 of the LCIA Rules and Article 13.5 of the ICC Rules.

If the parties want no arbitrator to be of the same nationality as any party, the following wording could be inserted into the arbitration clause: "No arbitrator shall be of the same nationality as any party."

2.6 Evidence and procedure

One advantage of international arbitration is the flexibility of the process. The parties are generally free to agree what procedure will be followed during the arbitration proceedings, including deciding on the procedural timetable. This will set out the dates for the filing of statements of case, witness statements (if any), requests for documents, when any hearing will be held and so on.

It is unusual for parties to set out in the arbitration clause the various procedural steps that will be followed. Most rules do not set out the arbitration process in detail either. This helps to preserve the flexibility of arbitration proceedings to be tailored to specific disputes when they arise. It will usually be up to the parties, therefore, to agree on the procedure once the arbitration has been commenced. Failing this, the arbitral tribunal will decide. For instance, Article 22.2 of the ICC Rules provides that the arbitral tribunal, after consulting the parties, may adopt such procedural measures as it considers appropriate, provided that they do not contradict any agreement of the parties. In contrast, Article 15 of the LCIA Rules sets out fairly detailed default provisions for the submission of written statements and documents which will apply unless the parties have agreed otherwise.

Cross-reference

A typical arbitration procedure is set out in detail in Chapter 9.

2.7 Privacy and confidentiality

Litigation before the courts is generally a public affair, judgments are publicly available and non-parties (including the press) are generally able to attend hearings and obtain copies of statements of case and other documents filed at court. In contrast, arbitration hearings are almost always held in private.

Some seats (eg, London and Hong Kong) and some institutional rules (eg, the LCIA (Article 30), the SIAC (Rule 39), the HKIAC (Article 42) and Swiss Rules (Article 44)) expressly provide for confidentiality. This means that neither documents produced or disclosed during an arbitration (including statements of case, witness statements and expert reports) nor the arbitral award can subsequently be made public. This can be particularly important if there is an ongoing commercial relationship.

TIP Although the ICC Rules are silent on confidentiality, the tribunal may make orders concerning the confidentiality of proceedings or of any other matters in connection with the arbitration. It may also take measures to protect trade secrets and confidential information (ICC Rules, Article 22.3).

If the confidentiality of the dispute or underlying transaction is particularly important (eg, in an intellectual property context), then it is worth also considering including an express confidentiality provision in the arbitration clause from the outset.

The following suggested clause imposes such confidentiality obligations upon the parties:

> *The existence and content of the arbitral proceedings and any rulings or award shall be kept confidential by the parties and members of the arbitral tribunal except (i) to the extent that disclosure may be required of a party to fulfil a legal duty, protect or pursue a legal right, or enforce or challenge an award in bona fide legal proceedings before a state court or other judicial authority, (ii) with the consent of all parties, (iii) where needed for the preparation or presentation of a claim or defence in this arbitration, (iv) where such information is already in the public domain other than as a result of a breach of this clause, or (v) by order of the arbitral tribunal upon application of a party.*

2.8 Default award

Where a party refuses or fails to participate in the arbitration proceedings (typically where a respondent does not file an answer to the Request for Arbitration and/or generally refuses or fails to take part in the arbitration), most arbitration rules[6] and legislation[7] have provisions which allow for the arbitration to proceed regardless. It is unusual, however, for parties to include provisions in arbitration clauses dealing with the consequences of a default by one party.

However, even when the respondent does not participate in an arbitration, the claimant is nevertheless required to prove its case. Unlike many national courts, arbitral tribunals do not have the power to issue default awards in favour of a claimant when the respondent fails to participate. Arbitrators must consider the evidence before them and, on that evidence, determine whether the claimed relief can be granted.

There is no reason why parties cannot include specific language in their arbitration agreement which empowers tribunals to issue awards on the basis of a failure to defend the case. However, this may not prevent a recalcitrant party from later raising a defence on enforcement or challenge that it was unable to present its case pursuant to Article V of the New York Convention. Any attempt to include such a clause would therefore have to include very clear language on the part of the respondent agreeing to the default award procedure. The concerns in relation to a default award would be similar to those in relation to any attempt to grant a summary award (discussed in Chapter 1). The parties may include language in an arbitration agreement that allows the arbitrators to grant a summary award – that is, where there is no reasonable prospect of successfully defending the case – and also the power to strike out a case where there is no reasonable prospect of success. There is no reason why parties cannot draft language to include these powers on the part of an arbitral tribunal. However, the wording must be clear that the parties are agreeing to a limitation on their rights in order to mitigate the possibility of a successful challenge to prevent enforcement of the award under the New York Convention.

2.9 Costs

Most arbitral rules include provisions regarding costs and give discretion to the arbitral tribunal as to who should bear them and in what proportion.[8] A distinction is often made between the fees and expenses of the arbitrators and the administrative expenses of the arbitral institution (in the case of institutional arbitration) on the one hand, and the legal and other costs incurred by the parties on the other.

Cross-reference This is dealt with in further detail in Chapter 13.

---

6 See, for example, Article 6.8 of the ICC Rules, Article 15.8 of the LCIA Rules, Article 28 of the Swiss Rules and Article 30 of the UNCITRAL Rules.

7 See, for example, Section 41(4) of the English Arbitration Act 1996, Section 1048 of the German Code of Civil Procedure, Article 1695 of the Belgian Judiciary Code and Section 24(3) of the Swedish Arbitration Act 1999.

8 See, for example, AAA Rules (Article 34), SCC Rules (Article 50), ICC Rules (Article 38.4), LCIA (Article 28.2–28.3), Swiss Rules (Article 40.1–40.2), SIAC (Article 35 and 37), UNCITRAL Rules (Articles 40.2(e) and 42.1).

> **TIP** If the seat is in England and Wales, any provision agreed before the dispute in question has arisen which requires a party to pay the whole or part of the costs of the arbitration in any event will be invalid. However, such an agreement made after the dispute has arisen would be valid.

2.10 Service of process clauses

A common mistake in many arbitration agreements is to include a clause providing for an agent for service of process where one or both of the parties are located outside the jurisdiction. Provided that the parties have not included an option to litigate within the arbitration agreement (as discussed above), a service of process clause is not required. In order for a successful claimant to be able to enforce an arbitral award, it must be shown that the respondent was given an opportunity to defend itself. Actual notice and service of the arbitration claim on the respondent are therefore essential.

3. Pathological arbitration agreements

A 'pathological' arbitration agreement is a badly drafted agreement which either does not make clear whether the parties have agreed to submit their disputes to arbitration, or is incapable of being satisfied.

A classic example of a pathological clause is when a contract includes both an exclusive court jurisdiction clause and an arbitration clause, with no indication as to how they interact.[9] The risk here is that when faced with inconsistent provisions which do not make clear what matters may be referred to arbitration, a court might decide that the parties never intended to arbitrate at all. However, in arbitration-friendly countries, the courts will often try to give effect to the arbitration agreement. In practice, this will deprive the court jurisdiction clause of any effect.

Other examples include where an arbitration agreement refers to an arbitral institution which does not exist, or refers to two separate arbitral institutions. Again, in such cases the courts in arbitration-friendly countries will usually construe the arbitration agreement and clarify its meaning so that the arbitration can proceed, although there would remain a risk that another court may refuse to enforce any resulting award at a later date.

In order to avoid drafting pathological arbitration clauses and mitigate the risk of losing time and money arguing what a clause means before the courts, it is a good idea to use, at least as a starting point, the clauses recommended by arbitration institutions (see section 2, above) and/or to seek advice from an arbitration specialist before finalising the agreement.

---

9 Outside the hybrid/optional dispute jurisdiction clauses discussed above.

4. Model arbitration clauses

The appendix to this chapter sets out some model arbitration clauses.

5. Expedited arbitration

One criticism of arbitration is that it can be too slow. In more complex and high-value cases it is not unusual for 18 to 24 months to pass between filing of the Request for Arbitration and receipt of the final award.

5.1 Institutional rules

Some institutions have expedited procedure provisions in their rules; however, they tend to apply to more minor disputes. The ICC Rules apply an expedited arbitration procedure for cases where the amount in dispute does not exceed US$2 million. The LCIA Rules do not include an expedited procedure. However, Article 14.4(b) of the LCIA Rules provides that the arbitral tribunal has a general duty to "adopt procedures suitable to the circumstances of the arbitration, avoiding unnecessary delay and expense, so as to provide a fair, efficient and expeditious means for the final resolution of the parties' dispute". Article 9A of the LCIA Rules also provides that any party may apply to the LCIA Court for the expedited formation of the arbitral tribunal, but this is in case of exceptional urgency only.

TIP The ICC has an expedited procedure for claims that do not exceed US$2 million (Article 30 and Appendix VI), and the HKIAC has an expedited procedure for claims that do not exceed HKD 25,000,000 (Article 41). The SCC has specific Expedited Rules of Arbitration for disputes regarding less complex issues and involving a smaller amount in dispute. The Swiss Rules have an expedited procedure which applies to cases in which the amount in dispute does not exceed Sfr1 million (Article 42). Finally, the SIAC has an expedited procedure which applies where the amount in dispute does not exceed the equivalent amount of S$6 million (Rule 5).

In the interests of efficiency, some expedited arbitration provisions impose procedures which purport to apply irrespective of contrary terms in the parties' arbitration agreement. These may include a requirement that a sole arbitrator hear the dispute, even when that does not accord with the parties' previous agreement.[10] The Chinese courts have refused to enforce an award made subject to such procedures on the basis that the tribunal was not constituted in accordance with the parties' agreement (as stipulated under Article 5(1)(d) of

10 See, for example, Article 5.3 of the SIAC Rules, and Article 30(1) and Article 2 of Appendix VI of the ICC Rules.

the New York Convention). Parties therefore need to be cautious that such provisions may give rise to difficulties on enforcement.

A further concern arises in relation to jurisdictions, like England and Wales, where relief from a national court in support of arbitration is only available if and to the extent it is not available from an arbitral tribunal. In circumstances where institutional rules permit the expedited formation of a tribunal and interim remedies including the ability to appoint an emergency arbitrator, it may be argued that national courts have no power to order interim relief (see Chapter 6 for discussion of emergency relief). Parties should consider whether they wish to exclude expedited arbitration procedures in order to mitigate that risk. The parties will need to decide whether urgent relief from a tribunal is likely to be sufficient, or whether they may be more likely to want to obtain urgent relief from a national court.

5.2 Other initiatives

There have been other initiatives designed to make arbitral procedures quicker and more efficient.

The Financial Sector Branch of The Arbitration Club has published the Financial Services Expedited Arbitration Procedure (EAP). The EAP was drafted following consultation with many key institutions, including the ICC, the LCIA, the International Centre for Dispute Resolution (ICDR), the HKIAC and PRIME Finance. The EAP provides a model set of clauses designed to supplement the standard arbitration rules of arbitral institutions. These clauses set out stricter parameters for procedural steps within the framework of existing institutional rules. For example, the time period for serving any response to a Request for Arbitration is limited to seven days; applications, directions and orders are made without any hearing; and there are strict page limits for pleadings. The EAP was designed for use by financial institutions, but the procedure could be adapted for use in other sectors.

The Chartered Institute of Arbitrators has published rules of controlled-cost arbitration. These apply to arbitrations under the English Arbitration Act 1996. The rules provide that the arbitrator should manage the arbitration procedure so that the total costs of the arbitration, including the arbitrator's fees and expenses, is not more than 20% of the amount in dispute, and that any costs one party can recover from the other are not more than 10% of the amount in dispute. In the context of managing costs, the arbitrator is expressly empowered to manage procedural steps (including the presentation of expert evidence) which could also expedite proceedings and encourage a swifter resolution.

The 2018 Vienna International Arbitration Centre (VIAC) Rules even empower the Secretary General of the VIAC to increase or decrease the arbitrators' fees by up to 40% in light of either efficient or inefficient conduct of the proceedings.

5.3 Suggested arbitration clause

When it is anticipated that the parties will require a quick decision on the merits should a dispute arise, a suitably drafted clause could expedite a resolution. The following is a suggested arbitration clause for expedited proceedings. Unless otherwise stated, each clause is 'standalone' and may be inserted separately from the others. The cross-references in italics should be kept where the clauses referred to in the cross-reference are also included.

To be inserted in the preamble to the contract:

The arbitration provision at clause [ ] has been drafted with a view to expediting the resolution of any arbitration between the parties. [The timetable in the arbitration clause can be achieved with the cooperation of each party, the [arbitration institution] and the sole arbitrator.]

To be inserted as the arbitration clause:

x.1 [Insert standard e.g. ICC or LCIA arbitration clause here specifying a sole arbitrator] [save that unless the parties agree otherwise expressly in writing:]

x.2 The parties shall agree on the identity of the sole arbitrator to be nominated. If the sole arbitrator is not so agreed and nominated to the [appointing authority e.g. the LCIA Court] for appointment within [ ] days of the date of service of the [request for arbitration], he/she shall be appointed by the [appointing authority]. [Keep time period concise.]

x.3 The sole arbitrator must be available to conduct a hearing and render the award in accordance with the timing provisions of clauses [x.4] and [x.5] below.

x.4 A single hearing shall be held if requested by a party and if deemed necessary by the arbitral tribunal. In the event that a hearing is to be held [, without prejudice to clause x.6 below,] the parties request that the arbitral tribunal attempt to hold a hearing on the merits (both liability and quantum) within [[ ] months from receipt of written notification to the parties of the formation of the arbitral tribunal]. The hearing should last a maximum of [ ] days.

x.5 [The arbitral tribunal shall not provide reasons for its award/state the reasons upon which the award is based in summary form.] [Without prejudice to clause x.6 below,] the tribunal shall endeavour to render the award within [ ] month[s] from the last day of the hearing or, if no hearing is to be held, from the date when the last party's pleadings have been served [or when the last addendum to a party's pleadings has been served in accordance with clause x.11 below,].

(Summary Award)

x.6 *At any time after the Arbitral Tribunal has been appointed, any party may apply to the arbitral tribunal and the Tribunal is hereby empowered to grant an order:*

x.6.1 *for an award against the other party on the ground that [the Claimant] has no real prospect of succeeding on the claim or that [the Respondent] has no real prospect of successfully defending the claim; and/or*

x.6.2 for the [request for arbitration], [answer/response] or any other pleadings to be struck out on the ground that such [request for arbitration], [answer/response] or pleading discloses no reasonable grounds for bringing or defending the claim. If the Tribunal strikes out a request or an answer/response then the Tribunal shall render an award in favour of the Respondent/Claimant respectively.

x.7 The time period specified in Article [x i.e. the provision relating to the service of the answer/response to the request of the arbitration] of the [ ] Rules is amended to be [ ] days.

x.8 There shall be no discovery or disclosure, [however the arbitral tribunal shall have the power to order the parties to produce such documents as are reasonably requested by another party or by the arbitral tribunal where the documents are manifestly relevant, specifically identified and the burden of production is not excessive. The arbitral tribunal shall draw upon Article 3 (including Article 9(2)) of the IBA Rules on the Taking of Evidence in International Commercial Arbitration in respect of any requests to produce.]

x.9 The parties' pleadings and witness statements (if any) shall be concise [consider adding page limits to keep concise]. [[Where there are related parties] to the extent practicable, [RELATED PARTIES] agree to be jointly represented and to file consolidated pleadings and evidence]

x.10 [Subject to the exemption in clause [x.11] below,] any documents or witness statements on which a party will seek to rely must be appended to that party's statement of case, statement of defence and counterclaim (if any), statement of reply/defence to the counterclaim or reply to the defence to counterclaim as the case may be.

x.11 [Should any documents be produced by a party upon the order of the arbitral tribunal after the receiving party's pleadings or witness statements have been served, the receiving party shall be allowed to serve an addendum to its pleadings and/or witness statements already served dealing solely with the impact of the new document(s) produced.]

x.12 Unless the arbitral tribunal orders otherwise, the time periods for service of pleadings shall be as follows:

x.12.1 Service of statement of case within 1 week from receipt of [written notification to the parties of the formation of the arbitral tribunal].

x.12.2 Service of statement of defence and counterclaim (if any) [within 4 [weeks] of the service of the statement of case].

x.12.3 Service of statement of reply (and defence to counterclaim, if any) [within 2 [weeks] from service of the statement of defence and counterclaim (if any)].

x.12.4 *Service of statement of reply to defence to counterclaim (if any) [within 2 [weeks] from service of the statement of reply].*

x.12.5 *Parties are not entitled to serve any pleadings or evidence outside of this timetable unless agreed with the other party or so ordered by the tribunal.*

x.13 *Any witness evidence on which a party seeks to rely must be presented by way of a written statement [as prescribed in clauses [x.9] [x.10], [x.11] and [x.12] above.] [Oral witness evidence in chief may only be admitted with the agreement of the other parties or if so ordered by the arbitral tribunal.]*

x.14 *The parties request that the arbitral tribunal expedite the arbitral procedure and avoid unnecessary delay as much as possible and note that this clause has been drafted to attempt to achieve this.*

Appendix: Model arbitration clauses

International Chamber of Commerce (ICC)

X.1 *All disputes arising out of or in connection with this Agreement shall be finally settled under the Rules of Arbitration of the International Chamber of Commerce by one or more arbitrators appointed in accordance with the said Rules.*

X.2 *The language to be used in the arbitration shall be [ ] and the seat of the arbitration shall be [city and/or country]. The governing law of the arbitration agreement shall be the substantive law of [ ].*

X.3 *Unless the parties expressly agree in writing to the contrary, the parties undertake to keep confidential all awards in their arbitration, together with all materials in the proceedings created for the purpose of the arbitration and all other documents produced by another party in the proceedings not otherwise in the public domain – save and to the extent that disclosure may be required of a party by legal duty, to protect or pursue a legal right or to enforce or challenge an award in bona fide legal proceedings before a state court or other judicial authority.*

Please Note: The ICC Rules applying to all arbitration agreements concluded after 1 January 2012 contain emergency arbitrator provisions providing for the granting of urgent conservatory or interim measures. Parties may however opt out of these provisions (Article 29.6(b) of the ICC Rules).

The London Court of International Arbitration (LCIA)

[EITHER 1 ARBITRATOR]

x.1 *Any dispute arising out of or in connection with this Agreement, including any question regarding the validity, existence or termination of this Agreement and/or this arbitration clause, shall be referred to and finally resolved by arbitration in [city and/or country] conducted in the [ ] language by a sole arbitrator pursuant to the LCIA Arbitration Rules which are deemed to be incorporated by reference into this clause. The governing law of this clause shall be the substantive law of [ ].*

[OR THREE ARBITRATORS – LCIA]

x.1 Any dispute arising out of or in connection with this Agreement, including any question regarding the validity, existence or termination of this Agreement and/or this arbitration clause, shall be referred to and finally resolved by arbitration in [city and/or country] conducted in the [ ] language by three arbitrators pursuant to the LCIA Arbitration Rules which are deemed to be incorporated by reference into this clause [, save that, unless the parties agree otherwise, each of the Respondent and Claimant shall nominate an arbitrator, and the third arbitrator, who shall act as chairman of the tribunal, shall be chosen by the two arbitrators appointed on behalf of the parties. If he is not chosen and nominated to the LCIA Court for appointment within 30 days of the date of appointment by the LCIA Court of the later of the two party-nominated arbitrators to be confirmed, he shall be appointed by the LCIA Court.] The governing law of this clause shall be the substantive law of [ ].

Please Note: The LCIA Rules provide for both privacy and confidentiality. The LCIA Rules also contain emergency arbitrator provisions providing for the granting of emergency relief. Parties may however opt out of these provisions (Article 9B.14 of the LCIA Rules).

Hong Kong International Arbitration Centre (HKIAC)

X.1 Any dispute, controversy or claim arising out of or relating to this Agreement, including the validity, invalidity, breach or termination thereof, shall be settled by arbitration in [city and/or country] under the Hong Kong International Arbitration Centre Administered Arbitration Rules in force when the Notice of Arbitration is submitted in accordance with these Rules.

X.2 The number of arbitrators shall be [one/three].

X.3 The arbitration proceedings shall be conducted in [insert language].

X.4 The governing law of the arbitration agreement shall be the substantive law of [ ].

Please Note: The HKIAC Administered Arbitration Rules provide for both privacy and confidentiality. The HKIAC Rules also contain emergency arbitrator provisions providing for the granting of urgent interim measures. Parties may however opt out of these provisions.

Singapore International Arbitration Centre (SIAC)

x.1 Any dispute arising out of or in connection with this Agreement, including any question regarding its existence, validity or termination, shall be referred to and finally resolved by arbitration in [city and/or country] in accordance with the Arbitration Rules of the Singapore International Arbitration Centre ("SIAC Rules") for the time being in force, which rules are deemed to be incorporated by reference in this clause.

x.2 *The Tribunal shall consist of [one/three] arbitrator(s).*

x.3 *The language of the arbitration shall be [insert language].*

x.4 *The governing law of the arbitration agreement shall be the substantive law of [ ].*

Please Note: The SIAC Rules provide for both privacy and confidentiality. The SIAC Rules also contain emergency arbitrator provisions providing for the granting of urgent interim measures. Parties may however opt out of these provisions.

Stockholm Chamber of Commerce (SCC Institute)

x.1 *Any dispute, controversy or claim arising out of or in connection with this Agreement, or the breach, termination or invalidity thereof, shall be finally settled by arbitration in accordance with the Arbitration Rules of the Arbitration Institute of the Stockholm Chamber of Commerce.*

x.2 *The arbitral tribunal shall be composed of [one/three] arbitrator(s).*

x.3 *The seat of arbitration shall be [insert city and/or country] and the language of the arbitration shall be [insert language].*

x.4 *The governing law of the arbitration agreement shall be the substantive law of [ ].*

x.5 *Unless the parties expressly agree in writing to the contrary, the parties undertake to keep confidential all awards in their arbitration, together with all materials in the proceedings created for the purpose of the arbitration and all other documents produced by another party in the proceedings not otherwise in the public domain – save and to the extent that disclosure may be required of a party by legal duty, to protect or pursue a legal right or to enforce or challenge an award in bona fide legal proceedings before a state court or other judicial authority.*

Please Note: The SCC Rules provide for privacy, and only the Tribunal is under obligation of confidentiality but the parties are not under such obligation unless otherwise agreed. The SCC Rules also contain emergency arbitrator provisions providing for the granting of urgent interim measures. Parties may however opt out of these provisions.

The Swiss Rules of International Arbitration (Swiss Rules)

x.1 *Any dispute, controversy or claim arising out of or in relation to this contract, including the validity, invalidity, breach or termination thereof, shall be settled by arbitration in accordance with the Swiss Rules of International Arbitration of the Swiss Chambers of Commerce in force on the date when the Notice of Arbitration is submitted in accordance with these Rules.*

x.2 *The number of arbitrators shall be [one/three].*

x.3 *The seat of the arbitration shall be in [city and/or country], and the arbitral proceedings shall be conducted in [insert language].*

x.4 *The governing law of the arbitration agreement shall be the substantive law of [ ].*

Please Note: The Swiss Rules provide for both privacy and confidentiality. The Swiss Rules also contain emergency arbitrator provisions providing for the granting of urgent interim measures. Parties may however opt out of these provisions.

Dubai International Financial Centre/LCIA Arbitration Centre's Arbitration Rules (DIFC)

x.1 *Any dispute arising out of or in connection with this Agreement, including any question regarding its existence, validity or termination, shall be referred to and finally resolved by arbitration under the Arbitration Rules of the DIFC-LCIA Arbitration Centre, which Rules are deemed to be incorporated by reference into this clause.*

x.2 *The number of arbitrators shall be [one/three].*

x.3 *The seat, or legal place, of arbitration shall be [insert city and/or country].*

x.4 *The language to be used in the arbitration shall be [insert language].*

x.5 *The governing law of the arbitration agreement shall be the substantive law of [ ].*

Please Note: The DIFC Rules provide for both privacy and confidentiality. The DIFC Rules also contain emergency arbitrator provisions providing for the granting of emergency relief. Parties may however opt out of these provisions (Article 9B.14 of the DIFC Rules).

United Nations Commission on International Trade Law (UNCITRAL)

x.1 *Any dispute, controversy or claim arising out of or relating to this Agreement, or the breach, termination or invalidity thereof, shall be settled by arbitration in accordance with the United Nations Commission on International Trade Law (UNCITRAL) Arbitration Rules as at present in force.*

x.2 *The appointing authority shall be [name of institution or person].*

x.3 *The number of arbitrators shall be [one/three].*

x.4 *The place of arbitration shall be [insert city and/or country], and the language to be used in the arbitral proceedings shall be [insert language].*

x.5 *The governing law of the arbitration agreement shall be the substantive law of [ ].*

x.6 *Unless the parties expressly agree in writing to the contrary, the parties undertake to keep confidential all awards in their arbitration, together with all materials in the proceedings created for the purpose of the arbitration and all other documents produced by another party in the proceedings not otherwise in the public domain – save and to the extent that disclosure may be required of a party by legal duty, to protect or pursue a legal right or to enforce or challenge an award in bona fide legal proceedings before a state court or other judicial authority.*

Please Note: As stated above, the UNCITRAL Rules are generally designed to be used when an arbitration is not administered by a particular arbitration institution. The UNCITRAL Rules provide for privacy but not for confidentiality.

5. Pre-commencement of arbitral proceedings

1. Introduction

When a dispute arises, a party should consider a number of things before deciding to commence formal arbitral proceedings. Most obviously, it will want to understand the likely outcome of the arbitration and the costs of achieving it. Proceedings, once started, may not be easy to stop. An early evaluation of the merits of the party's case and consideration of the alternatives should help a party to decide.

There may be certain contractual or statutory conditions precedent with which a party must comply before commencing arbitral proceedings. These may, for instance, oblige parties to take alternative steps first to attempt to resolve the dispute, or to commence proceedings within a certain period of time. A party may also need to take certain steps, such as seeking preliminary measures through the courts, before commencing proceedings to protect its position, the assets it is seeking to recover or key pieces of evidence.

> *Cross-reference*
> More on the interim measures that a party may seek both before and during arbitration proceedings can be found in Chapter 10.

On a practical level, a party will need to consider how to manage arbitration proceedings if and when they are commenced. It will need to consider, for instance, the documentary evidence it will need (including how and from where such evidence is to be collated), the counsel it will retain, the potential witnesses (factual and expert) required, whether insurers (or other third parties) will need to be involved and how it intends to fund the proceedings.

2. When to commence arbitration

2.1 Compliance with 'escalation' or 'tiered' clauses

One of the first steps to take when a dispute becomes apparent is to obtain and review a copy of the contract from which the dispute arises. The dispute resolution clause, which may be contained in the contract or in a separate arbitration agreement, should make clear whether particular steps are required before arbitration can be commenced. Common requirements include issuing a notice of the dispute to the other party, attempting to resolve the dispute through negotiations or even conducting a mediation first. Construction industry contracts, for example, often require a dispute to be submitted to the engineer, architect or some other third person before arbitration can be initiated by a party.

TIP Although not all disputes will be contractual in nature (eg, tort, negligence, breach of duty), an arbitration agreement that covers the relevant dispute is still needed in order for it to be possible to refer that dispute to arbitration.

Dispute resolution clauses may specify a tiered process that requires the parties to take increasingly formal steps to resolve the dispute only if prior, less formal steps have been unsuccessful. For example, a clause may require the parties to submit the dispute first to particular senior managers or directors with appropriate authority with a view to these decision-makers negotiating and agreeing a settlement of the dispute. If these negotiations fail to achieve a settlement, the clause may then require the parties to submit the dispute to mediation, with the mediator to be selected by agreement or appointed by an independent third party. If mediation fails to result in a settlement, then the clause may permit the parties to resort to arbitration in the usual way. These are often called 'tiered' or 'escalation' clauses.

One difficulty with tiered dispute resolution clauses, which require parties to negotiate or mediate before referring their disputes to arbitration, is that they often do not set out exactly what each party must do in order to comply with the different steps. The general principle is that a contractual provision must be sufficiently clear, obligatory and certain to be enforceable. Hence, agreements merely to 'negotiate' or to 'attempt to settle disputes amicably' before commencing arbitration proceedings could be held to be unenforceable due to insufficient certainty to have binding force – for example, because the monitoring and enforcement of such a vague obligation would be fraught with practical and legal difficulties. The English courts, for example, have refused to uphold an agreement to negotiate in good faith for an unspecified period on grounds of uncertainty. However, this does not preclude negotiations or friendly discussions from being treated as a condition precedent provided that it is an obligatory and identifiable step, and there is case law supporting this. If the dispute clause does not clearly set out the various dispute resolution stages and pre-conditions, with specific deadlines or timetables for each stage, confusion and delay can easily occur as a result of challenges to the validity of that clause.

There is, however, a growing trend in the English courts towards supporting methods of alternative dispute resolution (ADR) and the enforcement of clauses which provide for ADR methods, such as negotiation or mediation in advance of arbitration or litigation.[1] The English courts have noted that it is in the interests of "the ordinary regulation of international commerce" to stay proceedings brought in breach of an agreement to decide a dispute in some other way, whether by ADR or arbitration. Section 9(2) of the English Arbitration Act 1996 enshrined this approach in statute by providing that a party's right to a stay of legal proceedings which have been commenced contrary to an agreement to arbitrate should not be affected by provisions that the dispute be referred to arbitration only after other dispute resolution procedures have been exhausted. While the courts or tribunal may be slow to decide that the clause is not enforceable in circumstances where the parties clearly intended this to be the case, they will do so if the clause is not sufficiently certain. Some of the key points to bear in mind when reviewing or drafting an escalation clause are set out below.

Cross-reference For more detailed examples of and tips on drafting escalation clauses, see Chapter 4.

(a) *Mandatory escalation clauses*

If the dispute resolution steps in an escalation clause are clearly expressed as mandatory (eg, the parties shall meet and negotiate) and the right to arbitrate is conditioned upon that requirement (eg, only if the parties are unable to resolve their dispute through good faith negotiations after 30 days), then either party may refer the dispute to arbitration) then they are likely to constitute conditions precedent with which the parties must comply before commencing arbitration proceedings. However, courts and tribunals are unlikely to look kindly on parties that seek to delay the commencement of substantive proceedings by demanding a dogmatic adherence to the required steps, while simultaneously obstructing them from being taken.

As discussed above, under English law, an escalation clause which requires the parties to agree to some vague application of an ADR process before commencing arbitration is likely to be deemed void for uncertainty. In several cases, however, English courts have expressed the view that an agreement to enter into a prescribed procedure for an ADR process can give rise to a binding obligation, provided that matters essential to the process are already agreed. To increase its prospects of enforceability (at least under English law), an escalation clause should stipulate, among other things:

---

1 The English courts take an active approach to case management and it is common for the courts to encourage or order the parties to use an ADR procedure if appropriate (see Rule 1.4 of the English Civil Procedure Rules); therefore, the enforcement of (sufficiently certain) escalation clauses providing for ADR is arguably consistent with public policy.

- an unequivocal undertaking by the parties to enter into the ADR process;
- clear provisions for the appointment of the neutral party (eg, mediator) if required; and
- a clearly defined procedure for the ADR process.

Specifying deadlines by which the various steps must be completed or longstop dates before which arbitral proceedings cannot begin unless the dispute has not been settled through ADR provides additional certainty and increases the prospects of enforceability of the various steps as conditions precedent to arbitration. If that is the intention, the clause should state in as much detail as possible the procedure which will apply to each ADR step proposed. For example, in respect of mediation or negotiation, the escalation clause could specify:

- a limited time period within which the procedure should be performed;
- who should participate or how to select a mediator (including a fall-back mechanism for selection in the event the parties cannot reach agreement);
- a limited number of sessions and/or participants;
- the applicable procedural rules; and/or
- an institution under whose auspices it is to be conducted (most leading arbitral institutions have published rules for non-binding conciliation or mediation).

As with an arbitration clause, the procedure for mediation or negotiation can be specified with reference to institutional procedural rules, such as those published by the Centre for Effective Dispute Resolution (CEDR), the International Mediation Institute, the Institute of Conflict Prevention and Resolution (CPR) or the International Chamber of Commerce (ICC) Mediation Rules.

By agreeing to a clearly drafted escalation clause which incorporates a number of conditions precedent for arbitration, the parties are removing some flexibility from the process. They are compelling themselves to pursue ADR even in circumstances where it is likely to prove fruitless and only delay matters. A complicated or poorly drafted escalation clause also opens the door to potential satellite litigation in the arbitration in the event that a party decides that it is no longer in its best interests to comply with the requirements it has agreed and moves to commence arbitration before all steps have been completed. Jurisdictional challenges on the basis that the tribunal was not properly constituted, as the prescribed preliminary steps contained within an escalation clause have not been undertaken, are a common result. The effect of such a challenge, if successful, is to reset the arbitration as it is impossible (absent party agreement) for the tribunal simply to stay proceedings in those circumstances to enable the escalation steps to take place as, unlike a court whose jurisdictional power is inherent, the tribunal derives its jurisdiction solely from the agreement of the parties While not fatal to the merits of the case, it can result in increased cost and delay in having to re-start arbitration once the mandatory steps in the escalation clause have been complied with – such additional cost could have a negative effect both on any third-party funding that is in place, and any insurance arrangement. Even if a jurisdiction challenge on these grounds is unsuccessful before the tribunal, the complaining party is likely to be able to challenge any resulting award in court on the basis that the tribunal had no jurisdiction, thus creating the risk that the entire costs of the arbitration will have been wasted if that challenge is subsequently upheld by the court.

Therefore, the greater the complexity of the escalation clause, the greater the chance of it being challenged and parties (particularly those who may be keen to commence arbitration) should therefore be careful and ensure that they take each step in the proscribed manner, or else reach agreement with the other parties that the steps do not need to complied with and that arbitration can be commenced.

Furthermore, there is a risk that a party may challenge the enforcement of an arbitral award on the basis that an escalation clause is not an agreement to submit disputes to arbitration which falls within the Convention on the Recognition and Enforcement of Foreign Arbitral Awards 1958 (the 'New York Convention'). However, clearly stating and separating each procedural step mandated by the clause (and particularly defining carefully and clearly when the right to arbitrate arises) will help to minimise this risk.

Finally, there is a significant risk under some national laws that an asymmetric mandatory escalation clause that provides only one party with rights to resort to ADR and/or arbitration will be deemed unenforceable. Examples of asymmetric clauses have been upheld in some English cases, provided that the party with the option, for example, to resort to ADR does not take steps that lead the other party to believe that such an option would not be exercised. The question of the enforceability of one-sided escalation clauses should nevertheless be considered carefully under the applicable law.

Cross-reference

For more guidance on the use and enforceability of asymmetric clauses, see Chapter 4.

(b) *Optional escalation clauses*

In contrast, an escalation clause that sets out the procedural steps as optional and/or enables arbitration to be commenced at any stage (eg, notwithstanding the ADR procedure above, each party shall have the right at any time to refer the dispute to arbitration) is unlikely to amount to a binding obligation to take such steps prior to the commencement of arbitration.

While this may mean that one party might begin arbitration while the other is still interested in trying to settle, optional escalation clauses provide parties with more flexibility in deciding which approach and timetable to adopt. They can also reduce the potential for satellite disputes regarding jurisdiction or the enforceability of the clause as outlined above. If the parties are prepared to explore negotiation and/or mediation, then it is possible to have a twin-track process whereby an ADR process is begun at the same time as arbitration proceedings. The fact that an arbitration is proceeding – with its concomitant costs – may give parties an incentive to settle promptly, and the ADR process provides a forum in which they can try to do so. The optional escalation clause at least ensures that possible ADR procedures are at the forefront of the parties' minds when considering commencing arbitration, but does not commit them to taking certain steps before initiating proceedings.

2.2 Alternatives to commencing arbitration

Even in the absence of an escalation clause, before incurring the significant costs of beginning an arbitration a party will want to consider whether alternative procedures are available that may be to its advantage. Such procedures could include ADR, as well as applying for interim measures in the courts, seeking remedies under an investment treaty (if applicable) or even commencing litigation (particularly if there is some doubt over the scope or validity of the arbitration clause).

Besides the savings in time and costs, there can be a strategic advantage to considering ADR at an early stage in a dispute. Once arbitration proceedings are commenced, the relationship between the parties is likely to deteriorate. Parties will become more entrenched in their respective positions once these have been formally advanced in pleadings or submissions before the tribunal. Furthermore, as the parties become more financially invested in proceedings, the cost of achieving a settlement will increase.

Contrary to common perceptions, making an offer to negotiate or mediate need not be a sign of weakness. An early offer can convey a party's confidence in its own position while demonstrating reasonableness by seeking a speedy compromise. After preparing an early case assessment (described further below), this might therefore be an appropriate early step, driving home the merits of the case to the other side and showing that you are fully prepared and ready to pursue (or defend) a claim in arbitration proceedings if necessary.

Even if it is unsuccessful, ADR can help parties to narrow the issues in dispute, prevent the dispute from widening and explore the options for settlement. The confidential nature of ADR and the provision of a private forum in which the parties can fully and frankly exchange their views and/or obtain the impartial view of a third party helps with this process. ADR can also help parties to reassess the merits of their own case before commencing potentially costly and lengthy proceedings. A rejection by one party of an offer to engage in ADR may, at a later point in proceedings, make that party appear unreasonable (eg, when it comes to the consideration of costs). Little will have been lost, however, by the party making the offer.

When there is no escalation clause that calls for ADR, parties that wish to use ADR will need to agree to this, and the terms on which it would operate, after the dispute has arisen. ADR requires mutual cooperation and initiative, and is likely to succeed only if both parties are willing to engage in the process and genuinely desire a negotiated settlement.

2.3 ADR and arbitration

Cross-reference The common forms of ADR used are set out briefly in Chapter 1.

It is usual for the parties to agree that a mediator or neutral whom they retain as part of an ADR process – and with whom they may each have had frank discussions about the merits of their own case and potentially the value at which they would be willing to settle – cannot be called as a witness, or appointed as a consultant or arbitrator in any subsequent or ongoing proceedings. This is consistent with the usual agreement between the parties that ADR proceedings should be confidential and privileged. It allows discussions and disclosure to occur more freely without the parties worrying about prejudicing their position in a future potential (or ongoing) arbitration or litigation.

However, in some jurisdictions, the parties may agree to a hybrid 'med-arb' process. Here, if mediation fails to achieve a settlement, the mediator becomes an arbitrator and issues a final and binding award on the outstanding matters.[2] A common concern is the risk that overseeing a mediation may threaten an arbitrator's impartiality – it may be difficult for a mediator-arbitrator not to be influenced by private discussions held with the parties and his or her knowledge of settlement proposals made during the mediation process. This risk is recognised in the International Bar Association (IBA) Guidelines on Conflicts of Interest in International Arbitration,[3] which state that an arbitrator may help the parties to reach a settlement, for instance through mediation, but before doing so should receive an express agreement from the parties that acting in such a manner will not disqualify him or her from continuing to serve as arbitrator. Such an agreement is considered to be a waiver of a party's right to

2 The China International Economic and Trade Arbitration (CIETAC) Rules, for example, provide for arbitrators to be able to act also as conciliators.

3 Guideline 4(d), IBA Guidelines on Conflicts of Interest in International Arbitration, 23 October 2014.

object to any potential conflict of interest that may arise from the arbitrator's participation in the mediation or from information that the arbitrator may learn in the process. If appropriate provisions are not incorporated in the arbitration clause, any parties considering using a med-arb process should enter into such an agreement at the start of any mediation and before disclosing any information to the arbitrator that they would not want to be taken into account in the arbitration process.

Notwithstanding such an agreement, the IBA Guidelines require that the arbitrator resign should he or she doubt his or her ability to remain impartial or independent in the future course of the arbitration proceedings as a result of his or her involvement in the mediation. Finding a replacement arbitrator will cause substantial delay and additional expense. In addition, parties may refrain from discussing their case frankly and openly with the mediator during the mediation stage if they know that he or she will go on to act as arbitrator. This removes one of the key benefits of mediation – the ability to discuss the dispute openly – and makes it less likely to succeed. In certain jurisdictions, such as Hong Kong, national laws dictate that a mediator-arbitrator must disclose all confidential information gathered during mediation proceedings which is relevant to the arbitration. This further dissuades the parties from approaching the mediation as openly as they might otherwise do, potentially limiting the usefulness of the parties participating in a mediation at all.

Some jurisdictions (eg, England and Wales) do not permit an arbitrator to act if he or she has been involved in a previous negotiation process that may compromise his or her impartiality or independence. Any med-arb process would, from the outset, need to be handled with the utmost caution so as to ensure that the proceedings maintain the objective appearance of fairness. For example, during the mediation phase information could not be imparted to the mediator without the knowledge of both parties (which effectively prevents the mediator caucusing), the parties must be aware that any information imparted to the mediator may later be used against them and the mediator must be careful not to express final views on either party's case. In practice, this removes many of the practical benefits of mediation and means that, even if both parties have agreed to the med-arb process, it may still give rise to grounds which require an arbitrator to resign, allow a party to challenge the arbitrator and/or allow a party to challenge the enforceability of an award.

Med-arb is more usually adopted in civil law jurisdictions, where the process of dispute resolution is more naturally inquisitorial than adversarial. The approach is thus more familiar to the parties and counsel involved. The advantage of the process advocated by civil law lawyers is that it can lead to a more efficient resolution of the dispute since, if it is submitted to arbitration, the arbitrator will already be familiar with the facts of the case, the parties and their counsel.

TIP One way around the difficulties described is for the identity of the mediator and arbitrator to be different. The parties therefore agree that if they cannot reach a mediated settlement within a certain period of time, the mediator's appointment will be terminated and the dispute will be submitted to arbitration with another independent person acting as arbitrator.

TIP ADR can be conducted in parallel to ongoing arbitration proceedings. For example, the parties could agree a suspension of the timetable to enable a mediation to take place, or they could fix the timetable in such a way as to provide for a relevant window where they may be an opportunity to engage in ADR should it be agreed.

3. Gathering evidence

The facts of the dispute are likely to be key to the tribunal's eventual decision, and very few arbitrations revolve entirely around principles of law. The relevant facts will be determined by the tribunal either as a result of the parties' presentation of documentary and/or oral evidence (as is the case in common law systems), or by the tribunal actively making its own enquiries of the parties to collect the relevant evidence (more typical in civil law systems). In reality, evidence presented to the tribunal will usually derive from a combination of parties autonomously producing documents and witness evidence, the tribunal's discretion to require document production and the supervision of national courts (eg, interim measures to preserve evidence).

3.1 Gathering key documents and evidence

Once the dispute has arisen, it is important to take early measures to preserve potential sources of evidence which may be necessary later to prove relevant facts. Depending on the nature of the procedure chosen by the parties (or adopted by the tribunal), the parties may also be obliged in subsequent arbitration proceedings to produce relevant and material documents. Although in arbitration proceedings such a duty is often more limited than the general duty of disclosure (or discovery) in litigation in common law jurisdictions, to avoid adverse inferences being drawn, it is important to ensure that documents which may fall within that duty are preserved.

The sooner that relevant evidence can be identified the better, as it might be crucial to forming a view on the merits of the case and the development of a strategy, including whether to commence proceedings (if claimant), how to defend a claim and/or whether to raise a counterclaim (if respondent) and the consideration of whether ADR options are worth exploring and if so when.

One of the most important sources of evidence is contemporaneous documents. This is not least because documents are easier and more straightforward to present to the tribunal, and usually more reliable than the testimony of witnesses of fact (who may be seeking to recall events which took place some years ago). In certain circumstances, it may also be necessary to inspect the subject matter of the dispute. If this is held by other parties, it may be necessary to seek interim measures to preserve it as described above.

At the outset it is important to inform a party of its obligation and set out a roadmap of the steps that need to be taken in a specific timeline. Sending a letter to the client outlining all of this at the commencement of the dispute, and starting data collection early can save costs in the long term and may also help secure funding (if sought) and enable a more accurate assessment of the chances of success. In this regard, there are a number of practical steps that should be regardless of the jurisdiction and the procedural laws governing the arbitration:

- inform the client that they should take steps to preserve all the relevant documentation which would include, but is not limited to, informing their IT department to stop any automatic deletions of emails, instant messages, other files and documents that may have relevance to the case (see further below);
- work with the client (and usually their IT department) to identify relevant types of documents, timeframes and custodians that may have access to or have generated information relevant to the dispute, and the sources and locations of that information, and in doing so therefore identify data hotspots;
- in conjunction with (i) and (ii) above, it may be sensible for a specialist e-disclosure firm to be brought in to assist with the identification of the hotspots as well as to run more detailed data analytics on the information provided; and
- coordinate the collection and organisation of the relevant documents, again where sensible using a specialist e-disclosure provider to ensure all relevant data is collected and potentially uploaded onto a review platform, thus maximising the efficiency of the subsequent document review process.

As at the time of writing, artificial intelligence (AI) has begun to impact the manner in which discovery and disclosure are performed. Predictive coding is just one of a number of techniques and it is expected that these will become increasingly sophisticated. To date, the Serious Fraud Office (SFO) in the United Kingdom has used AI in a number of matters and it appears that this use will develop across the market in the future. As such, practitioners should remain aware of the relevant best practice and raise such issues with the tribunal as necessary when considering the procedure for document production. When determining the scope of disclosure in future hearings, what may be considered reasonable will in no small part be dictated by the capabilities of the available technology, both in relation to driving down costs and examining the data.

TIP Creating a sensible filing system, whether in hard copy or in an electronic data room, to handle documents as and when they are located will make it significantly easier to manage the dispute when proceedings commence.

TIP At an early stage (ie, during the preparation of pleadings):

- List all relevant custodians and key words or phrases which will likely form the basis for searches and requests.
- Make a list of the documents held by either party (or third parties) which you might expect to see and which you might expect to be useful in respect of the client's position. This can help identify the documents that the client should search for and what documents you may wish to request from the other party.

3.2 Preserving documents

Given the preponderance with which records, especially electronic documents, are created and the requirements of national legislation – particularly tax and regulatory laws – with regard to record keeping, it is common for companies to have a document retention policy in place. Such policies aim to ensure the preservation of records for the minimum required periods, as well as the routine destruction of records which are irrelevant and no longer required, or which must not be retained in accordance with data protection laws. Such policies usually provide for these destruction processes to be suspended once there is a prospect of litigation or arbitration proceedings, but it is important to instigate this suspension as soon as the dispute becomes apparent by notifying all employees likely to be affected, and by suspending automatic deletion routines for electronic documents.

It is good practice to send a standard notice to all employees who may be connected with the dispute, explaining the steps that they are required to undertake to ensure that documents are not destroyed. Employees should also be reminded not to rearrange or edit any of the relevant files, alter or amend any documents, or alter or destroy any automatically created information (the 'metadata') – such as details of the date of creation, author and details of previous saved versions.

TIP An example of such a notice is set out in the appendix to this chapter.

Documents in this context should include all electronic records (including databases, emails, voicemails, data on mobile devices) as well as hard-copy records (even if these are informal, manuscript notes). It may not be possible at this early stage to determine precisely what may be relevant to the dispute so the net should be cast widely to preserve as many potentially relevant categories as possible. It may be sensible for counsel or in-house counsel to brief employees face to face to ensure that they properly understand this requirement and that the message is duly disseminated.

Failure to preserve documents in the manner described above not only will make the process of initially gathering evidence more difficult, but may be prejudicial to a party's case if documents which support it have not been preserved or if, in subsequent proceedings, the party is ordered to produce types of documents which it appears have been destroyed or altered since the dispute arose.

Cross-reference For more on document production during arbitration proceedings, see Chapter 11.

In practice, a tribunal can order a party to produce documents under its control. This may include documents held by companies within the same corporate group as a party (particularly if the party has already disclosed or relied on documents of such companies). It is therefore important that any companies within the same corporate group that are likely to hold relevant documents also take the steps detailed above to preserve documents. That said, in order to avoid prejudicing potential arguments to resist document production, any such companies should avoid transferring documents to the company which is the party to the arbitration, at least until the relevant legal position has been considered.

3.3 Avoid creating adverse evidence

At the same time, it is also important to make sure that employees are aware of the risk of creating documents which adversely harm the client's case and which the client may later be ordered to disclose by the tribunal. Although arbitration proceedings do not necessarily follow the common law approach to disclosure – which usually requires parties to conduct an extensive search for and to disclose the existence of all relevant documents (whether helpful or harmful) – it is not unusual for the parties to make requests for the specific disclosure of documents. Clients from civil law jurisdictions may be unfamiliar with this sort of process or the potential risk of their continued creation of documents.

For example, adverse evidence could be created in the form of internal documents, such as memos or emails between employees, which may speculate on the causes and possible ramifications of the dispute. A party is unlikely to be able to claim privilege over such documents unless they are created specifically for the purpose of obtaining legal advice from counsel or assisting in the conduct of the potential proceedings. To the extent that memos on the factual background to the dispute must be prepared as part of the evidence-gathering exercise described above, this should be effected through either external or in-house counsel so as to ensure that any relevant legal privilege applies as far as possible.

Adverse evidence might also be created in the form of external documents, such as correspondence with the other party to the dispute. Even though a dispute has arisen, it may still be appropriate to communicate with the other party, for instance to fulfil continuing contractual obligations and/or keep open a dialogue and the possibility of negotiations. However, such communications will likely be produced by one or other party at some point during the proceedings, so it is advisable for employees to be made aware of this. A process should be put in place so that correspondence potentially sensitive to the issues in dispute can be reviewed by counsel. The early involvement of counsel can also help to ensure that metadata (which may potentially contain privileged information, such as amendments or comments from counsel) is not inadvertently disclosed. Copies of documents should also not be requested from any third parties in relation to the dispute until consideration can be given to the information they may contain.

TIP When sending documents to the other side, try to send as a portable document format (PDF) or else as a newly saved document so that potentially harmful metadata is not inadvertently disclosed.

3.4 Privilege

In general terms, privilege is a right to withhold certain confidential documents from production to the tribunal or court. In international arbitration, interesting issues can arise as to the extent to which this right should apply. Disputes frequently involve parties from different jurisdictions, and contracts which may have a governing law and/or a seat of arbitration from yet further jurisdictions, and in each of them the approach to questions of privilege may be significantly different.

In many jurisdictions privilege is an established principle of public policy. This is based on the principle that for the effective administration of justice, a party must be able to seek and receive legal advice; if a party feels unable to communicate openly and frankly with its legal representatives for fear that such communications would be produced to the court/tribunal or the opponent, then the provision of advice would inevitably be fettered.

Under English law, the two most common types of privilege are confidential documents created for the purpose of obtaining legal advice (legal advice privilege) and confidential documents that are created for the dominant purpose of assisting in existing or reasonably contemplated 'litigation' (litigation privilege). It is generally accepted that litigation privilege applies by analogy to other forms of adversarial dispute resolution, including arbitration. Other common law jurisdictions have similar rules – in the United States, for example, confidential attorney-client communications made in the course of the provision of legal services and the work product prepared in anticipation of litigation are both privileged.

The position in civil law jurisdictions varies considerably. In civil law jurisdictions parties do not generally face (or therefore need protection from) wide-ranging obligations to produce documents, and thus a doctrine of legal privilege akin to that in common law jurisdictions has not developed. In civil law jurisdictions confidential information entrusted to an independent legal adviser by a client is nevertheless protected. This is usually based on the adviser's professional obligations under statute and codes of conduct which compel him or her (sometimes with concomitant criminal sanctions) to keep secret confidential information obtained as a result of his or her professional relationship with the client.

In the absence of a prior agreement by the parties, an arbitral tribunal is not bound to determine privilege in any particular way,[4] and the flexibility of the arbitral process allows the tribunal to adopt an appropriate solution depending on the applicable law and procedural rules of the arbitration. Only if a party or the tribunal demands production of documents that have not been produced voluntarily will the issue of privilege tend to arise. Where a party has a legitimate expectation of privilege under the rules of its own jurisdiction, the tribunal is likely to want to preserve this (although in marginal cases each arbitrator's own legal background is likely to influence the extent to which he or she considers that privilege protection should trump production). As the tribunal is obliged to treat the parties fairly and equally, this means that in most cases a tribunal will apply the least onerous disclosure rules of those that might otherwise be applicable to the particular dispute, with the result that both parties will be able to rely on a wide definition of privilege in accordance with such rules.

At the pre-commencement stage, the primary consideration should be to maintain any privilege protection which applies to documents already in existence or which could apply to documents that are to be produced in relation to the pending arbitration. It is important, therefore, to investigate and consider at an early stage the relevant rules and laws on privilege, taking into account the jurisdictions relevant to the dispute, and then put in place a mechanism for

4 In respect of English seated arbitrations this is confirmed by Section 34(1) of the English Arbitration Act 1996.

exchanging documents between legal counsel and the client, witnesses and relevant third-party advisers that maximises their chances of retaining privilege protection.

Assumptions should not be made as to what may or may not be privileged. Communications with in-house counsel in particular should be treated with the utmost care. In common law jurisdictions, communications between in-house counsel and their clients within the same organisation usually attract privilege protection if they meet the relevant requirements. However, in certain civil law jurisdictions, in-house counsel are not considered to be in the same professional category as external counsel and are therefore not covered by the same professional obligations to keep secret any confidential information which they receive. This distinction is often a cause of privilege disputes in international arbitration. In any case, complex issues can arise when external counsel are instructed by in-house counsel as to which individuals within the instructing organisation are 'the client' for the purposes of privilege protection. It is important to consider this point at an early stage so that lines of communication can be established with external counsel that preserve privilege protection as far as possible.

To address these risks, employees should be advised to take great care in relation to the creation of any new documents relating to or concerning the matter, including internal memos, reports, minutes and emails. Ideally, employees should not create documents that contain anything that you would not want the other party to see at a future date, unless it is clear that the document will benefit from privilege protection. For instance, as it will be necessary to interview witnesses at an early stage (as described below), consideration should be given to who will conduct these interviews so that notes of the interview remain privileged. Similarly, if it is necessary to instruct third parties, such as experts, to provide advice relevant to the pending proceedings, consider whether to instruct external counsel to handle this process from the outset. Existing documents should also not be copied or distributed indiscriminately, as this may result in loss of any privilege protection which may apply. It is a sensible precaution for privileged documents between legal adviser and client to state that they are privileged legal advice and confidential. While this label alone will not ensure that privilege protection applies, it will flag to the recipients that the document should be circulated with care.

To avoid potential difficulties concerning privilege in arbitration proceedings, parties may also want to consider trying to agree on the applicable privilege rules before commencing the arbitration (or shortly thereafter). In some cases, it may not be practical to do so. Seeking direction from the tribunal as part of the first procedural order may therefore be a sensible alternative.

3.5 Contacting key witnesses

In preparing for potential arbitration proceedings and pursuing or defending a claim, a party may require input from its employees, agents, third-party advisers, and its senior managers and directors. These people will be able to provide relevant details surrounding the documentary record described above, and can help to brief counsel by identifying and focusing on the key issues, and explaining the general background. If any individuals are particularly close to the facts, it may be desirable to ask them to submit witness evidence during arbitration proceedings.

It is a good idea to contact these people and take a full 'proof' of their evidence at an early stage; that is, to take an account of the entire story, regardless of whether the particular details are helpful or harmful. This not only provides a useful documentary record of the evidence for future reference, but might be important if there is a risk that the witness may be difficult to contact or uncooperative in the future.

It is therefore important to identify and contact the relevant people at an early stage. Since few, if any, of them are likely to have had prior experience of arbitration proceedings (or any form of dispute resolution) and the steps involved, it might be helpful for managers and human resources personnel to provide reassurance and support to ensure that they are not overwhelmed by the additional demands of the dispute.

With regard to relevant people who have left the business, it may be appropriate to make contact at an early stage to ensure that they will be available to assist with the dispute. Equally importantly, it may be necessary to ensure that they will not improperly cooperate with the other side, for instance by reminding them of the terms of any confidentiality provisions in their employment or severance contract. However, it should be remembered that there is no property in a witness, and any party has as much right as the other to present evidence from any potential witnesses.

TIP Where the dispute relates to the sale of a business (or part of it) and relevant employees or documents may now be in the hands of the opponent, you should check the terms of the sale agreement to see if they require the buyer to provide continued access to staff and/or documents in the event of a dispute.

TIP If any employees are likely to leave the business in the near future, it is important to obtain from them all relevant information and documents before they do so and, where possible, to ensure that they leave on favourable terms which provide for continued support with the dispute.

4. Other pre-commencement steps

4.1 Instructing external counsel

Parties will usually instruct and retain external counsel to advise on a dispute which is subject to arbitration, particularly if they feel that they do not have the expertise in-house or sufficient personnel to manage a dispute of a certain complexity and size. In-house counsel will benefit from having an intimate knowledge of the internal processes and personnel of the relevant party, and may even have been involved with the negotiation of the disputed contract. However, it is likely to be necessary to appoint counsel with specialist expertise of international or domestic arbitration law and procedure, knowledge of what may be particularly technical areas of law and the resources to manage the proceedings, particularly in terms of marshalling evidence and preparing pleadings and submissions.

It is therefore important to consider whether to appoint external counsel at the outset, not least to assist with and advise on the various pre-commencement steps described above. Counsel can also help to conduct an early case assessment, described in more detail below, which will provide management with an indication of the merits of the dispute and inform strategic decisions that may be needed at an early stage, such as whether to attempt settlement or engage in ADR.

It is often necessary to weigh up a number of potential factors when instructing counsel, such as the appropriate skills and experience for the particular dispute, geographical location and relevant language experience, available resources and, of course, cost. It is sensible for an in-house legal team or management to take the time at an early stage to obtain information from and evaluate possible options as to external counsel, in order to make a decision that best fits the company's interests for the dispute in question.

In international disputes, which may span a number of different jurisdictions, the governing law of the dispute and location of the company's offices may not necessarily be the most important factors in determining which counsel are the most suitable to instruct. In reality, experience of international arbitration procedure, familiarity with similar disputes, a good understanding and experience of the company's business and sector, and the capability and project management experience to coordinate the case across several countries are likely to be more relevant. Potential costs and budgeting (including any consideration of external funding, whether from insurers or professional litigation funders – see below) are also important factors to consider, as these may drive a party's early strategic decisions. Counsel's geographical location and working culture are relevant, particularly as it is likely to be necessary for a party to work closely with counsel over an extended period.

TIP If the dispute is covered by insurance, the insurer may well require at least input into (and in some cases express approval of) the external counsel to be appointed, and so you should be careful to check the requirements of the relevant policy.

4.2 Early case assessment

One question which will naturally arise at the beginning of any dispute is whether the risks of pursuing (or defending) potential arbitration proceedings outweigh what might be gained from (or lost by) a quick settlement. One of the first tasks to undertake, therefore, is an early case assessment of the likely outcome and prospect of success, the potential costs of arbitration proceedings, as well as the significant factual or legal issues that may arise and what evidence may exist or may be needed to deal with them. Depending on the time available, this assessment can range from a guideline review based on the available preliminary documents to a more forensic examination and quantification of the issues and potential liability involved. The scope of the initial review should be proportionate to the complexity and scale of the dispute and may, in the first instance, be dictated by the time available before certain steps need to be taken (eg, in accordance with contractual dispute resolution procedures).

No matter how thorough, no early case assessment will be able to predict precisely the outcome of the dispute. However, what it should provide is an indication of the likely range of outcomes and the general probability with which they may occur. It should also highlight key risk areas and points for further investigation. Case assessment should be an ongoing exercise throughout the dispute and one which, particularly in the early stages, can be refined as new information comes to light – for instance, from more extensive document searches, talking with potential witnesses or information obtained from the other side.

One main advantage of an early case assessment is that it helps to formulate a strategy at the start of the dispute. A good early case assessment should evaluate, in commercial terms, whether it will be more beneficial to seek to achieve a settlement in the short term (possibly before proceedings commence) than to pursue the result that the client may end up with in arbitration (taking into account the risks involved). This will inform the client's decision as to whether to engage in one of the ADR processes described above and allow it to evaluate the potential terms on which a settlement might be reached. It is important to brief the client, and possibly its senior management team, about the conclusions of the early case assessment and the likely course of proceedings. This way they can be properly informed before taking important strategy decisions, and can justify those decisions to more senior management and shareholders if necessary.

4.3 Assessing the potential cost of arbitration

The potential cost of any arbitration proceedings will be a significant factor in determining strategy at an early stage. Even a strong case may not justify the risks of a company engaging in arbitration proceedings if the upfront costs comprise a significant proportion of its working capital or it would face liquidation should it lose the proceedings and be ordered to pay the other side's costs. From a commercial perspective, the money that a company uses to fund arbitration proceedings is money that might otherwise have been invested in the business. Furthermore, even if external counsel are engaged, arbitration proceedings will typically require significant time commitments from individuals in the relevant commercial and legal teams who are most familiar with the facts of the dispute. These individuals will, for instance, need to spend time locating relevant documentary evidence and, if they are to be called as witnesses, preparing witness statements with counsel and attending hearings. A company therefore has to be satisfied that the potential costs justify the potential outcome of any arbitration proceedings over and above what could be gained from (or lost by) reaching an early settlement.

Even if a company may ultimately recover a proportion of its costs from the other side if it is successful in the arbitration, it should factor in the risk that it may still have to pay the shortfall. Worse still, if it is not successful, a company may have to pay a significant portion of the other side's costs (in addition to any damages that may have been awarded).

TIP It may be possible to obtain insurance against the risk of being required to pay such costs, see section 4.4 below.

Cross-reference For more on costs in arbitration proceedings, see Chapter 13.

In addition, a company may be required under applicable accounting rules to set aside provision in its accounts for the potential costs of the arbitration proceedings, as well as any damages that it might be ordered to pay. While it may not be necessary to include such reserve in external accounts until proceedings have actually commenced and preliminary issues are addressed – so that the amounts can be quantified with greater certainty – for management reporting and internal accounting purposes a company may still require this information sooner.

It can be very difficult for counsel to estimate the potential costs of arbitral proceedings at an early stage. As noted above, an early case assessment will not predict with certainty the outcome of the dispute or all of the issues that might arise during its resolution. In particular, the full scope of the dispute and the position taken by the other side may not be apparent until pre-action correspondence or more detailed pleadings are exchanged between the parties. Similarly, it may be unclear to what extent preliminary issues, such as the validity of the arbitration agreement or jurisdiction of the tribunal, will be raised, or interim measures sought, whether through the courts or from the tribunal.

In addition, unless provided for in the arbitration agreement between the parties, the detailed procedure to be adopted – for instance, in respect of disclosure of documents, exchange of witness evidence, expert evidence and the hearing (if in fact an oral hearing will be required) – will be uncertain. *Ad hoc* arbitrations, conducted without institutional support and possibly only a limited set of rules agreed in advance between the parties, may be more protracted as the parties may have to agree additional issues as they go along.

The amount of work required at each stage may depend on whether the tribunal and parties prefer to adopt a more common law style or a more civil law style approach. The common law approach places a greater emphasis on witness testimony, disclosure of documents and evidentiary hearings. However, it is likely to increase the cost of certain elements of the proceedings, albeit with the potential benefit that such steps may allow a party to examine and test in more detail the other side's case as the proceedings progress. The civil law approach, in contrast, places greater weight on documentary evidence produced by the party with the burden of proving the relevant issue, with less emphasis on witness evidence and disclosure, which may result in a less costly arbitration in the long run. Many international arbitration proceedings these days adopt a hybrid of rules and procedures from the different approaches, which are aimed at ensuring that each party has a full opportunity to present its case and respond to the case put to it (eg, through the use of evidentiary hearings), yet in a more cost and time efficient manner (eg, by limiting the scope and obligation of disclosure).

Cross-reference For more on the procedure that may be adopted in an international arbitration proceeding, see Chapter 9.

The usual approach to estimating costs at an initial stage is to make assumptions about the steps that are likely to be involved in potential arbitration proceedings, drawing upon experience of similar disputes and the conclusions reached in the early case assessment. As counsel, it is helpful to state these assumptions expressly to the client, so that it has a clear understanding of not only the basis on which future costs are likely to be incurred, but also the basis on which the estimate may change as the dispute unfolds.

TIP Clients often prefer to have a big-picture overview of the total costs of dealing with the dispute and when these will be incurred, depending on the strategy that they have chosen to adopt and/or the stage at which the dispute can be resolved, as opposed to lots of detailed and potentially confusing information.

As a starting point, it is helpful to work through each stage of the proceedings (eg, pleadings, document production, witness evidence, expert evidence and the hearing), and consider the amount of work and level of expertise likely to be required at each stage. In terms of legal fees, matters to consider include:

- the number of issues identified in the early case assessment as likely to form part of the dispute;
- the overall complexity of the dispute;
- the likely process and timetable for the proceedings;
- the potential number of factual witnesses;
- whether expert evidence will be required and, if so, in what areas;
- the likely number of documents held by the client that will form part of any document search (eg, by considering the time period relevant to the facts in dispute, the number of individuals (or custodians) who would have created or sent relevant electronic documents, the size of electronic or hard-copy filing systems);
- the likely document production procedure to be followed;
- the possible need for interim measures and/or determination of preliminary issues (and whether any court proceedings will be necessary in this regard); and
- the likely length of any final hearing.

In addition, likely disbursements should be estimated where possible. Potential heads of disbursements could include:

- arbitrators' fees;
- the fees of any institution involved;
- experts' fees (which will depend on the level of expertise and number of experts required); and
- potential travel expenses, if witnesses and/or the client and/or counsel are located in different jurisdictions.

Cross-reference

For more on arbitrators' fees, which in an institutional setting are likely to be specified by the institution, see Chapter 13.

Any estimate of costs should be kept under active review so that the client can make an informed decision as to whether the cost of continuing with the arbitration justifies the potential reward. Indeed, in many jurisdictions it is a regulatory requirement that clients are given up-to-date information on the actual and anticipated costs of the work required. This is an important part of the project management of any dispute.

4.4 Third-party funding and ATE insurance

In general, third-party funding essentially involves a claimant entering into an agreement with a funder that the funder will provide money to the claimant to enable them to fund the costs of the arbitration, in return for a significant stake in the underlying claim. Usually this involves the funder receiving either a multiple of the committed amount or a percentage of the damages awarded (usually whichever is the greater) in the event that the case is successful. While this means that the claimant will often end up with less at the end of a successful case than if no funder had been involved, the availability of funding in the first place may enable a claimant to pursue proceedings that it may otherwise not have been able to afford. Further, if the case is unsuccessful, the claimant is not required to repay the funder (and this is the risk that the funder takes). There is an increasing trend for third-party funding to be used to fund at least some of the legal and other costs involved in arbitrations, in those jurisdictions where third-party funding is permitted.

It will be necessary to demonstrate to any funders why the amount they could recover justifies the risk of no recovery at all if the case is not successful – for instance, by showing that the claim is sufficiently strong, that there is likely to be a significant award of damages (ie, several millions of pounds) to the party seeking the coverage if it is successful, and that assets will be available to recover this award. This may in itself require a significant amount of work. In this regard, the overwhelming majority of funders, save for those who offer off the shelf products, will normally require the following information before agreeing to fund the case:

- a clear budget for the solicitors, counsel, external expert (including foreign law) and tribunal fees up to and including the hearing;
- a timeline for when each tranche of funding is expected to be drawn down;
- a breakdown on the merits of the case and counsel's opinion on the same (as they will only tend to fund cases with a good prospect of success);
- confirmation that monetary damages are the objective (as opposed to a non- monetary remedy such as an injunction or seeking to control shares);
- details of the case strategy up to and including enforcement and the likelihood of successful enforcement; and
- details of any non-conventional/contingent fee arrangements between the lawyers and the client.

Funders may differ both on the level of funding that they are willing to commit (which is usually pegged to the level of damages) and the cost of that funding (which is typically calculated on a drawdown/ringfenced amount versus time basis).

Once funding is in place, the funders typically require regular updates on the progress of the case and its costs. Different funders differ on both the frequency of these updates and the level of detail, but all expect accurate accounts of how the cash invested is being spent. A funder should not, however, have any direct control over the proceedings.

There are two principal ways the funding market can be accessed: (i) via a broker; or (ii) directly applying to the funders. There are advantages to both, but typically the more specialised the claim the fewer the funders and therefore the less need for a broker. Despite this, engaging a broker may drive down the funding costs as funders will know they are one of a number that is being contacted and this creates competitive tension.

As a corollary to funding, insurance may be required both to backstop the funder's investment, and to provide protection to the client. If the client does not have already an insurance policy that is likely to cover the costs of commencing proceedings and/or any potential liability to the other side (including adverse costs liability), the outset of the dispute is the appropriate time to consider whether an after the event (ATE) policy can be purchased.

There are a large number of ATE products on the market. Typically, they are broken down into three categories according to when the premium is paid: (i) upfront; (ii) partially deferred; and (iii) fully deferred. Generally, fully deferred premiums are more expensive than the upfront premiums as the insurer is taking risk in the outcome of the case. Regardless of how the premium is dealt with, most insurers (as with funders) require a legal opinion that there is good prospect that the case will have a successful outcome, whether that would be via settlement or in a final award.

TIP In April 2018, the International Council for Commercial Arbitration and Queen Mary University published a joint report on third-party funding which includes a section on 'best practice' in Chapter 7. This may be a helpful guide to some of the issues that practitioners may wish to consider when pursuing funding options with their clients. However, it should be noted that the best practices are not obligatory, and practitioners should consider whether they are in the interests of their clients in any given set of circumstances.

4.5 Notification of claim to interested parties

(a) Insurers

Most insurance policies will require potential claims against the insured to be notified soon after the insured becomes aware of the dispute. This gives the insurer an opportunity to become involved in the conduct of any defence or settlement of the claim. This is an important step and one which, if not complied with, could prejudice coverage under the insurance policy.

It is therefore important at the start of the dispute to consider whether there are any relevant insurance policies (eg, covering liability and/or legal defence costs) and to review their provisions. Even if this is unclear, the best course of action is to preserve the right to claim coverage later. Save to the extent required under the relevant policy, notice to any insurer can usually be relatively brief, simply explaining why coverage may exist in respect of the costs of the dealing with the dispute and/or any potential liability.

(b) Third parties

Under share or business acquisition agreements the seller may give certain warranties or indemnities in respect of the company or assets being sold. This might include a warranty that the seller is not aware of anything that might cause proceedings to be brought against the company or the business, and that no such proceedings are pending or threatened. Accordingly, the buyer may find that it has a claim for breach of such warranty against the seller, or at the very least there may be provisions that it can rely on to require the seller to cooperate as necessary in relation to the dispute. Such agreements tend, however, to strictly limit the scope of what may be claimed and often impose short limitation periods for bringing such claims. In each case where the dispute relates to a recently acquired company or business, it will therefore be necessary to review the relevant acquisition agreement carefully and to comply with its notification provisions to preserve any potential claim that may be possible against the seller under that agreement.

(c) Public accounts

As mentioned above, once a party becomes aware of a potential liability that it may incur in respect of a dispute, it may be necessary – subject to the applicable accounting rules – for it to make provision in its public accounts. A party's appointed auditors should therefore be informed at an early stage, particularly if they are in the process of preparing public accounts, so that they may consider the extent to which this is or may be required and advise on such provision accordingly. This may particularly be the case if the party is a listed company, as it may have strict notification obligations.

(d) Potential media enquiries

Parties typically agree that disputes which they have agreed to arbitrate, and their associated arbitration proceedings, should be confidential. Many institutional rules (eg, the London Court of International Arbitration (LCIA), the Singapore International Arbitration Centre (SIAC), the Hong Kong International Arbitration Centre (HKIAC) or Swiss Rules) expressly provide for this. Enquiries from the media for comment should be treated with considerable caution and the response prepared in accordance with any applicable confidentiality obligations.

In any case, although commercial disputes may be of great significance to the parties concerned, most of them are unlikely to generate much attention from the media, at least outside niche trade publications.

One exception is international investment arbitrations involving state counterparties, where for example access to natural resources or the development of key infrastructure projects may be at stake. These are a matter of public interest and, as such, the existence and status of such proceedings, as well as the awards rendered and even the submissions filed by the parties, are increasingly being made public in response to calls for greater transparency in such disputes. For example, the International Centre for Settlement of Investment Disputes (ICSID) matters contain a presumption of openness and transparency and it is up to the parties to highlight which documents/what information they desire to keep confidential as well as agreeing other details concerning whether the hearing should be public or private. This process is also subject to any relevant treaty provisions that may govern the dispute, but ultimately if the parties cannot agree the tribunal has the power to decide what information to make public, including whether to make the award public. Any information that the tribunal does publicise is posted on the ICSID website which may include the details of the parties and their representatives, the procedural listing and any materials, including awards, which fall outside any confidentiality agreements reached. As such, there is often a significant amount of material available to the public which may result in significant media attention in the ongoing dispute. In responding to any such enquiries, however, practitioners and parties should be cognisant of what is and is not covered by any confidentiality decisions or agreements.

A similar approach to transparency in bilateral investment treaty (BIT) investor state arbitrations are contained in the 2013 amendment to the United Nations Commission on International Trade Law (UNCITRAL) Rules which apply to treaties concluded on or after 21 April 2014, unless the parties agree otherwise, and to treaties preceding this date with the agreement of the parties. As with the ICSID rules, the UNCITRAL Rules contain a presumption of openness unless otherwise determined by the tribunal on application by the parties. The ICC has also followed suit and on 1 January 2016 it agreed to publish the names and nationalities of all arbitrators and instituted a policy where all information would be publicised after the constitution of the tribunal subject to the parties agreeing whether or not to opt out of this transparency rule.

Disputes that affect a significant number of people, such as large numbers of employees or consumers, may also draw media attention.

Even where there is media attention and the dispute is not confidential, a party should consider the potential consequences before fighting its dispute in the media. Taking an aggressive position in public may prompt the other party to do likewise, thereby forcing the adoption of extreme positions and reducing the likelihood of reaching a compromise (which would inevitably involve public concessions) in the future. Because the media are unlikely to share a party's particular view of the dispute – and may well decide to put a different spin on the issues – this adds to the risk of this strategy. It may lead to the wide publication of potentially damaging statements that misinterpret a party's position. Furthermore, certain public statements might breach confidentiality provisions applicable to the arbitration. If it is necessary to make extensive media communications and these are permitted under the parties' agreement to arbitrate, public relations experts should be brought in at an early stage.

In instances where media attention is likely, it is advisable to prepare a general public statement of your client's position to use in response to media enquiries and any public statements made by the other parties. This need not be detailed: a short holding statement could be prepared to summarise your client's position, or simply acknowledge the existence of the dispute. To reduce the need for further statements, it could also note that because the dispute is confidential your client does not intend to make any further public statements until it has been resolved.

4.6 Preliminary correspondence

Once the above factors have been considered and a strategy for dealing with the dispute formulated, it may be appropriate (or even necessary under the applicable law or procedural rules) to send a letter to the other side which sets out your client's position before commencing proceedings. This correspondence will form part of the evidence in any subsequent arbitration, and care should be taken in its drafting and counsel's advice sought. Ideally, the letter should summarise your client's case in a well-balanced and matter-of-fact way, and set out exactly what steps your client is requesting and by when. Care should be taken when sending any notice required by contract or statute to ensure that it is sent to the correct parties in the correct manner.

If it is close to the expiry of any relevant limitation period, a claimant party may wish to consider, if permitted under the applicable law, agreeing with the other party to suspend time for limitation purposes before formally issuing a notice of arbitration and taking steps to appoint an arbitral tribunal. This might give a party time to protect its position through precautionary settlement discussions without it having to commence proceedings.

At the same time as sending open preliminary correspondence, it may also be sensible to attempt further settlement at this early stage in correspondence by proposing an ADR process or making an offer to settle (regardless of whether the arbitration agreement requires any preliminary ADR steps to be taken). Any such correspondence should be clearly marked as being 'without prejudice', 'confidential' and 'not to be sent to the arbitral tribunal. For disputes conducted across different systems of law and cultures, it is important to consider the extent to which even correspondence marked in this way will be privileged from disclosure in subsequent proceedings.

If pre-action correspondence (and the threat of commencing arbitration proceedings), or the use of ADR processes – whether undertaken voluntary or under an escalation clause – do not lead to a satisfactory resolution to the dispute, then the next step is likely to be to commence proceedings.

Appendix: Standard preservation of documents notice to employees

This notice confirms the immediate steps that you should take to avoid unnecessarily prejudicing your position through the creation or destruction of documents.

Any relevant document that is created or held by or on behalf of any member of your organisation (including in overseas offices), whether in hard copy or electronic form and whether for internal or external circulation and whether in draft or not, could have to be disclosed to the other party(ies) in this case if it progresses to arbitration. This includes notes, memos, reports, minutes, letters, emails and texts (no matter how informal). It may also extend to information contained outside the office eg, on relevant persons' smart phones, laptops and home computers.

You should ensure immediately that no existing documents relating to this dispute are destroyed. This includes all forms of electronic documents (and versions of documents) and their metadata (the history of an electronic document including when it was created, opened or amended and by whom). Any routine document or electronic data destruction policies within the organisation should be suspended until all relevant material has been secured (this includes stopping the over-writing of back-up tapes etc). All documents and electronic information held by relevant persons leaving the organisation must also be preserved.

We appreciate that this may cause some problems in practice but the duty to preserve evidence is very strict. The duty to search for and disclose documents in all forms may be restricted by considerations of cost and proportionality and we will need to discuss the potential scope of this exercise with you in detail so that we can advise on the best approach (including the need to agree this with the other party(ies)).

Please do not ask any third party to send you documents at this stage, until we have had a chance to consider what they have in their possession.

It is vital that you advise all relevant members of staff of the need to retain and preserve existing documents and of the risks of creating new documents now (ideally by briefing them orally, rather than sending them any note/email), along the following lines:

- Take great care in relation to the creation of any new documents relating to or concerning the matter, including internal memoranda, reports, minutes and emails.
- Ideally, no document should be created by you which contains anything which you would not want the other party to see at a future date, unless that document is created specifically for the purpose of obtaining legal advice from us or assisting in the conduct of litigation.
- Do not commission or produce reports unless absolutely necessary and, if it is absolutely necessary, consider commissioning any such report via external legal counsel, to increase the prospects of this being protected by privilege and not subsequently having to be disclosed to the other party.
- Do not copy documents indiscriminately, as this may result in loss of protection.
- Do not make manuscript notes on relevant documents or amend or alter them.
- Do not rearrange or edit relevant files (both hard copy and electronic).
- Do not destroy any documentation relating to the matter (including electronic information and databases).
- Do not alter or destroy the information automatically created by the production and delivery of electronic documents (the metadata).
- Do not approach third parties for documents or copies relating to the matter or give instructions to any third parties such as experts or potential experts without seeking advice first.
- If approached by third parties seeking documents (eg, subsidiary companies, insurers, auditors, accountants, police, regulatory or similar bodies, the press etc), please seek advice from us first.

We will give you more detailed advice on managing the disclosure process as the matter progresses. In the meantime, we hope the above is helpful. If you have any queries or concerns in relation to this, please contact us on [CONTACT DETAILS].

6. Commencing an arbitration

When a party wants to initiate an arbitration, it simply sends the other side a written document explaining that it wishes to avail of the arbitration mechanism in the contract. This document is commonly called a 'Request for Arbitration' or a 'Notice of Arbitration'. This chapter refers to it as a Request for Arbitration.

A Request for Arbitration must comply with any requirements set out in the arbitration agreement or in any relevant arbitration rules. In an institutional arbitration, apart from filing it with the relevant institution and paying any relevant filing fee, there are generally no formal requirements or detailed code or procedure on the manner of service of the Request for Arbitration on the respondent. What is required is to give the other side proper notice of the arbitration proceedings so that it is in a position to answer the case put against it, and present its own case in response.

It is advisable to set out in the Request for Arbitration at least the general nature of the claims and the relief that is being sought. Often further details are provided later in a statement of case, statement of claim or detailed memorandum. The reasons for this are set out below.

1. Whether to be claimant or respondent

The 'choice' of whether to be claimant or respondent is often not a choice at all. If a Request for Arbitration is served in accordance with a pre-existing arbitration agreement, then the party serving it is the claimant, and the recipient is the respondent.

Assuming the usual circumstances – that the parties have previously disagreed on the issues at a commercial level and that each side has made statements indicative of a legal dispute and the prospect of proceedings – a party should consider whether it would be advantageous to be the claimant or respondent to those proceedings.

In particular, a party faced with demands which it considered baseless or excessive might itself issue a Request for Arbitration seeking a declaration from the arbitral tribunal, such as a declaration that it is not liable in respect of a particular dispute.

One of the most common reasons for a party to initiate arbitration when it would normally be the respondent is to engage the jurisdiction of the arbitral tribunal if there was a concern that the other side may otherwise seek to commence court proceedings in breach of the arbitration agreement. For example, the other party may not accept that the dispute is governed by an arbitration agreement or may otherwise want to try to commence court proceedings in a jurisdiction where the judicial system may be more favourable to that party. Arbitration may therefore be started in order to try to head off any negative foreign court proceedings. Or it may be started to ensure that the 'correct' decision-making body is the first constituted and, all things being equal, likely to be the first to issue a decision on the dispute.

Claimants and respondents may also have different procedural advantages under the different rules and procedures that may be adopted by the tribunal. In some instances, for example, the respondent is entitled to file a rejoinder to the claimant's reply (and accordingly get the final say); in other cases, it is not. However, virtually all tribunals will involve the claimant having the first pleading (and opportunity to shape the dispute), and the respondent having the first opportunity to respond to a fully articulated case (and therefore be in a better position to gauge with which issues it must engage).

Where a dispute is inevitable, it is sometimes perceived to be an advantage to be the claimant, particularly where either the arbitration agreement or the relevant rules provide the respondent with a limited amount of time to respond to the claimant's case. For example, Article 15.3 of the London Court of International Arbitration (LCIA) Rules gives a respondent 28 days from receipt of the 'Statement of Case' to file its 'Statement of Defence'. Given that the respondent's job is to respond to the case made against it, a claimant may use the time before it has to file its statement of case to prepare a very detailed, comprehensive case against the other party, while the respondent will then have to act very quickly in response. It may therefore be to a party's advantage to initiate the proceedings as claimant. It should be noted though that in many international arbitration proceedings any default timetable in the institutional rules is often varied by agreement between the parties and tribunal, or by order of the tribunal, in order to ensure that all parties are given a fair and reasonable opportunity to present their case.

2. How to start an arbitration proceeding

An arbitration starts when one party requests that a dispute be referred to arbitration. The procedure for commencing an arbitration is typically specified in the arbitration agreement.

An arbitration agreement will typically involve three connected contracts. The first is the underlying contract (eg, a joint venture agreement or sales contract), which contains the arbitration agreement. The second is the arbitration agreement itself, often a clause referring to and incorporating detailed arbitral rules. The third is the contract formed by the arbitral reference – the further agreement formed between the parties to arbitrate a given dispute in accordance with the arbitration agreement.

Whether framed as a 'notice', 'claim', 'request' or otherwise, a Request for Arbitration is a contractual notice under both the underlying contract and the arbitration agreement. It will draw its content from the provisions of the contract.

It is important that the Request for Arbitration is broad enough to cover all of the claims and disputes which are to be covered in the arbitration. If the initial Request for Arbitration is not wide enough to cover a claim which would nevertheless be subject to the arbitration agreement, then subject to any rules on amending a claim, it will fall outside the jurisdiction of the tribunal.

Beyond that, what is required from a Request for Arbitration will depend on whether the arbitration agreement specifies *ad hoc* or institutional arbitration. Arbitral institutions such as the International Chamber of Commerce (ICC) or the LCIA have specified what is required in a Request for Arbitration under their respective rules. *Ad hoc* arbitration (ie, an arbitration not controlled by an institution and in accordance with its rules) is typically governed by the United Nations Commission on International Trade Law (UNCITRAL) Rules or else by the arbitration legislation of the seat. These will set out what is required to commence arbitration. In some cases, an arbitral institution may act as an appointing authority for *ad hoc* proceedings, constituting a tribunal under the applicable (usually UNCITRAL) rules.

The core features of a Request for Arbitration are the same in both institutional and *ad hoc* arbitration. However, in institutional arbitration, the notice is filed with the institution and served on the counterparty, by either the institution or the requesting party. In *ad hoc* proceedings, which have no 'registry', the notice is simply served on the counterparty.

2.1 Request for Arbitration

A Request for Arbitration, as an initiating document, must give the respondent (and the arbitrators to be appointed) sufficient information to understand the dispute and the claims put against it. It need not, however, be a detailed statement of claim of every issue and argument that the claimant may wish to plead in the arbitration. Those more detailed pleadings are generally issued only after the tribunal has been constituted (and, possibly, after certain procedural directions have been agreed). That being said, many institutional rules do allow parties to treat their Request for Arbitration as the statement of case (eg, LCIA Rules Article 15.2, Singapore International Arbitration Centre (SIAC) Rule 3.2, UNCITRAL Article 20.1, Hong Kong International Arbitration Centre (HKIAC) Article 16.1). This may be appropriate in cases where, for example, the claim is very simple with little evidence and so there is no real need for a separate more detailed pleading, or else if the claimant party is keen to speed up the process and so cut out the time that would be spent on further detailed submissions. An example where this approach could be taken would be a claim for the simple enforcement of a debt. There is also the added advantage in such cases of being able to put time pressure on the respondent as they will not have the luxury of the time during which the detailed statement of case is being prepared to build their case in defence. In the majority of cases, however, a claimant will want to serve a relatively simple Request for Arbitration with a more detailed pleading to follow.

The Request for Arbitration must also specify the authority of the tribunal to determine the dispute (by reference to the arbitration agreement) and the method by which arbitrators will be appointed.

By way of example, the UNCITRAL Rules require that a 'Notice of Arbitration' submitted in accordance with those rules include:

- a demand that the dispute be referred to arbitration;
- the names and contact details of the parties;
- identification of the arbitration agreement that is invoked;
- identification of any contract or other legal instrument out of or in relation to which the dispute arises, or in the absence of such contract or instrument, a brief description of the relevant relationship;
- a brief description of the claim and an indication of the amount involved, if any;
- the relief or remedy sought; and
- a proposal as to the number of arbitrators, language and place of arbitration, if these have not previously been agreed by the parties.

The Notice of Arbitration may also include:

- a proposal for the designation of an appointing authority;
- a proposal for the appointment of a sole arbitrator; and/or
- notification of the appointment of an arbitrator.

Similarly, as an example of the requirements of institutional arbitration, the LCIA Rules require a Request for Arbitration to include:

- the names, addresses, telephone, fax and email numbers (if known) of the parties to the arbitration and of their legal representatives;
- a copy of the written arbitration clause or separate written arbitration agreement invoked by the claimant, together with a copy of the contractual documentation in which the arbitration clause is contained or in respect of which the arbitration arises;
- a brief statement describing the nature and circumstances of the dispute including the estimated monetary amount or value, and specifying the

claims advanced by the claimant against the other party or parties to the arbitration;

- a statement of any procedural matters (eg, the seat or language(s) of the arbitration, the number of arbitrators or their qualifications or identities) on which the parties have already agreed in writing for the arbitration or in respect of which the claimant wishes to make a proposal;
- the name, address, telephone, fax and email details (if known) of the claimant's nominated arbitrator, if the arbitration agreement calls for parties to nominate arbitrators;
- the fee prescribed in the LCIA Schedule of Costs (without which the Request for Arbitration will be treated as not having been received by the registrar and the arbitration as not having been commenced); and
- confirmation that copies of the Request for Arbitration (including all accompanying documents) have been or are being served simultaneously on all other parties to the arbitration. This confirmation is to be followed by documentary proof of actual delivery of the Request for Arbitration.

Both examples contain the same core features: a description of the dispute and claims, reference to the arbitration agreement and a method of constituting the tribunal. Institutional rules, though, tend to be more prescriptive.

TIP A template for a typical institutional Request for Arbitration is set out in the appendix to this chapter.

TIP When filing a Request for Arbitration in institutional arbitration, it is important to take note of how many copies must be filed, and the registration fee to be paid, as the institution may not formally accept the request and commence the proceedings until these are provided.

TIP When effecting service of any document commencing arbitration proceedings, it is advisable to obtain proof of delivery and receipt (for example in the form of a courier delivery note and recipient signature for the delivery).

It is important to note for the purpose of limitation periods that, unless there is a special agreement, service of the Request for Arbitration will generally stop time running for limitation periods. This should always be checked against both the law of the arbitral seat and the law of the underlying contract.

An additional point of importance is the correct commencement of proceedings in instances where there are multiple-parties and/or multiple related contracts containing arbitration clauses. Where there are multiple parties to the arbitration agreement, it will be important to identify correctly the rights of each party with respect to the establishment of the procedure for the arbitration. Where there are multiple contracts involved in the dispute, close attention will need to be paid to whether the arbitration agreement, and the applicable rules, permit claims arising out of or in connection with more than one contract to be made in a single arbitration. For instance, Article 9 of the ICC Rules allows for a single arbitration to be commenced: "claims arising out of or in connection with more than one contract may be made in a single arbitration, irrespective of whether such claims are made under one or more than one arbitration agreement under the Rules." The same approach is also found in the SIAC Rules (Article 6), HKIAC Rules (Article 29) and the Stockholm Chamber of Commerce (SCC) Rules (Article 14).

In contrast, the LCIA Rules do not provide for arbitration being commenced under multiple contracts. This was confirmed in the case of *A v B* [2017] EWHC 3417 (Comm) where it was held that the consolidation provisions under Article 22.1(ix) are intended to address the situation of a dispute concerning multiple contracts.

Issues where there are multiple parties are dealt with differently under each of the principal arbitration rules. Under the LCIA Rules 2014 the joinder provision states that a party may be joined only on application by a party and that it requires the consent of the applicant and the new party for them to join the application (Article 22.1(viii) LCIA Rules 2014). In contrast to this, the ICC Rules state that new parties can be joined on the simple request of a party prior to the confirmation/appointment of any arbitrator (although after that date no additional party can be joined unless all parties, including the new parties, agree: Article 7.1 ICC Rules 2017). The SCC Rules state that a party may apply for another party to be joined until the submission of the Answer, but that after that date no request will be considered unless the SCC Board decides otherwise (Article 13 (2) SCC Rules 2017). The UNCITRAL Rules 2013 state that parties may only be joined on request by a party and only if the third party is a party to the arbitration agreement (Article 17.5 UNCITRAL Rules 2013).

Consolidation rules also vary between the institutions. Under the LCIA Rules, subject to the approval of the LCIA, where all the parties consent or there are multiple LCIA arbitrations that are being commenced under the same or a compatible arbitration agreement, and no arbitration tribunal has been appointed, or where it has been appointed the tribunal is composed of the same arbitrators, the proceedings may be consolidated (Article 22.1(x) LCIA Rules 2014). Under the ICC Rules arbitrations may be consolidated on the request of a party where either the parties agree or all the claims are made under the same arbitration agreement or involve the same parties with the same legal relationship and the ICC finds that the arbitration agreements are compatible (Article 10 ICC Rules 2017). Under the

SCC Rules 2017, similarly to the ICC Rules 2017, arbitrations may be consolidated on request by a party and agreement by the parties where the claims are made under more than one arbitration agreement, the relief sought arises out of the same transaction or series of transactions and the Tribunal considers the arbitration agreements to be compatible (Article 15 SCC Rules 2017). In contrast, the UNCITRAL Rules 2013 contain no consolidation provisions.

TIP If in any doubt with respect to commencement-related issues (such as whether one Request for Arbitration will suffice or whether separate requests are required), contacting the institution to confirm can be a helpful step.

2.2 Response to Request for Arbitration

Institutional arbitration rules typically require the respondent to provide an initial 'answer' (or 'response') to the Request for Arbitration. The response should contain the respondent's contact details (including its legal counsel representing it in the proceedings), its proposals for constituting the tribunal and any counterclaims to be made (along with the supporting documentation that would be required for those counterclaims as if made via a Request for Arbitration). Whilst there is typically no requirement on the respondent to set out any more than a bare denial of the claims made by the claimant in the Request for Arbitration, many respondents will take the opportunity to set out at least the brief details of their defence and comments on the relief sought by the claimant, in order that the Tribunal is aware from the outset that they intend to defend fully the claim being made against them.

The timeframe for making a response is typically 28 or 30 days from receipt of the Request for Arbitration or commencement of the arbitration. That said, most institutional rules will provide that if no response is made, then the arbitration will nonetheless continue, and that this does not mean that the claims made by the claimant's claims are deemed to be accepted by the respondent.

An example of such a provision is contained in Article 5 of the ICC Rules:

(1) Within 30 days from the receipt of the Request from the Secretariat, the respondent shall submit an Answer (the 'Answer') which shall contain the following information:

(a) its name in full, description, address and other contact details;

(b) the name in full, address and other contact details of any person(s) representing the respondent in the arbitration;

(c) its comments as to the nature and circumstances of the dispute giving rise to the claims and the basis upon which the claims are made;

(d) its response to the relief sought;

(e) any observations or proposals concerning the number of arbitrators and their choice in light of the claimant's proposals…and any nomination of an arbitrator required thereby; and

(f) any observations or proposals as to the place of the arbitration, the applicable rules of law and the language of the arbitration.

The respondent may submit such other documents or information with the Answer as it considers appropriate or as may contribute to the efficient resolution of the dispute.

…

(5) Any counterclaims made by the respondent shall be submitted with the Answer and shall provide:

(a) a description of the nature and circumstances of the dispute giving rise to the counterclaims and of the basis upon which the counterclaims are made;

(b) a statement of the relief sought together with the amounts of any quantified counterclaims and, to the extent possible, an estimate of the monetary value of any other counterclaims;

(c) any relevant agreements and, in particular, the arbitration agreement(s); and

(d) where counterclaims are made under more than one arbitration agreement, an indication of the arbitration agreement under which each counterclaim is made.

The respondent may submit such other documents or information with the counterclaims as it considers appropriate or as may contribute to the efficient resolution of the dispute.

The claimant shall submit a reply to any counterclaim within 30 days from the date of receipt of the counterclaims communicated by the Secretariat. Prior to the transmission of the file to the tribunal, the Secretariat may grant the claimant an extension of time for submitting the reply.

A response under the UNCITRAL Rules (see Article 4) is in similar terms, save that a discussion of any counterclaims in the response is only optional (as are jurisdictional challenges and any claims against non-claimant parties to the arbitration agreement).

It is worth noting that the 'response' or 'answer' does not mean that the Respondent has submitted to the jurisdiction of the Tribunal. The respondent may engage with the arbitral process with regards to the appointment of the tribunal while making it clear that it reserves its right to challenge the Tribunal's jurisdiction. Challenges to the jurisdiction of the tribunal can then be raised once the tribunal is constituted, provided that they are made by the time that the substantive defence is filed. This enables the process to continue and to be self-adjudicating.

2.3 Practical matters

An arbitration is a legal proceeding. Accordingly, there are certain formalities and procedures which must be complied with.

Where a Request for Arbitration is made in respect of an *ad hoc* arbitration, as discussed above, it is nothing more than a contractual notice sent to the counterparty. Although the request will need to contain the information required by any applicable rules (eg, the UNCITRAL Rules), there is no specific form or template document. The request is then sent, with a brief cover letter, to the proposed respondent. Like any contractual notice, however, this could be subject to any specific requirements of form, content or service that may be specified in the contract (for example, in a notices provision) or arbitration agreement. The response (if any) will be sent to the claimant in a similar form.

If institutional arbitration is requested, or where an arbitration agreement specifically provides that an institution will act as an administering or appointing authority, then the Request for Arbitration should be sent to the arbitral institution. Each institution has its own requirements for filing such a request. This usually involves a certain number of written copies (usually one for the institution, one for each proposed arbitrator and one for each opposing party), and, critically, the institution's filing fee. As a matter of practice, it is usual to serve a copy of the Request for Arbitration on the proposed respondent simultaneously with filing the Request for Arbitration with the institution, even if the institution's rules require the institution to provide a copy to the respondent directly before it will be considered served (eg, Article 4.5 ICC Rules).

TIP Some institutions provide for online filing of requests for arbitration (eg, LCIA). Others permit requests for arbitration to be submitted by email or fax provided that the requisite number of hard copies follows by post, courier or hand delivery (eg, ICC and Vienna International Arbitral Centre (VIAC)).

TIP In addition, practitioners should be mindful of the technological limits of submitting extremely large files. Typically preparing file transfer protocol (FTP) files well in advance of the deadline is essential in order to ensure that both the institutions, parties and the arbitrators will have ready access to the relevant documents at the correct time.

3. Jurisdictional challenges

3.1 Challenging the applicability of the arbitration agreement

An arbitral tribunal can determine only those disputes within its jurisdiction. That jurisdiction is determined by the parties' agreement. However, because the parties' agreement may be contained in multiple documents agreed well before any dispute had arisen, there is often disagreement as to whether claims advanced in a Request for Arbitration are within the jurisdiction of the arbitral tribunal.

This effectively leaves a party that is disputing an arbitral tribunal's jurisdiction with three choices:

- It can ignore the Request for Arbitration (and subsequent proceedings which will continue without its participation), and argue before any court in subsequent recognition and enforcement proceedings that the award resulting from the arbitral tribunal is invalid because the tribunal lacked jurisdiction. This is a risky strategy, particularly if the party disputing jurisdiction has assets across many jurisdictions (and consequently might face multiple enforcement proceedings), as the courts in New York Convention states have only limited grounds on which to refuse to enforce an arbitral award. Furthermore, different courts in different jurisdictions may come to opposite conclusions. As such, this path is almost always inadvisable.
- It can take no part in the arbitral proceedings, but instead seek an immediate declaration from the courts of the seat of the arbitration that the tribunal does not have jurisdiction to determine the claims advanced. However, as noted in Chapter 4, the courts in some jurisdictions will generally leave the question of jurisdiction to the tribunal to determine. Even in those jurisdictions where the courts will determine the question themselves, such as England and Wales, this is often only the case where the relevant claim has been brought before the court in the first instance and the respondent party is seeking a stay of these proceedings in favour of arbitration. Where arbitration has already been commenced, and particularly if a tribunal has been constituted, the courts may await the decision of the tribunal on its own jurisdiction before considering the question: see Article 16(3) of the UNCITRAL Model Law and, for English-seat arbitrations, Section 67 of the Arbitration Act 1996.
- It can participate in the arbitration and ask the tribunal to determine its objection to the tribunal's jurisdiction. This allows the party to bring its challenge before the tribunal, yet at the same time reserves its right to renew its jurisdictional objections before the relevant court (ie, either the court of the seat of arbitration, or the court of the jurisdiction where the enforcement is sought) in the event that such objections are not accepted by the tribunal. This is the advisable course in most cases, because it gives the respondent at least two opportunities to have jurisdiction overturned: before the tribunal and, if unsuccessful, again before a court. Under English law, the court can determine the question of jurisdiction afresh and is not bound by a tribunal's findings of fact. The Singaporean courts take the same approach; where the court is presented with a jurisdiction challenge, it is not bound to accept or consider the tribunal's findings and will consider it *de novo*.

Each of these approaches can be combined with commencing parallel proceedings in what the party claims is an appropriate forum with jurisdiction over the dispute. A party disputing jurisdiction may also ask a court or other tribunal to issue an anti-suit injunction (or anti-arbitration injunction) calling on the other party to stay or withdraw the arbitral proceedings said to have been brought without jurisdiction.

Cross-reference For more on pre-commencement of arbitral proceedings, see Chapter 5; for more information concerning interlocutory applications and provisional measures, including asking a court or other tribunal to issue an anti-suit or anti-arbitration injunction, see Chapter 10.

3.2 Grounds for challenging the applicability of the arbitration agreement

There are several possible objections to the jurisdiction of an arbitral tribunal. The most common are detailed below.

(a) *Not a party to the arbitration agreement*

The parties' consent to arbitrate may be straightforward; for example: a demand for payment from Party A to Party B under a supply contract between them that contains the arbitration clause. It may, however, be much less straightforward. A party may allege that it is not party to the arbitration agreement – for example, because:

- there is no arbitration agreement;
- any agreement was with some other entity – perhaps a different entity within the respondent's corporate group;
- the purported arbitration agreement was not validly incorporated by reference into the contract governing the dispute, and accordingly there is no valid arbitration agreement;
- the arbitration agreement was not validly assigned or novated to the claimant or respondent; or
- the claimant (often an insurer) is not subrogated to the insured's rights and obligations under the arbitration agreement.

Many other examples are possible. They are all, in effect, arguments that the challenging party did not agree to arbitrate at all (or at least in any relevant way). Accordingly, they are objections to the party's participation in the whole of the proceedings.

(b) *Challenging the scope of the arbitration agreement*

Alternatively, a party challenging jurisdiction may accept the existence of the arbitration agreement between the parties, but challenge whether the agreement extends to the matters in dispute.

For example, a party may accept that contractual disputes are arbitrable, but argue that other claims (eg, claims in tort, breaches of fiduciary duty or claims in respect of immovable property) are outside the scope of an arbitration clause. Generally, and subject to the provisions of each individual contract, commercial parties are presumed to have intended that all connected disputes would be determined by the one decision-making body.

Alternatively, in a situation involving more than one contract between the parties, a party may argue that the arbitration agreement relied on by the claimant covers only disputes arising under some other contract(s) between the parties, and was not incorporated into the contract from which the matters in dispute arise. For example, a party might argue that a joint venture agreement is governed by an arbitration clause, but a discrete contract for the supply of services from one joint venture party to the other, silent on the issue, is properly subject to the jurisdiction of the appropriate court.

(c) Challenging arbitrability of the dispute

A party might also challenge the fundamental arbitrability of a matter. This is an argument that, regardless of what the parties might have attempted to agree in an otherwise valid arbitration agreement, the tribunal cannot determine the subject matter of the arbitration. A clear example of such a matter is a person's criminal guilt, which can be determined only by a state's criminal court. This category is narrowing, however, following a general trend within states (and the courts of those states) to adopt more pro-arbitration stances.

The precise scope of what is and is not considered arbitrable varies across jurisdictions. However, it is generally invoked, aside from in relation to criminal guilt, in the context of questions of competition/antitrust law, corruption or insolvency. Each of these questions either is a matter of inherent public interest or requires the special authority of a court to administer. Some jurisdictions also specify that consumer law or employment disputes cannot be arbitrated (at least in a conventional arbitration), in a bid to protect consumers and employees from what is perceived as an uneven playing field.

These restrictions, however, are confined to the particular questions of criminal guilt, breaches of competition policy and so on. There is no reason why a contractual dispute which is factually linked with criminal acts or anti-competitive behaviour would necessarily be found not to be arbitrable.

Cross-reference For more on arbitrability, see Chapter 3.

3.3 Bringing the challenge

Where a party (invariably the respondent) wishes to challenge the jurisdiction of the tribunal, it must do so at an early stage in proceedings. A party is not entitled to participate in the merits of a hearing and then raise a jurisdictional objection late in the day if it perceives that the award is unlikely to fall in its favour. It is generally (although not universally) accepted that any jurisdictional objection must be made prior to, or together with, the first substantive pleadings on the merits filed by the party challenging jurisdiction. In practice, such objections are often made (or at least signalled) in a response to a Request for Arbitration (with the full details following in the subsequent comprehensive pleading).

Whether fully set out in the initial response, or outlined and fully substantiated later, a jurisdictional challenge must set out the grounds on which the respondent is challenging the tribunal's jurisdiction, and refer to the evidence supporting its arguments. It should also address whether the respondent seeks to bifurcate the proceedings – that is, to have the tribunal determine the jurisdictional challenge as a separate and preliminary issue to the merits of the dispute. Although this may seem an obvious course (since if the tribunal does not have jurisdiction to determine the merits, there seems little point in expending time and money arguing them), it may be that the issues, evidence and witnesses relevant to a jurisdictional challenge are inextricably wound up in the merits of the case, and that it is actually more time and cost effective for both jurisdiction and the merits to be heard together. The original UNCITRAL Rules adopted in 1976 assumed that a tribunal would ordinarily determine jurisdiction as a preliminary issue (see Article 21(4)), whereas the 2013 UNCITRAL Rules (with new article 1, paragraph 4, as adopted in 2013) have no presumption in either direction (see Article 23(3)).

From a procedural point of view, when an objection to jurisdiction is signalled in a response or in the correspondence surrounding the Terms of Reference (where applicable) or setting of the procedure, it is not yet necessary to prove or even fully articulate the grounds and supporting evidence for the challenge (eg, by annexing a complete record of the correspondence which is said to disprove the applicability of an arbitration agreement) – those will follow in the substantive challenge submissions. However, the challenge must still be sufficiently detailed at this stage to allow the claimant (and tribunal) to understand the basis of the respondent's objection, and to allow the tribunal to determine how it should proceed with the challenge when deciding the procedure for the arbitration.

3.4 *Prima facie* review under the ICC Rules

Articles 6(3) and 6(4) of the ICC Rules provide that a *prima facie* review of the tribunal's jurisdiction may be carried out by the ICC Court where a challenge to the existence of an arbitration agreement between the parties is set out in the response, or where no response is filed.

Before a tribunal is convened, the ICC Secretary General may refer a proposed arbitration to the ICC Court to determine whether, *prima facie*, an arbitration agreement under the ICC Rules may exist. This is a high-level threshold test and is not intended to replace substantive challenges before the tribunal, which are still heard by the arbitral tribunal once it has been convened in the manner described above. Rather, it is designed to keep out claims which are clearly outside the jurisdiction of any tribunal that might be convened. For example, for a proposed arbitration between parties A and B, the ICC may decline to convene a tribunal if B alleges that no arbitration agreement exists between A and B, and A has provided no evidence of such an agreement beyond its own assertion. However, if A were to provide an arbitration agreement which was on its face between A and B2 (a related company of B), and assert that in reality the agreement was also between A and B, this would usually satisfy the prima facie standard. The arbitral tribunal would then be convened and would proceed to determine the challenge to its jurisdiction.

4. Urgent interlocutory relief: emergency measures and emergency arbitrators

Although arbitral tribunals can offer swift, effective and adaptable resolution of disputes, it can sometimes take a significant amount of time for the parties to establish the tribunal. This is particularly the case if they are unable to agree where required to do so, or if the intervention of the courts of the seat is required. In the ordinary course of events, it may take many months to move from a Request for Arbitration to constituting the arbitral tribunal and holding a first procedural conference.

There is therefore a significant amount of time in which parties that have agreed to submit a dispute to arbitration, and are in the process of constituting the tribunal, are not yet able to seek and obtain interim orders (eg, freezing or preservation orders, anti-suit injunctions or security for costs), from the yet to be established tribunal.

Parties (and arbitral rules) have traditionally circumvented this problem by providing that parties were entitled to seek interim relief from a relevant court prior to the establishment of the arbitral tribunal to preserve their rights, and that such conduct would not constitute a breach or waiver of the agreement to arbitrate. All major arbitral institutions, and the UNCITRAL Rules, contain provisions to this effect.

However, depending on the nature and location of the dispute and the relief sought, the disputants may not have access to an appropriate court. Moreover, if the arbitration agreement contains what in England and Wales is referred to as a Scott v Avery clause, which precludes access to other dispute resolution bodies prior to the issue of an arbitral award, a court may interpret this wording as excluding access to interim relief from the courts.

Several prominent institutions (including the ICC, LCIA, SCC, Swiss Chambers of Commerce, SIAC, HKIAC, International Centre for Dispute

Resolution (ICDR) and American Arbitration Association (AAA)) have adopted 'emergency arbitrator' provisions within their rules, which allow a party to seek the appointment of an emergency arbitrator at very short notice prior to the constitution of a tribunal. The ICC Rules, for example, envisage appointment of an arbitrator within two days of the Request for Arbitration, setting down a procedural timetable within a further two days, and an order no later than 15 days after the appointment of the emergency arbitrator (see Article 29 and Appendix V). Those orders are not binding on any subsequently appointed tribunal and can be sought only in respect of urgent, interim or conservatory measures. The requesting party must establish that these cannot wait until the main arbitral tribunal is constituted.

Although these timeframes are impressive in comparison to full arbitral proceedings, they may still be significantly slower (and less responsive) than those possible for urgent applications brought before most major commercial courts, and certainly than, say, the courts in London. They also require that notice be given to the other party: there is no scope for an *ex-parte* application.

Furthermore, it is unclear to what extent the interim orders (or 'interim awards' as they are referred to in some institutional rules) will be enforceable by a court. If they are treated as an interim order rather than an award, both that and the award of any associated costs may prove difficult to enforce. This may be particularly true if the other side refuses to proceed with a full arbitration or disputes the existence of a binding arbitration agreement.

However, in jurisdictions where parties consider the courts to be either less responsive or less reliable, emergency arbitrator provisions provide a welcome alternative forum for urgent orders.

The statistics released by some of the prominent arbitral institutions show that there is variation in the prevalence and success of applications to appoint emergency arbitrators. For instance, SIAC appears to be the most popular rules under which to make an emergency arbitrator application; 19 applications were made in 2017 (of a total 452 cases filed) with 16 of those application resulting in an award/order and with one application being withdrawn (two applications remained pending at the time of SIAC publishing its 2017 statistics). Since SIAC introduced emergency arbitrator provisions in 2010 (the first arbitral institution to do so), 57 emergency applications were received between 1 July 2010 and 31 March 2017. Of those applications 33 (ie, 58%) were granted either in full or in part, six (ie, 10%) were withdrawn and 16 (ie, 28%) were rejected (two remained pending at the time of SIAC's publication of its statistics). This is to be contrasted with the statistics released by the LCIA which record that since introducing emergency arbitrator provisions in 2014, as at the time of publishing the 2017 LCIA statistics, only two applications had been made for an emergency arbitration to be appointed, and both were rejected.

There are varied reasons for why emergency arbitrator provisions are used more frequently under certain rules; confidence in local courts, tradition in seeking urgent relief through the courts and a culture of maintaining privacy in certain jurisdictions being just some of the potential reasons.

When considering emergency relief, it is also important to bear in mind local case law and any local idiosyncrasies of the *lex arbitri*, as in certain jurisdictions it seems that the availability of effective and timely relief from an emergency arbitrator may operate to curtail the powers of the local court to grant such relief. For instance, in the interesting (and factually unusual) recent case of *Gerald Metals S.A. v Timis & Ors* [2016] EWHC 2327 (Ch), the English High Court held that where there is sufficient time for an applicant to obtain interim relief by way of an expedited tribunal or from an emergency arbitrator under the applicable institutional rules (in this case LCIA Rules Articles 9A and 9B), the court does not have power to grant urgent relief (as section 44(5) of the *Arbitration Act 1996* provides that the court may only act to the extent that the tribunal has no power or is unable at that time to act).

It should also be noted that once the Tribunal is established, the parties are normally required to seek any interim relief from the Tribunal save for in exceptional circumstances where urgent *ex parte* relief or relief against third parties is required (eg, ICC Rules Article 28(2), SIAC Rule 30.3). In fact, even in those exceptional circumstances, the rules may still require the party seeking the relief to obtain permission from the Tribunal first before it can go to the relevant court (eg, LCIA Rules, Art 25.3) – this may, however, defeat the object of seeking an *ex parte* order.

Cross-reference For more on seeking interim relief from the Tribunal, see Chapter 10.

TIP When drafting arbitration agreements and considering the seat and/or the rules to adopt, it is worth bearing in mind how easy it may be to obtain urgent interim measures from the courts of the relevant seat and, thus, whether emergency arbitrator provisions may be necessary.

Appendix: Template Request for Arbitration

[NAME OF ARBITRAL INSTITUTION]

CASE NO.

[NAME OF CLAIMANT(S)]
Claimant(s)

- v -

[NAME OF RESPONDENT(S)]
Respondent(s)

REQUEST FOR ARBITRATION

[DATE]

[LAW FIRM]
[ADDRESS]
Ref:
Counsel to the Claimant

Table of Contents

Page

I. **Introduction**

II. **The Parties**

A. [Claimant(s)]
B. [Respondent(s)]

III. **Contractual And Factual Background**

IV. **Arbitration**

V. **The Place Of Arbitration**

VI. **The Language Of Arbitration**

VII. **The Arbitral Tribunal**

VIII. **Applicable Law**

IX. **Representation**

A. Claimant(s)
B. Respondent(s)

X. **Service And Costs Advance**

[NAME OF ARBITRAL INSTITUTION]

CASE NO.

[NAME OF CLAIMANT(S)]
Claimant(s)

- v -

[NAME OF RESPONDENT(S)]
Respondent(s)

REQUEST FOR ARBITRATION

I. Introduction

Pursuant to Article [NUMBER] of the [NAME OF RULES] ('[NAME] Rules') the Claimant, [NAME OF CLAIMANT] ('[CLAIMANT]'), hereby submits its Request for Arbitration against the Respondent, [NAME OF RESPONDENT] ('[RESPONDENT]').

Dispute arise out of contractual arrangements between the parties in relation to [COMPLETE BRIEF SUMMARY].

II. The Parties

A. [CLAIMANT]

[CLAIMANT] is a company incorporated and existing under the laws of [COUNTRY]. [BRIEF SUMMARY OF COMPANY'S FUNCTION].

[CLAIMANT]'s details are as follows:

[CLAIMANT NAME AND ADDRESS, TEL, FAX AND EMAIL]

B. [RESPONDENT]

[RESPONDENT] is a company incorporated and existing under the laws of [COUNTRY]. [BRIEF SUMMARY OF COMPANY'S FUNCTION].

[RESPONDENT]'s details are as follows:

[RESPONDENT NAME AND ADDRESS, TEL, FAX, EMAIL]

III. Contractual and Factual Background

[COMPLETE WITH DETAIL OF AGREEMENTS, PERFORMANCE, BREACH ETC] .

Relief Sought

Accordingly, the Claimant seeks the following relief:

[SET OUT DETAILS OF RELIEF SOUGHT, INCLUDING INTEREST, LEGAL COSTS AND EXPENSES, AND MANAGEMENT COSTS AND EXPENSES].

IV. Arbitration

[SET OUT ARBITRATION CLAUSE OF THE AGREEMENT]:

[SET OUT SATISFACTION OF ANY CONDITIONS PRECEDENT TO THE ARBITRATION CLAUSE]. The matters in dispute are, accordingly, properly referred to arbitration.

V. The Place of Arbitration

[IF IN THE CLAUSE, STATE PLACE OF ARBITRATION. OTHERWISE, STATE PREFERENCE DEPENDING ON WHAT RULES ALLOW].

VI. The Language of Arbitration

[IF IN THE CLAUSE, STATE LANGUAGE OF ARBITRATION. OTHERWISE, STATE PREFERENCE DEPENDING ON WHAT RULES ALLOW].

VII. The Arbitral Tribunal

[IF IN THE CLAUSE, STATE NUMBER OF ARBITRATORS. OTHERWISE, STATE PREFERENCE DEPENDING ON WHAT RULES ALLOW. IF NOMINATION PERMITTED AND DESIRABLE, SET OUT NOMINATION].

VIII. Applicable Law

[STATE GOVERNING LAW OF THE CONTRACT].

IX. Representation

A. Claimant

The Claimant is represented in this arbitration by:

[LAW FIRM]

[ADDRESS]

Attn:

Tel:

Fax:

Email:

B. Respondent

[To the best of our knowledge, the Respondent has not to date instructed legal representatives in relation to this arbitration] OR [SET OUT LEGAL REPRESENTATIVE FOR THE RESPONDENT].

X. Service and Costs Advance

[RESPONDENT]'s postal address is [ADDRESS].

The Claimant confirms that, in accordance with [PROVISION IN RULES], [NUMBER OF] copies of this Request for Arbitration have been served on [INSTITUTION]. Further, a [bank transfer/cheque] has been made to the [INSTITUTION] for the advance of [AMOUNT].

The Claimant has also directly served a copy of this Request for Arbitration on [RESPONDENT] at the above address [CHECK NOTICE PROVISIONS IN CONTRACT FOR ANY VARIATIONS HERE].

Respectfully submitted

[LAW FIRM]
Counsel for the Claimant
[CLAIMANT]

[NAME OF ARBITRAL INSTITUTION]

CASE NO.

[NAME OF CLAIMANT(S)]
Claimant(s)

- v -

[NAME OF RESPONDENT(S)]
Respondent(s)

INDEX OF EXHIBITS

[LIST EXHIBITS]

7. Selecting the tribunal or arbitrator

Constituting a tribunal is the process of selecting and appointing the arbitrator (or arbitrators) as set out in the relevant arbitration agreement.

Choosing an arbitrator is one of the most important steps in the arbitration process. In making such a choice it is possible for the parties to influence the entire course of the arbitration process, and to influence the administration, efficiency, tone and even final decision of the tribunal.

As the arbitration process is based on agreement between the parties, both have some influence over the identity of the arbitrators. This is one of the major differences between arbitration and litigation, and a key advantage of the arbitration process. This influence may be exercised directly by the appointment of an arbitrator of the party's choice, or a party may be able to veto an appointment that it deems unsuitable.

1. Criteria required from arbitrators

In addition to choosing an arbitrator that they trust, in whom they have confidence and who will run the arbitration properly, the parties should bear in mind the following considerations when selecting an arbitrator.

1.1 Independence and conflicts of interest

The first question to be asked about a potential arbitrator is whether accepting the appointment will lead to a conflict of interest. Under all arbitration rules, arbitrators have duties to be independent of the parties and avoid potential conflicts of interest. The International Bar Association (IBA) has produced guidance on the effect of situations that may lead to conflicts of interest in the form of a red, orange and green traffic light system (see the 2014 IBA Guidelines on Conflicts of Interest in International Arbitration[1]). Among other things, the guidelines make it clear that parties should consider whether it is appropriate to appoint the same arbitrator in multiple cases. Queries relating to conflicts should thus be among the first questions asked of any potential appointee.

1 www.ibanet.org/Publications/publications_IBA_guides_and_free_materials.aspx.

> **TIP** When seeking to determine a potential arbitrator's availability, you should provide the parties' names, the names of their counsel and a very brief description of the dispute in question in order that the potential appointee can check whether he or she would have any conflict of interest.

1.2 Partiality and bias

Strongly linked to the consideration of conflict of interest is the question of whether a candidate could be accused of partiality or bias. If such an accusation is upheld, it may mean an arbitrator being disqualified or barred from acting. It may also make any award made by that arbitrator susceptible to challenge.

In addition, if an arbitrator acts in such a way that he or she could be accused of partiality, the other arbitrators may simply ignore or give less weight to any views expressed. Therefore, if there is any relationship between the arbitrator and the party that appointed him or her, that party should consider seriously whether it would be appropriate or in its best interests to appoint that arbitrator, even if there is no conflict of interest.

1.3 Pre-disposition towards the dispute

It is equally possible for parties to identify perceived pre-dispositions of arbitrators towards the subject matter of a dispute. A pre-disposition has been variously described as a tendency towards certain kinds of decisions, a discernible opinion on a certain issue, or a like or dislike of commonly held positions in a dispute. This is often one of the most important elements that parties consider when choosing an arbitrator and, although slightly controversial, it can greatly affect a party's chances of succeeding.

A pre-disposition may be ascertained from an arbitrator's previous decisions or writings on similar issues. Or it may arise from his or her opinion on a particular area of law or commercial practice. As long as an arbitrator's position on such matters is justifiable and is not perceived to be a bias outside his or her professional duties, then it can certainly be an advantage for a party to appoint an arbitrator who is more likely to push for a decision on his or her side of a dispute.

However, any such perception can be dangerous: it may be incorrect, or the opinion of the arbitrator may change. It should also be recognised that each dispute has differing facts and issues, which may lead an arbitrator to reach a decision that is contrary to expectations.

1.4 Nationality and language

Arbitration rules often contain provisions determining the nationality of arbitrators. The importance of nationality is significant. Arbitrators' views on determining a dispute or the procedure for running the arbitration will often depend on the traditions, norms or politics of the country in which they have trained, worked or lived. A good example of this in the legal sphere is the difference in interpretation that exists between lawyers from the common law and civil law traditions.

It is important that arbitrators can work together efficiently and understand the dispute and the positions of the parties. Nationality may help an arbitrator to understand the context of a dispute or the background of the business of the parties.

However, there may also be difficulties (and perhaps even an appearance of bias) if a national of the same jurisdiction as one of the parties finds in favour of that party. For this reason, a number of institutional rules provide that the nationality of the chairman or of a sole arbitrator must be different from that of the parties. This is thought to help balance the arbitration and should be considered when choosing the nationality of any party-nominated arbitrators.

Language must also be considered. If a panel of arbitrators, or the arbitrators and the parties, do not share a common language, then it may be difficult to ensure that communication is quick and clear. Translation necessarily slows any proceedings and often fails to pass on all of the information and nuances that knowledge of a common language would provide.

1.5 Formal qualifications

Some arbitration agreements stipulate that arbitrators must possess certain formal qualifications. These may be legal qualifications for a number of years or membership of a particular industry or trade body. It may also be the case that, under the rules of a particular arbitral institution, only arbitrators registered with or approved by that institution may be appointed. A lack of qualifications specified by an arbitration agreement or by an arbitral institution may lead to a challenge to an arbitrator's appointment or his or her removal from a tribunal.

1.6 Expertise in a particular area

A number of industry sectors traditionally appoint arbitrators with expertise and experience within that sector. Even if such a tradition does not exist, it may benefit an arbitrator's understanding or analysis of a dispute to have relevant expertise. Common examples of arbitrators selected with professional expertise as a prerequisite are arbitrators concerned with construction or shipping.

1.7 Lawyers versus non-lawyers

In almost all circumstances, arbitrators are required to give reasons for their decisions. These may be subject to appeal or challenge through a national court system and must stand up to scrutiny. Nominating a legally trained and experienced arbitrator increases the chances that he or she will be able to handle these tasks properly. Lawyers are also familiar with the procedural and administrative concerns of a contentious dispute, and may also have professional experience in arbitration. It is not unusual for questions of statutory or contractual interpretation to arise in the course of an arbitration, together with conflict of laws and jurisdiction issues.

TIP If you want particular expertise which requires a non-lawyer, consider appointing a party-appointed arbitrator who is a professional expert, but a chairman who is a lawyer with arbitration experience. That way, you can benefit from both disciplines.

1.8 Diversity

Choosing arbitrators with diverse backgrounds and characteristics can ensure that a tribunal reflects and understands the parties' own diversity and wider social norms. Having more diverse panels can also help to improve the overall quality of decision-making.

One characteristic which has received particular attention is gender. In 2015, members of the arbitration community drew up a pledge to address the under-representation of women on international arbitral tribunals. The Pledge seeks to increase, on an equal opportunity basis, the number of women appointed as arbitrators in order to achieve a fair representation as soon as practically possible, with the ultimate goal of full parity. All the major arbitral institutions, international law firms, and arbitrators and practitioners have signed the Pledge.

1.9 Different kinds of lawyer

If it is decided that a lawyer is appropriate, you may wish to consider whether an academic or practising lawyer is more suited to the dispute. In certain circumstances, knowledge of business practicalities or technical knowledge of a particular area of law may be desirable. Lawyers experienced in different legal systems may also have qualities that place them above other options. For example, it may be preferable to have a lawyer trained in a civil legal system as part of the arbitral tribunal rather than one trained in a common law system, or vice versa.

1.10 Practical considerations

Just as important as the qualifications and professional abilities of a potential arbitrator are his or her practical skills. These will ensure that the arbitration is run properly and effectively.

(a) Caseload and availability

The most well-known and sought-after arbitrators tend to have diaries that are booked up months or years in advance. These individuals may be at the peak of their profession, but they may be unable to ensure that the parties' dispute is heard quickly. Parties should consider whether the arbitrator in question will be able and willing to spend the necessary time and effort to conduct the arbitration, or whether other commitments will interfere.

TIP When checking conflicts, it is a good idea to check whether the candidate would be sufficiently available to handle the arbitration in a timely manner. Having an idea at this early stage of when you think the matter might be heard and for how long can help to avoid unnecessary delay.

(b) *Cost*

In large international arbitrations the cost of the arbitrator's time may be small in comparison to the sums in dispute. However, in those arbitrations where the arbitrator charges on an hourly rate basis (eg, the London Court of International Arbitration (LCIA)), clients will always expect their legal counsel to be aware of different cost options and to minimise any costs where possible.

(c) ***Management and communication skills***

Being an arbitrator includes managing the arbitration process. If the arbitrators do not or cannot run the arbitration effectively – including the use of office staff, transcribers, printers and other support – then the parties will find their dispute resolution long-winded and costly.

Where there is a panel of three arbitrators, each party appointing its member of the panel and considering a chairman must think carefully about the appointees' skills in communication and persuasion. Even an arbitrator who supports your case will be of no use unless he or she can communicate that support to the rest of the panel coherently and in such a manner that his or her view is respected and given significant weight.

(d) ***Enthusiasm***

It is sometimes worth considering candidates who are less established in the arbitration community. A young or relatively inexperienced, energetic arbitrator may bring fresh ideas and an interested approach to the dispute. He or she may also be more available and less expensive. However, your client may be more comfortable with one of the experienced arbitrators who is better known and more established in the field.

2. How to choose an arbitrator

Given the vast amount of information necessary to make an informed choice of arbitrators, what sources are available to legal professionals or businesspeople to help them to differentiate between individuals?

2.1 **Recommendations**

Personal or professional recommendations have traditionally been, and remain, the most common method of choosing an arbitrator. Arbitrators who are used regularly are more likely to be the subject of recommendations. Personal recommendations are often highly useful, especially if they come from a person whose opinion and judgement is respected.

> **TIP** Remember, a recommendation is based on experience of a particular arbitration – what is right for one arbitration may be wrong for yours. Recommendations are no substitute, therefore, for careful consideration of your needs and the requirements of your arbitration.

2.2 **Reputation**

If an individual is known as the leading arbitrator in his or her field, then you may be fairly comfortable that his or her appointment will not be a bad decision. However, you will not be able to discern his or her engagement with your dispute or any pre-disposition towards the issues.

Choosing an arbitrator based on reputation, rather than first-hand knowledge or recommendation, will usually mean greater expense. However, an arbitrator with a good reputation among his or her peers will likely be respected by the rest of the panel and have persuasive views in that context.

2.3 ***Curriculum vitae***

Experienced arbitrators will usually have a CV that they can send to interested parties, which will include details of their expertise and availability.

2.4 **Interviews**

Parties increasingly ask for interviews with potential arbitrators before making a recommendation or appointment. However, due to the possibility of accusations of partiality or related issues, some arbitrators refuse to be interviewed or to meet with the parties prior to appointments, or significantly limit the information that may be discussed at any interview. The Chartered Institute of Arbitrators (CIArb) has produced a widely used practice guideline on interviewing prospective arbitrators. This includes a prohibition on discussing, whether directly or indirectly, the circumstances around the dispute, the positions of the parties or the merits of the case.

> **TIP** The CIArb guidelines can be found at www.ciarb.org/guidelines-and-ethics/guidelines/arbitration-guidelines.

If an interview is possible, any description of the case should be balanced and neutral, and must not go into the relative strengths and weaknesses of the case, or the matters at issue between the parties. A summary of the dispute will often be prepared in writing prior to the interview and made available to all parties, or a transcript of the interview will be taken in order to ward off any future challenges based on accusations of partiality or bias.

2.5 Arbitrator databases

There are a number of online databases and resources to help with arbitrator selection. Some of these require the payment of a fee to access information, while others are offered free of charge. For example, Global Arbitration Review provides an Arbitrator Research Tool (ART) with information on awards, CVs and procedural preferences, on payment of a fee, while the Equal Representation in Arbitration (ERA) Search Committee offers a free online service for female arbitrators.

These databases can provide information and suggestions to help with a search, but they cannot provide the same level of insight as a personal or professional recommendation.

2.6 Research

It may be possible to identify the position which may be adopted by a potential arbitrator by researching if they have published any commentary on issues pertinent to the matters in dispute. If they are a retired judge or have previously been an arbitrator in a published award, reviewing these materials may give an insight into their views on certain issues.

3. Number of arbitrators

For obvious reasons, it is presumed in most rules and arbitration agreements that there should be an odd number of arbitrators sitting on any particular tribunal. By far the most common are arbitrations with either a single arbitrator or a panel of three. While complex or specialist disputes may have more arbitrators, this is rare and can result in otherwise unnecessary duplication of work and lengthy deliberations.

3.1 Sole arbitrators

Appointing a sole arbitrator is less costly than having three and will normally mean less delay. After all, there will be only one diary to consider. A sole arbitrator will often make his or her award and set out the reasoning more quickly, avoiding the need for lengthy consultation or debate. Sole arbitrators are almost always appointed by agreement or by an institution.

3.2 Three arbitrators

It is often argued that a panel of three arbitrators will produce an award and a decision that is more certain, of higher quality and less open to challenge than one produced by a sole arbitrator. Parties tend to agree on three arbitrators when it is anticipated that the arbitration will be high value or complex. Where it is likely that a dispute will involve very detailed or technical evidence, it may be an advantage for the tribunal to have three members. It may also be useful to have one or more of the panel appointed because of their particular technical or industry expertise.

Having three arbitrators, with one nominated by either side, may alleviate or eliminate problems of differing experience or legal traditions that might otherwise cause significant issues. Where each side comes from a different professional, legal or cultural background, appointing one arbitrator to represent each background can mean that a common ground is more likely to be reached. One of the most important advantages of a three-person tribunal is that the process, and ultimately the award rendered, will benefit from the arbitrators being able to discuss the evidence and legal arguments with their colleagues. Three heads considering a problem can often be preferable to one.

3.3 Chairman

Where three arbitrators are appointed to a tribunal, one will act as a chairman. It may be permissible for the party-nominated arbitrators to consult the party that nominated them about the choice of a chairman. On procedural matters, the other two arbitrators may grant – with the parties' agreement – the chairman the power to make decisions. This can ensure the smooth running of the arbitration.

The chairman will engage in the process like the other two arbitrators, and will take part in all hearings and discussions.

Cross-reference For more on choosing one or three arbitrators, please see Chapter 4.

4. Methods of selection

4.1 Appointment by institution or other body

The parties may opt in their arbitration agreement for an arbitral institution to appoint a chairman or sole arbitrator of its choice. In rare cases, the parties may agree to an institution or other neutral body selecting the entire tribunal. This has been suggested as a way of addressing concerns about the appointment of partisan arbitrators. It may also have the advantage of improving diversity on tribunals. However, large numbers of users favour party appointments, as the ability to select an arbitrator gives the parties a sense of control and trust in the proceedings.

Even where an arbitration clause does not provide for an institution to be involved in the appointment process, parties may ask the institution for a list of names for consideration or for the institution to appoint an arbitrator of its choice. It is worth noting that even when the parties choose an arbitrator, institutional rules may reserve the right to confirm an appointee. For example, under the LCIA Rules, all arbitrators are actually appointed by the LCIA Court.

TIP If you wish to avoid the institution choosing any of the arbitrators, it is important to specify this in the arbitration agreement.

Arbitration agreements may also provide that a separate, unconnected individual should appoint an arbitrator, particularly in the event of a disagreement between the parties. For example, an arbitral institution, the Chairman of the Law Society or respected individuals in relevant industry sectors may be named as the appointing authority in these circumstances.

4.2 Arbitrator nominated in the agreement

It is also possible, although rare, for the parties to have agreed to nominate a particular arbitrator in their arbitration agreement. In these circumstances the arbitrator (or arbitrators) so nominated will probably constitute the tribunal. However, there are obvious problems with using such a method.

Arbitrators nominated in an agreement executed perhaps years in the past may be unavailable for a wide variety of reasons – from leaving the profession to having no diary availability to having died in the meantime. It may also be that the arbitrators nominated are unsuitable to form a judgment on the dispute in question. In such circumstances, the parties will have to come to a new agreement on how to select their arbitrator.

4.3 Agreement between the parties

Where only one arbitrator is required, it is common for the arbitration agreement to provide that the arbitrator should be selected by agreement between the parties. Selecting an arbitrator is one area where parties can influence the arbitration process.

Once a dispute has reached the stage where arbitration is necessary, however, the parties may be unable to agree on an appointee. One party may even refuse to engage in the process. At this point institutional arbitration can be a real advantage, as it will ensure that the process progresses.

If agreement is not reached in an institutional arbitration, the institution will usually appoint a sole arbitrator. The institution will also step in if a respondent does not appoint its party-appointed arbitrator when the parties have agreed on a tribunal of three. In *ad hoc* arbitrations, however, the parties (or, more likely, the claimant party) may have to apply to court to resolve the stalemate.

TIP If you are having trouble agreeing with the other party on the identity of the arbitrator(s), consider suggesting the use of a strike list (as discussed below).

4.4 Party-appointed arbitrators nominate chairman

In a three-member tribunal, it is usual for each party to nominate an arbitrator. These nominees are then usually confirmed (or rejected) by the relevant appointing authority or arbitral institution, which will then appoint them as party-nominated arbitrators. The two appointees may then agree on a chairman between them.

The party-appointed arbitrators may be required to have certain qualifications, or be chosen from a list. The parties may not, of course, choose a biased arbitrator, or one with a conflict of interest. The party-nominated arbitrators should not act as advocates for their party. However, beyond any requirements set out in the arbitration agreement or the relevant institutional rules, a party may pick the arbitrator who it believes will be the best both for the arbitration process and who will be open to its case.

The chairman may also be required to be one of a specific group or class of individuals. It is possible that the parties may influence the choice of chairman through discussion with their appointee or by objecting to or vetoing the choice. However, if these rights exist at all, they are usually extremely limited.

4.5 Strike list

A strike list is an option that is increasingly being used to select arbitrators in international arbitration. A list is produced either by an arbitral institution or as a compilation of all individuals considered appropriate by either party. This is then considered by both parties, which can each veto names on the list and rank the remainder in order of preference. The arbitral institution, or another third party, will then appoint the arbitrators with the highest preference ratings from the combined lists. This method is used under the current United Nations Commission on International Trade Law (UNCITRAL) Rules when the parties are unable to agree on the arbitrator(s), and is useful in *ad hoc* arbitrations as an alternative to applying to the relevant court.

The strike-list method has a number of advantages. It does not allow arguments to interfere with proceedings, it can be quick and it is likely to produce a tribunal with which both parties are reasonably happy. It is, of course, possible that a party will veto all of the names on a list. However, since each party does not see the preferences of the other, this is unlikely. Each party will mark its preferences based on its objective analysis of the individuals concerned.

It is possible that the list system will take more time than direct appointment by an institution. However, an expedited process may be adopted.

It is also a potential disadvantage that the parties must choose from a list that has been set out by an arbitral institution. However, institutions will very often have approved arbitrators or a veto on appointment in any event, and the arbitrators nominated on a list will ordinarily all have the levels of skill, knowledge, experience and impartiality expected by the institution.

5. Frustration, delay and default

Where the relevant agreement or rules require the parties either to agree on an arbitrator or to nominate an arbitrator, either party can derail the process. Should one party disagree that the dispute should be settled by arbitration, be unwilling to engage in communication or merely wish to increase the delay and expense caused by the dispute, this may present an opportunity for it to halt proceedings before they have begun.

This may be an acceptable tactical move. Arbitration is rarely cheap and, as in any form of litigation, significant delays or expense can wear your opponent down, financially and in terms of its commitment to the cause. These tactics may be used in particular where the defaulting party has a much weaker case and considers it might lose an arbitration, or where the financial strength or willingness to prosecute the dispute of an opponent is in doubt.

A party that is asked to appoint or agree an arbitrator may also simply not engage, or not consider the particular arbitration seat, rules or concept applicable or appropriate.

In these circumstances the various arbitral institutional rules, UNCITRAL Rules or national statute – whichever is appropriate – provides methods to minimise delay. If necessary, there are ways to constitute the tribunal without agreement or to force a defaulting party to engage with the process. These methods include appointing a party-nominated arbitrator as a sole arbitrator or asking the relevant institution or appointing authority to nominate an arbitrator in place of the party in default. The notice and delay requirements will depend on the rules used, although experienced arbitrators or institutions will be aware of the fine balance between allowing a party a fair opportunity to defend itself and efficiently moving the arbitration process on. A party that is seeking to use default or delay provisions should ensure that it has not caused any delay itself, or the relevant authority may be less willing to assist.

6. Confirmation of appointment and constitution of the tribunal

If the arbitration agreement sets out the method for appointing the arbitrators and the qualifications that they must have, the parties should take care to follow the agreement closely. Any breach or failure to adhere to its stipulations may lead to the validity of the appointment of the tribunal being challenged. This may in turn lead to challenges to jurisdiction and therefore to the enforceability of the decision.

6.1 Institutional arbitrations

Where the parties have agreed to arbitrate under the auspices of an arbitral institution, the rules of that institution will govern the procedure for constituting the tribunal. In these circumstances it is generally the parties that nominate the arbitrators. These in turn are then appointed by the institution. The institution will organise the constitution of the tribunal and will often act as the appointing authority in the event of any dispute between the parties or a failure to agree on the arbitrators or chairman.

Institutions will almost always require some level of influence over the appointment of arbitrators and the procedures necessary to constitute a tribunal. The institution is contracted by the parties to appoint arbitrators and produce a tribunal that is capable of resolving the dispute. Any failure to do so may have contractual implications even where the fault lies with a particular member of the tribunal.

6.2 *Ad hoc* arbitrations

Where there is no arbitral institution, the parties will choose the tribunal themselves. Where there is no agreement on the choice of arbitrators, the parties commonly refer to an appointing authority to resolve the issue, or ultimately to the courts of the seat.

In an *ad hoc* arbitration the parties may use whatever procedure they see fit to constitute the tribunal. However, the UNCITRAL Rules are often used as a guideline or starting point. Under these rules, if there is no agreement on an appointing authority, the parties must apply to the Secretary General of the Permanent Court of Arbitration at The Hague to select one.

The flexibility that the *ad hoc* system allows the parties in appointing their arbitrators can be an advantage. However, many parties consider it outweighed by the uncertainty of being able to reach agreement on the appointment in a timely and cost-effective manner.

Under an *ad hoc* system, the tribunal can be considered constituted once all nominees have accepted their appointment and all parties have been notified. Once constituted, the tribunal is a body independent of and separate from the parties.

8. Dealing with the tribunal

1. Contacting the tribunal

Once the tribunal has been constituted, it will normally take control of the arbitral process, in consultation with the parties. If the parties have chosen an institutional arbitration, the institution will at this stage transfer the file to the arbitrators. This is often the first opportunity for all members of the tribunal to review the claimant's Request for Arbitration, the respondent's answer to that Request for Arbitration and key documentation. These documents should enable the tribunal to understand the issues that are likely to require determination in the course of the arbitration, in order that an appropriate procedure for the arbitration can be established.

After the tribunal has been constituted, all correspondence addressed to the tribunal should be sent to each tribunal member, and copied to the arbitral institution if applicable. Communications with the tribunal must never be made *ex parte* – that is, without the knowledge of the other parties – and copies of all correspondence to and from the tribunal must be copied to all parties.

This does not mean, however, that the parties should copy all correspondence between themselves to the tribunal. This will inundate the tribunal with documents that often have little bearing on any decision required from them. It also adds to the cost of the arbitration. When the parties have reached an impasse that cannot be resolved between themselves and there are issues that require the tribunal's input, it is appropriate at that stage to make an application to the tribunal that clearly identifies the issues for determination and that includes the documentation that is necessary and relevant for the tribunal to decide the issue at stake. In this way, the tribunal can efficiently decide whether the issue can be determined on the papers or whether oral submissions on the issue are required. It can then make appropriate directions.

It also goes without saying that any without prejudice communications between the parties (eg, concerning potential settlement) should not be copied to the tribunal.

From a practical perspective, most international tribunals now work electronically, and it has become the norm for correspondence to be sent by email. The appropriate methods of communication should, however, be considered by the parties and tribunal at the outset and recorded in the first procedural order. For example, it may be agreed that all communications should be sent by email, with submissions of over 20 pages also to be sent in hard copy. Except where specifically directed or requested, parties should avoid sending the same communications by several methods – for example, email, fax and post. This is so as to avoid over-burdening the tribunal.

With this increasing use of email for all communications between the parties and the tribunal, however, comes the additional risks posed by hacking and other threats to cybersecurity. It is thus also appropriate for the parties and the tribunal to consider at the outset any safeguards that may need to be put in place to try to mitigate those risks (for example, avoiding the use of non-secure email addresses). This may be particularly relevant where there is highly sensitive or confidential information contained in submissions, exhibits or other communications which need to be protected. In those circumstances, it may be advisable to consider setting up a secure site for the relevant documents to be uploaded to/downloaded from rather than simply sending by email.

TIP Given the extensive use of mobile devices it is worth trying, where possible, to record the text of the communication in the body of an email rather than in an attachment.

TIP When emailing the tribunal, include a clear description of the relevant proceeding in the subject line (as the tribunal is likely to have a number of matters at any one time), followed by a brief description of the subject matter of the correspondence. This way, emails relevant to specific issues may easily be found at a later date. An email that only states "Please find attached letter" is not helpful. It is better to state "Please find attached letter relating to [XYZ]".

TIP Do not send all correspondence to the tribunal with a copy to the counterparty and then send the same correspondence addressed to the counterparty with a copy to the tribunal. The tribunal does not need to receive multiple copies of the same email as that only adds to its administrative burden.

TIP Try to avoid adding to long email chains of correspondence as these can become unwieldy if they need to be printed in hard copy. Start a new email chain when you can.

2. Administrative secretaries

In some cases, particularly in *ad hoc* arbitrations with a sole arbitrator, the arbitrator may seek the parties' agreement to appoint an administrative secretary. The administrative secretary does not have, and should not be given, any decision-making authority – this remains at all times with the arbitrator. The administrative secretary's role is to assist in the administration of the arbitration, including the management of documents and correspondence received from the parties, the monitoring of procedural timetables and the facilitation of smooth communication between the parties and the arbitrator. Appointing an administrative secretary can save the parties significant costs (as they will generally be much cheaper than the arbitrator(s)), particularly in a complex arbitration involving difficult legal issues, many witnesses, multiple parties and large volumes of documents. Sometimes the cost of an administrative secretary will be borne by the parties and sometimes by the arbitrator(s) themselves, depending on what the parties and the tribunal agree.

Where an administrative secretary is appointed, he or she will often be the first point of contact between the parties and the arbitrator. Accordingly, it is very important that all correspondence and documents filed with the tribunal be copied to the administrative secretary. In many cases the administrative secretary will be content to receive copies of all correspondence and documentation by email and will not require hard copies unless otherwise advised. This is a matter that should be confirmed with the administrative secretary and the tribunal.

Recognising the potential significance of the role tribunal secretaries play, some institutions have provided guidance on their use. For instance, section XVII of the 2017 ICC Note to the Parties and Arbitral Tribunals on the Conduct of Arbitration provides guidance relating to the appointment, duties, and disbursements and remuneration of administrative secretaries. Similarly, section 8 of the 2017 LCIA Notes for Arbitrators sets out the role of the tribunal secretary; the process for proposing the use of a tribunal secretary; and the approval, removal and replacement of a tribunal secretary.

3. Keeping the tribunal informed

Throughout the course of an arbitration proceeding, it is important to keep the tribunal informed about the status of the arbitration and the relative positions of the parties. Whether under institutional rules or national legislation, the tribunal has a duty to give each party a reasonable opportunity to present its case and deal with that of its opponent. It is also obliged to adopt procedures that are suitable to the circumstances of the arbitration and that avoid unnecessary delay or expense, so as to provide an efficient means for resolving the dispute.[1]

1 See, for example, Article 14 of the LCIA Rules, Article 22 of the ICC Rules, Section 33 of the English Arbitration Act 1996 and so on.

Communicating clearly with the tribunal will help it to make important timetabling and procedural decisions, help it to focus on the issues that remain in dispute and ensure that it is available for hearings when required. A failure to communicate with the tribunal may quickly lead to the arbitral procedure going awry. From a practical point of view, it will not help the defaulting party to gain the tribunal's confidence. While a tribunal has a duty to act fairly and impartially, the behaviour of a party can adversely affect the tribunal's impression of that party and may result in adverse decisions on costs. The tribunal retains wide discretion to award costs against a party that improperly causes additional cost and expense during the proceedings.

If the parties have reached agreement on particular issues, whether substantive or procedural, a letter outlining these should be sent to the tribunal and copied to the other party or parties. The tribunal should always seek confirmation from all parties that an agreement has been reached on procedural or substantive issues. In deference to the autonomy of the parties, where the parties reasonably agree on a particular course of action, the arbitral tribunal is very likely to adopt the suggested course and will issue an appropriate procedural order or direction to record any changes in the timetable, or issue a consent award where the parties have agreed settlement terms.[2] For this reason it is almost always sensible to seek agreement with the counterparty on any issues which can reasonably be agreed before making an application to the tribunal. This will save the cost of engaging the tribunal on those issues.

By way of example, if the parties have entered into discussions to settle some or all of the claims, both parties should ordinarily inform the tribunal that such discussions are taking place, if they are likely to result in settlement of the arbitration or otherwise affect the procedural timetable. In this case it is likely that the tribunal will order a stay of the arbitral proceedings pending the outcome of the settlement negotiations. The tribunal will also cease work on any pending awards. Where the tribunal is being paid by the hour, such as in LCIA institutional arbitrations or *ad hoc* arbitrations, informing the tribunal of a likely settlement in order that it "downs tools" will also lead to significant savings in the tribunal's fees.

Where the parties cannot agree on an issue, it is appropriate to write to the tribunal to seek its decision. This letter should set out the party's position and the preferred method of resolution – for example, whether the issue can be resolved "on the papers" filed to date, whether full written submissions are needed, whether a teleconference or oral hearing is needed and whether a written formal decision (with reasons) is required. The tribunal may itself call

---

2 However, the tribunal is not required to sign off on any such decisions or awards if, for example, it has reason to believe that they may be being used to perpetrate fraud or money laundering (see below).

for written submissions on the particular issue, may call a procedural teleconference or order an in-person hearing, or a combination of the above, depending on the complexity of the issue involved.

4. Unresponsive tribunals

Occasionally a busy tribunal may be silent for a long period, particularly during the award drafting stage. At this stage the parties may become anxious regarding when the award will be released. Where the tribunal has not given an approximate date on which it expects to deliver the award, and has not done so within a reasonable time after all submissions have been received from the parties, it is appropriate to ask the tribunal to indicate a date on which the award will be finalised. If the tribunal remains unresponsive and fails to render the award, most arbitration laws allow the parties to apply to the relevant court in the seat of the arbitration or relevant arbitral institution to have the arbitrator removed or replaced. In such cases a party may also seek damages against the arbitrator for breach of contract for failing to carry out his or her arbitral mandate. Such action is, however, very much a last resort as it may result in the entire arbitration being re-run before a new arbitrator.

Unresponsive tribunals and delays are less likely when the arbitration is administered by an arbitral institution, since the institution prompts arbitrators to render awards within the time limits set out in the relevant rules or otherwise agreed between the parties. The institution will usually monitor the arbitrator's performance and compliance with stated deadlines, and the parties can ask the institution to chase the tribunal where they may be reluctant to do so themselves. In cases of serious or repeated defaults, the institution may remove or replace the arbitrator and/or, more likely, may refuse to confirm the appointment of the arbitrator in future cases.

> **TIP** It is proper to remind politely the tribunal to provide an update on the expected date of delivery of the award if the award is not rendered in a timely manner within the expectations of the parties. However, before blaming the tribunal for any delay, it is wise to keep in mind that there may be many legitimate reasons why an award has been delayed. For example, one or both parties may have filed unclear or overly long submissions or untidy document bundles, or the case may have involved particularly numerous or complex issues, or large volumes of technical evidence. In other cases, the tribunal may be endeavouring to resolve its own internal disagreements. All communications should therefore be courteous and polite. Good manners are more likely to receive a response.

5. Suspicions of bribery, corruption or money laundering

Bribery is the offer, gift or promise of a benefit in exchange for a person to act or refrain from acting in the exercise of official duties. An example would be a payment to a government official in order to win a tender bid for a contract. Corruption is the improper use of entrusted power for private gain, such as fraud, embezzlement or the payment of bribes. Money laundering is transferring, concealing or disguising the proceeds of criminal activities. It usually involves reintegrating the proceeds of crime into the legitimate economy.

Bribery, corruption and money laundering are increasingly recognised as issues of transnational public policy. As such, many state governments have taken steps to criminalise and counter the effects of these activities.

Bribery, corruption and money laundering may affect international arbitration proceedings in a number of ways. Bribery or corruption may affect the legality of the substantive contract between the parties. Arguments may also arise as to whether an arbitration clause contained in a contract tainted by bribery is rendered invalid, thereby depriving the tribunal of jurisdiction. The contemporary view, based on the doctrine of separability (ie, that the agreement to arbitrate is a separate and distinct contract from the substantive contract), is that issues of bribery do not affect the tribunal's jurisdiction to determine the effect of allegations of bribery on a contract, unless bribery directly affects the arbitration agreement. Whether or not bribery renders the contract illegal and unenforceable is a matter of the law applicable to the contract. However, a tribunal is likely also to consider whether the contract is illegal at the place of performance of the contract, the requirements imposed by the law at the seat of the arbitration and issues of international public policy.

From a more practical point of view, arbitration practitioners should also be aware of how parties may use international arbitration proceedings to facilitate money laundering. For example, money launderers may establish Company A and make a number of small deposits of proceeds of criminal activity into its bank account. Company A then commences a 'sham' arbitration by issuing a claim against a related entity, Company B. Shortly after the arbitration commences, Company A and Company B ask the tribunal to issue an award recording the settlement of the arbitration by consent, with a payment to be made to Company B. In this manner, Company B receives the proceeds of crime and has an apparently legitimate award which it may enforce against Company A. Company B may launder this money further by requiring Company A to make the payment into the client account of Company B's (unsuspecting) lawyers, who then pay it on to Company B.

A quite different set of issues arises when it is alleged that one or more of the arbitral tribunal members are corrupt. Where there is strong evidence that a tribunal member has been bribed, it is appropriate to make a challenge under the applicable institution rules or procedural law. There may also be public policy grounds for challenging any award rendered by that tribunal, or resisting enforcement thereof. However, extreme caution should be exercised before any allegations of bribery or corruption are levelled at the tribunal, as the tribunal is likely to take an adverse view of such allegations unless they are supported by very strong evidence. An unsuccessful challenge is very likely to damage that party's position when the tribunal comes to determine both the substantive issues and issues of costs.

TIP Where there is a suspicion of bribery or corruption affecting the contract or arbitral proceedings, it is important to consider carefully all available evidence that substantiates the allegation, and to assess whether there is sufficient evidence to raise the allegation before a tribunal or court. Specific evidence that proves the allegations must be available. Improperly brought allegations of bribery or corruption not only are very likely to prejudice the alleging party's case, but may also contravene any professional rules of conduct to which that party's lawyers may be subject.

9. Establishing procedure

1. Establishing the procedural timetable and conduct of the arbitration

The chair of the tribunal is usually responsible for contacting his or her co-arbitrators and making initial contact with the parties. He or she will often write an introductory letter (or, more commonly these days, an email) on behalf of the tribunal to the parties. This will usually set out the next steps that the parties should take. The approach adopted will vary depending on the terms of the arbitration agreement and the applicable procedural rules. Ordinarily, however, the parties will be invited to agree on a procedural timetable that allows the dispute to be resolved in an effective, efficient and cost-effective manner while giving each party a fair opportunity to present its case. In some cases, the tribunal will prepare a draft procedural order that sets out the procedural steps that it would like the parties to consider when attempting to agree on an appropriate procedure.

TIP The tribunal will be looking for clear and realistic input from the parties at an early stage regarding the arbitration's expected duration and any procedural steps or issues that are particular to this dispute. It will want to establish an orderly and fair process and will not be impressed if the parties cannot agree on relatively straightforward matters or if a party seems to be making unreasonable objections to the counterparty's proposals. Where agreement cannot be reached, write to the tribunal for guidance, setting out the reasons for the position taken.

It is important to set a realistic timetable for the gathering and preparation of statements of claim and defence and subsequent pleadings. Where possible, the tribunal will invite the parties to agree on a suitable date for an in-person preliminary procedural/case management meeting. Indeed, many of the institutional arbitration rules includes express provisions for such a meeting to take place (for example, International Chamber of Commerce (ICC) Rules Article 24, London Court of International Arbitration (LCIA) Rules Article 14.1, International Dispute Resolution Centre (IDRC) Rules Article 20(2), Conflict

Prevention and Resolution (CPR) Rules for Administered Arbitration of International Disputes Rule 9.2, German Institution for Arbitration (DIS) Rules Article 27.2 and Singapore International Arbitration Centre (SIAC) Rules Article 19.3). This allows the tribunal and the parties to meet face to face at an early stage and gives the tribunal an opportunity to resolve and finalise any procedural issues upon which the parties could not agree or that could not be resolved by correspondence. It also reassures the tribunal that all parties are aware of the arbitration proceedings and that they have been given the opportunity to present their case on the procedure to be adopted. This is particularly important since a lack of proper notice of the arbitration or an inability to present one's case is grounds under Article V(1)(b) of the Convention on the Recognition and Enforcement of Foreign Arbitral Awards 1958 (the 'New York Convention') for resisting the enforcement of any award. Where the arbitration is conducted under the ICC Rules, the preliminary procedural meeting also gives the parties and the tribunal a chance to agree and sign off on the Terms of Reference.

TIP When considering the procedure, it is worth bearing in mind the typical steps on the following page. (Not all of these may be relevant, and others not included may be required.)

TIP Useful guidance on organising the arbitration procedure can also be found in the following:

- 2016 United Nations Commission on International Trade Law (UNCITRAL) Notes on Organising Arbitral Proceedings (see www.uncitral.org/uncitral/en/uncitral_texts/arbitration.html);
- LCIA's 2017 Notes for Parties (www.lcia.org/adr-services/guidance-notes.aspx); and
- ICC's 2017 Note to Parties and Arbitral Tribunals on the Conduct of the Arbitration (https://iccwbo.org/publication/note-parties-arbitral-tribunals-conduct-arbitration).

2. ICC Terms of Reference

2.1 Purpose and effect

Where the ICC Rules of Arbitration apply, the tribunal is usually required to draw up the Terms of Reference and have them signed by the parties within 30 days of the ICC Secretariat transferring the file to the tribunal: see Article 23(2) of the 2017 ICC Rules which apply to arbitrations commenced on or after 1 March 2017. This date can be extended by the ICC Court.

The Terms of Reference are mandatory under the ICC Rules. Their purpose is

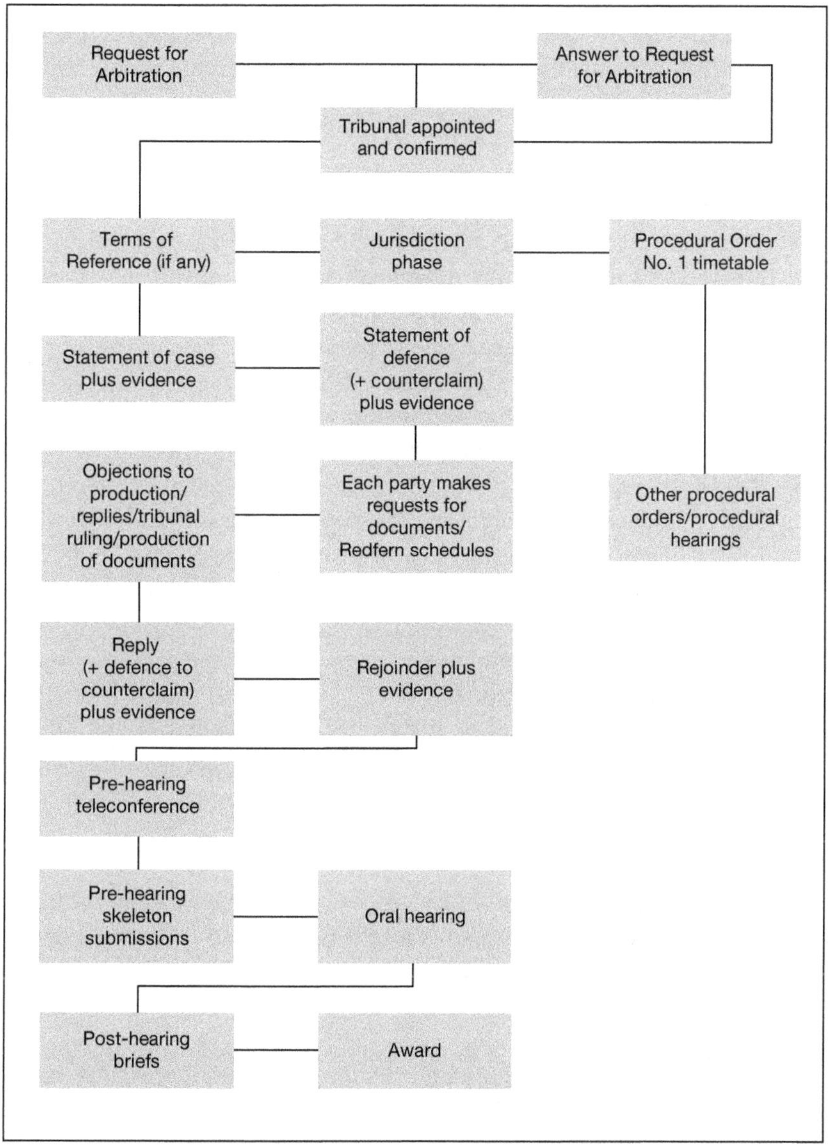

to ensure that at an early stage the parties and the tribunal consider the scope of the issues to be determined and the procedural timetable to be adopted. Once the Terms of Reference have been signed or approved by the ICC Court, no party can make any new claims that fall outside the limits of the Terms of Reference without authorisation from the arbitral tribunal. In making such a decision the tribunal should consider the nature of the new claim(s), the stage of the arbitration and other relevant circumstances. If the parties agree that new claims or defences should be included in the arbitration, the tribunal will ordinarily admit and decide them, and should issue a procedural order recording the parties' agreement and the tribunal's decision to admit the new claims.

2.2 Preparing the Terms of Reference

Under the ICC Rules of Arbitration, it is the tribunal that must prepare the Terms of Reference. Nevertheless, the tribunal will often ask the parties to summarise their respective claims and defences and the relief sought, along with the amounts of any quantified claims. These summaries are subject to analysis and review by the tribunal, but they will be used as a basis for the matters to be included in the Terms of Reference.

There are at least five reasons for this approach:

- at this early stage the parties will have a better knowledge of their respective case than the tribunal;
- it ensures that the Terms of Reference accurately reflect the parties' claims and defences and the scope of the issues to be decided;
- allowing the parties to participate in drawing up the Terms of Reference is more likely to result in a document that they find agreeable than one drafted by the tribunal alone;
- it allows the arbitrators at an early stage to identify any issues that can be resolved swiftly; and
- where the parties are represented by experienced lawyers, it is generally more time and cost effective for the parties to draft these aspects of the Terms of Reference than to leave the tribunal to construct the whole thing from scratch.

Once the draft Terms of Reference have been prepared by the tribunal, they may be circulated to the parties for their agreement. The parties may then make any additional recommendations or amendments, which the tribunal may or may not adopt.

TIP Writing a clear and concise summary of the case and issues involved for inclusion in the Terms of Reference will help focus the tribunal and the parties on the issues that need to be resolved.

2.3 Matters that must be included in the Terms of Reference

Article 23 of the 2017 ICC Rules provides that the Terms of Reference must include:

- the full names, descriptions, addresses and other contact details of each of the parties and of any person(s) representing a party in the arbitration;
- the addresses to which notifications and communications arising in the course of the arbitration may be sent;

- a summary of the parties' respective claims and relief sought, together with the amounts of any quantified claims and, as far as possible, an estimate of the monetary value of any other claims;
- a list of issues to be determined, unless the arbitral tribunal considers it inappropriate;
- the full names, addresses and other contact details of each of the arbitrators;
- the place of the arbitration; and
- particulars of the applicable procedural rules and, if such is the case, reference to the power conferred upon the tribunal to give effect to general considerations of equity (ie, the power to act as amiable compositeur or to decide *ex aequo et bono*).

2.4 Matters that may be included in the Terms of Reference

In addition to the above matters, which must be included in the Terms of Reference in accordance with Article 23 of the 2017 ICC Rules, the tribunal may include the following matters to reduce the risk of disputes between the parties and of challenges to any subsequent award.

Arbitration agreement: The arbitration agreement forms the jurisdictional basis on which the arbitrators may determine the issues between the parties. It is useful, therefore, to include a reference to the underlying contract in which it appears and provide a verbatim quotation.

TIP Once signed, the Terms of Reference act like a submission agreement, confirming that the parties have agreed to submit the dispute described to arbitration. If a party wants to challenge the jurisdiction of the tribunal, it must include reference to such a challenge (although not the detailed grounds) and a sufficient reservation of rights, to ensure that the Terms of Reference are not used against it as an agreement to submit to the tribunal's jurisdiction.

Procedural background: A summary of the procedural background that led to the tribunal being constituted ensures that no issues will arise from the preliminary stages of the arbitration. It confirms that the tribunal was properly constituted, and that no challenges have been made to any of the arbitrators.

Addresses for service and modes of communication: At an early stage in the arbitration the tribunal may want to impose rules regarding valid service and modes of service. For example, it may include provisions for service by email and hard-copy documents. In international arbitrations where parties are located in different jurisdictions and time zones, the tribunal may also impose rules on complying with time limits. For example, a tribunal may impose a rule that the time for meeting applicable deadlines is that at the sender's place of business, or that at the seat of the arbitration.

Venue and place of procedural hearings: It is important to keep in mind that the legal 'seat' of the arbitration is distinct from the physical place where the arbitration is held. Ordinarily, the substantive hearing of the arbitration will be held at the place of the seat (although this is not normally a strict requirement). However, to facilitate efficient conduct of the arbitration and to keep costs to a minimum, the tribunal may include provisions that enable procedural hearings to be held anywhere that is convenient to the parties and the tribunal, including by teleconference or video link. Alternatively, and to avoid doubt, provision may be included to deem that the procedural hearings must take place at the seat of the arbitration. Where the parties agree on the place and mode of hearings, the tribunal will seek to abide by their choice. Where the parties cannot agree, the tribunal will usually reserve the right to determine an appropriate place and mode of procedural hearings.

Chair's authority to issue procedural orders: The chair of the tribunal may reserve the right to make and sign procedural orders on behalf of the tribunal after consultation with the co-arbitrators. Where procedural decisions are urgently required, the Terms of Reference may permit the chair to make procedural orders alone.

Interim, partial or final awards: The Terms of Reference may consider whether all issues should be dealt with in a final award or whether they can or should be determined on an interim or partial basis. This will depend greatly on the nature of the issues in dispute and the parties' views on issuing partial awards on discrete issues. It may be appropriate, for example, to bifurcate the proceedings between liability and quantum stages. In such case, at the liability stage the tribunal will determine whether any of the claims and counterclaims in the arbitration succeed. At the quantum stage, the tribunal will assess the amount of the loss and relief to be ordered in the award. In a large and complex commercial arbitration, the costs of assessing the amount of losses can be great, and often involve instructing professional accounting or other firms to provide expert opinion on the value of the loss. Bifurcating the arbitration into stages prevents these costs from being incurred unnecessarily (if, for example, the claim is unsuccessful at the liability stage). Similarly, any objection to jurisdiction may be bifurcated from the merits of the dispute and dealt with in advance.

Default: The tribunal may retain the right to continue with the arbitration and make an award if one party to the arbitration fails to comply with procedural orders or to appear at any hearing, provided that they have been given reasonable notice and opportunity to comply.

The following table sets out the items that are typically included in the Terms of Reference.

Contents of ICC Terms of Reference

I. The full names and descriptions of the parties	This section includes the full names and addresses of all parties. If a corporate party, this will include the company description, address, registered office, registration number and legal representatives' contact details.
II. Details of commencement of the arbitration	This section records the date on which the Request for Arbitration and the Answer to the Request for Arbitration were filed, with a quotation of the relevant arbitration clause and choice of law provisions upon which the tribunal's jurisdiction is said to be founded.
III. Address for service and mode of service to be used	This section includes the full postal address and alternative email and/or fax addresses for sending documents and sets out the method and timing of service.
IV. Summary of background facts	This section states the material background facts, such as when and why the parties entered into the transaction, what its purpose was and anything else that might affect the legal relationship between the parties, such as termination or assignment of any relevant agreements.
V. Summary of the parties' claims and defences	This section summarises each party's case and briefly outlines the issues in contention. The tribunal will often ask the parties to draft and submit their own case summaries.

continued on next page

VI. Statement of relief sought	This section sets out what it is that the parties want the tribunal to order in its award. For example, payment of a specific sum of money, plus interest and an award of costs.
VII. Issues to be determined	This section sets out the issues that must be determined in the arbitration. It may not always be possible to do this at the outset, when only brief details of the claims and defences have been filed, and so this is often determined at a later stage in the proceedings.
VIII. The arbitral tribunal	This section includes the names and contact details for the members of the arbitral tribunal and the dates on which each arbitrator was appointed.
IX. Applicable substantive law	This section sets out the substantive law applicable to the arbitration and any express choice of law provisions contained in the agreement between the parties.
X. Applicable procedural rules	This section sets out the procedural law applicable to the arbitration and how this will be determined if not agreed between the parties.
XI. Other procedural issues and directions	The tribunal may seek the parties' agreement to measures that improve the efficiency of the arbitration process; for example, a provision that allows the chair to make procedural orders alone, after consultation with the co-arbitrators and the parties.
XII. Tax liability issues	The tribunal may include a provision that deals with the parties' liability for any value added tax that may be payable on arbitrators' fees.

continued on next page

XIII. Agreement to the Terms of Reference	This section provides for the date of execution of the Terms of Reference and allows for the signatures of each arbitrator and the parties. To avoid argument between the parties at a later date it should also state the legal seat of the arbitration; for example, 'place of arbitration: Paris; France'.

TIP For further guidance concerning the drafting of ICC Terms of Reference, see the model Terms of Reference published by the ICC at https://iccwbo.org/publication/model-icc-terms-reference/.

3. Agreeing the procedural timetable

3.1 Procedural order

The first procedural order in an arbitration normally sets out a number of matters that are fundamental to its ongoing conduct. The first procedural order is effectively a road map of the future conduct of the arbitration. This should be set out in a standalone order and not contained in any Terms of Reference, to avoid any difficulty in altering that procedure at a later date.

A typical first procedural order will deal with the following issues:

- the number of rounds of pleadings;
- the content and style of pleadings;
- the timetable for the filing of pleadings;
- general document production including the approach to be taken with respect to electronic records;
- requests for specific document production/Redfern Schedules;
- inclusion of rules of evidence, such as the International Bar Association (IBA) Rules on Taking of Evidence in International Arbitration 2010 or the Prague Rules on the Efficient Conduct of Proceedings in International Arbitration (Prague Rules);
- timetable for the filing of factual witness statements and expert reports (if any) and dates by which each party must advise the other party of their intention to call expert evidence;
- whether factual witness and expert evidence will be filed with the pleadings (in a 'memorial' style) or whether they will follow sequentially after pleadings have been filed;
- whether written witness statements will be treated by the tribunal as direct evidence;
- whether the tribunal has the power to have experts in specific disciplines

examined together (ie, expert witness conferencing, also referred to as 'hot tubbing') and/or to instruct its own experts;
- who bears the costs of experts and witnesses;
- whether the tribunal will follow the principle of *iure novit curia* ('the court knows the law');
- the presentation of hearing bundles and witness statements, and their organisation and numbering;
- a date for final agreement between the parties on the contents of the hearing bundles;
- requirements for certifying any translated documents;
- the venue and date of the oral hearing as well as the payment of any venue fees;
- arrangements for transcription services and payment of their fees;
- arrangements for interpreters and payment of their fees;
- whether documents, correspondence and pleadings may be submitted and filed electronically by email or by other means;
- how the parties should communicate with the tribunal; and
- whether there will be post-hearing briefs or whether the need for them will be decided at the hearing.

It should be noted that the above list, and the guidance set out in this chapter, are examples only of the types of procedures that are frequently discussed and/or used. However, as discussed in Chapter 1 above, one of the key advantages of international arbitration is flexibility, and the majority of arbitral rules and laws do not include a fixed procedure in order to allow the parties and the tribunal to adopt the procedure that is most appropriate to each case. Parties should avoid adopting a 'standard' or 'typical' procedure simply because it is one with which they, their counsel and/or the tribunal is most familiar, and should instead consider which procedural steps are in fact necessary for the case at hand, bearing in mind the issues in dispute, the amount in dispute, and the likely costs and time involved.

Several useful publications have been created by various arbitration bodies and institutions that set out guidelines for the efficient conduct of arbitration proceedings. Some of the guidelines referred to in this book, and used regularly in arbitration proceedings, include the IBA Rules on the Taking of Evidence in International Arbitration, the UNCITRAL Rules on Organising Arbitral Proceedings, the Chartered Institute of Arbitrators' guidelines on interviewing arbitrators, the ICC Secretariat's Guide to ICC Arbitration, and the LCIA Guidance Notes. The Prague Rules aim to provide similar guidance where the parties wish to follow the inquisitorial approach of the civil law tradition.

TIP Many more such guidelines exist (most of them free) and can be found on the websites of the various arbitration bodies. They include:

- UNCITRAL: www.uncitral.org/uncitral/en/uncitral_texts/arbitration.html;
- IBA: www.ibanet.org/Publications/publications_IBA_guides_and_free_ materials.aspx;
- Chartered Institute of Arbitrators (CIArb): www.ciarb.org/ guidelines-andethics/guidelines/arbitration-guidelines; and
- ICC: https://iccwbo.org/publication/note-parties-arbitral-tribunals-conduct-arbitration/ and www.adr.org/adr-resources.

TIP A template Procedural Order No. 1 is set out in the appendix to this chapter.

3.2 Number of pleadings

A typical English court-style proceeding usually includes three core pleadings: a statement of claim, a statement of defence and a reply. If a counterclaim is filed with the defence, this is treated as if it were a statement of claim, with the defendant to the counterclaim (ie, the main claimant) filing its defence with its reply, and the counter-claimant filing a separate reply on the counterclaim only. In civil law systems there are typically four sets of pleadings: the claimant's statement of claim, the respondent's statement of defence, the claimant's reply to the defence and finally the respondent's rejoinder.

In international arbitration the parties are free to agree on the number of pleadings that will be presented to the tribunal. However, a typical arbitration will usually involve filing three or four pleadings, similar to either the common or civil law system, depending on the case and the nationality and experience of the parties and the tribunal.

Cross-reference For more on the content of pleadings, see Chapter 11.

3.3 Factual and expert witnesses

Whilst the parties are free to decide on the procedural rules applicable to the presentation of evidence by factual and expert witnesses, the procedure adopted with respect to the submission of pleadings is likely to influence the procedure concerning witness evidence. For instance, the parties may choose to adopt a 'memorial' style process for pleadings, whereby witness evidence (factual and/or expert) is submitted at the same time as the pleadings, so that a party's case as to the facts, law and evidence is all put forward together. Alternatively, a sequential process may be adopted with the parties only exchanging witness statements and expert reports after all pleadings have been filed (and possibly also after any document production phase), followed by any reply witness statements or reply expert reports which the parties may wish to submit in order to respond to the evidence filed by the other side.

Other procedural issues which might be addressed at the outset of the arbitration concerning witness evidence include: whether a written factual witness statement will serve as the witness' evidence in chief; any directions on what form any witness statement and/or expert report should take or what it should contain (eg, name, address, background/relevant qualifications and experience, affirmation of truth, date and place of signature); if expert evidence is required and, if so, what disciplines of expert evidence are appropriate (or a procedure for this to be determined in due course); and, where reply witness statements or reply expert reports are permitted, whether these ought to be limited to responding only to points arising in the other side's first witness statements and expert reports.

TIP Further suggestions of procedural issues concerning factual and expert witnesses are contained in the template Procedural Order No. 1 appended to this chapter.

Cross-reference See further discussion of the content of factual and expert witness evidence in Chapter 11.

3.4 Documentary evidence

In international arbitration the parties are free to decide on the procedural rules applicable to the discovery process and the obtaining of evidence. The choice of rules will depend on the preferences of the parties and the tribunal. Approaches to discovery and the obtaining of documentary evidence differ greatly around the world. In the courts of common law countries, particularly in the United States, each party is required to search for and disclose all documents that are within its control, that are relevant to the issues and that may be harmful to its case or support the opponent's case. The objective of this extensive discovery process is to discover the 'truth'. Unfortunately, this process can be very expensive and time consuming in large cases involving potentially millions of documents. On the other hand, in many civil law systems, the parties have much more limited discovery powers, reflecting the inquisitorial role of the courts in the civil law system. It is often expected that a party bringing a claim will have gathered sufficient evidence to substantiate its case before filing any claims.

In an international arbitration it may benefit the claimant or respondent to adopt one system or another. In an international fraud case, for example, where all parties are represented by English lawyers and the arbitrator is a former English High Court judge, the claimant may wish to adopt the more extensive disclosure rules in the English Civil Procedure Rules. The respondent may (unwisely, if it is in possession of information that may be harmful to its case) agree to this approach simply because these rules are familiar to the lawyers and the arbitrator. However, this situation is unusual. A typical international arbitration will often involve a three-person tribunal, some of whom may be from common law backgrounds and others from civil law backgrounds. The parties often come from different legal systems as well. Often, parties' preferences will be shaped by their experiences within their own systems. The time and cost involved in an extensive disclosure process may also be a relevant factor to be considered. It is necessary to choose a system of procedural rules of evidence and discovery that is acceptable to both parties.

Once a dispute arises it may be difficult to agree on the appropriate rules to adopt. For this reason, the IBA developed its Rules on Taking of Evidence in International Arbitration. The objective of these rules is to strike a workable balance between the very different discovery approaches taken by civil and common courts and lawyers. These rules are adopted in many arbitrations and provide a useful framework and objective standards to be applied during the evidence gathering and discovery process including the approach to electronic documents.

It is now more likely that relevant documents will be in electronic form and those which were in hard copy, may have also been saved electronically. It is important, therefore, to consider early the approach to be taken with respect to the production of electronic documents. The IBA Rules on Taking of Evidence in International Arbitration defines 'document' as "writing, communication, picture, drawing, program or data of any kind, whether recorded or maintained on paper or by electronic, audio, visual or any other means". This broad definition of 'document' can lead to high costs in searching for and producing such materials. It can prove helpful in terms of both time and costs to consider the scope and issues associated with electronic document production at an early stage in proceedings and to seek to agree with the counterparty what approach will be taken during the course of proceedings with respect to the scope of document production.

TIP When first instructed, investigate with your client its document retention policies and actual practices. This may involve speaking with your client's IT department to establish the best way to search for and collate relevant documents as well as what, if any, residual back-up and metadata they hold. For more on this, see Chapter 5.

Whilst international arbitration does not generally place an obligation on parties to preserve potentially relevant documents from the time an arbitration is in the party's contemplation, the tribunal can draw an adverse inference from the failure to produce documents where the party is unable to provide a satisfactory explanation as to why it cannot produce the documents as ordered by the tribunal.

TIP Further guidance on how best to approach the issue of the production of electronic documents can be found at the following:

- the 2010 IBA Rules on the Taking of Evidence in International Arbitration: www.ibanet.org/Document/Default.aspx?DocumentUid=68336C49-4106-46BF-A1C6-A8F0880444DC;
- the 2013 IBA Guidelines on Party Representation in International Arbitration: www.ibanet.org/Document/Default.aspx?DocumentUid=6F0C57D7-E7A0-43AF-B76E-714D9FE74D7F;
- the 2012 ICC Arbitration Commission Report on Managing E-Document Production: https://iccwbo.org/publication/icc-arbitration-commission-report-on-managing-e-document-production/
- the 2009 Conflict Prevention and Resolution Protocol on Disclosure of Documents and Presentation of Witnesses in Commercial Arbitration: www.cpradr.org/resource-center/protocols-guidelines/protocol-on-disclosure-of-documents-presentation-of-witnesses-in-commercial-arbitration; and
- the 2008 CIArb Protocol for E-Disclosure in Arbitration: www.ciarb.org/docs/default-source/practice-guidelines-protocols-and-rules/e-discolusure-in-arbitration.pdf?sfvrsn=2.

Another issue to consider with regard to document production is the timing of production. Most of the time parties will be required to produce the documents they rely on with their initial pleading (this is the position adopted in, for example, the IBA Rules on Taking of Evidence in International Arbitration, and the LCIA Rules Article 15.2). There will then ordinarily be a period for an exchange of further documents, pursuant to whichever disclosure regime is chosen (eg, a specific document request procedure such as in the IBA Rules, or a more extensive disclosure process akin to English or US court proceedings). Often this document exchange process will be simultaneous, occurring either after the Statement of Defence (this tends to be more popular where there will be four pleadings so that any documents exchanged can be referred to by both parties in the Statement of Reply and Statement of Rejoinder) or after all pleadings have been filed (this tends to be more popular where there are only three pleadings, so that the claimant does not have an unfair advantage prior to the filing of its Statement of Reply). Alternatively, document production may be staggered. For instance, if there are likely to be large amounts of documents across several categories, it may prove more efficient to conduct searches and reviews by categories rather than one large exercise leading to the production of a single, large-scale set of documents. Or a sequential exchange may be appropriate, where for example the claimant is required to produce any additional documents requested by the respondent prior to the respondent filing its Statement of Defence (with the respondent being required to produce any additional documents the claimant requests after that filing has taken place). This can be helpful in situations where one party has the majority of relevant documents in its custody, possession or control (for example, the buyer in an mergers and acquisitions (M&A) transaction, if the seller has handed over all documents with the business) in order that the opposing party can fairly have access to relevant documents prior to being required to set out its case.

In response to the concern amongst those users, practitioners and arbitrators from the civil law tradition that the IBA Rules on the Taking of Evidence does not properly cater for the civil law approach, the Prague Rules have been developed. The Prague Rules follow an inquisitorial approach, providing a more proactive role for the tribunal in connection with issues concerning fact finding, documentary evidence, witnesses of fact, expert witnesses and assistance in amicable settlement.

Consideration should also be given to issues of data protection and cybersecurity to ensure that the transmission of electronic documents is not in breach of any applicable regulatory regimes and is carried out in a secure manner. In April 2018, the International Council for Commercial Arbitration (ICCA), the New York City Bar and the International Institute for Conflict Prevention and Resolution (CPR) published a draft Cybersecurity Protocol for International Arbitration which has been developed with a view to identifying reasonable cybersecurity measures to protect the information exchanged during international arbitrations (available at: www.arbitration-icca.org/media/10/43322709923070/draft_cybersecurity_protocol_final_10_april.pdf).

Cybersecurity and data protection issues should be raised and dealt with at the case management stage in order that any appropriate or necessary procedures can be agreed with the tribunal and put in place.

Cross-reference For more on managing document production, see Chapter 11.

3.5 Document presentation: hearing bundles

Each tribunal or arbitrator will have its own preferred numbering system and method of organising documents and hearing bundles. The tribunal may specify how it wants the bundles to be prepared in the first procedural order. If specific instructions are included, they are given for a reason and the parties should do their best to comply with them. The key objective of a hearing bundle is to make it as easy as possible for the tribunal to access and identify the submissions, evidence and the law so as to help it when drafting the award. It is very important to ensure that the bundle is logically and clearly organised and well indexed, and that all references in the submissions and the bundle are accurate. It is both costly for the parties and frustrating for the tribunal to have to search for a document that is being relied on by a party because the reference is incorrect. Such errors may also detract from the strength of the submission. To assist the tribunal, parties may want to include a chronology of key events (agreed between the parties where possible) and/or an entity relationship diagram where complex interrelated company structures are involved.

It is common when filing 'memorial' style pleadings to separately, consecutively and uniquely number each document filed in support of each party's submissions. For example, the claimant's factual exhibits could be numbered 'C-[#]', the respondent's exhibits 'R-[#]' and legal authorities numbered 'CLA-[#]' and 'RLA-[#]', respectively. When it comes to the oral hearing, the tribunal may be content to leave the documents ordered in this fashion. More frequently, however, it will prefer a consolidated chronological bundle (at least of the contemporaneous factual documents). If so, references to the original numbering (eg, C-16 etc) should be included in the index.

TIP Where the hearing bundle consists of several volumes, it is also helpful if each file includes a copy of the consolidated index to all of the hearing bundles, rather than just to the documents in that specific folder.

TIP Global Arbitration Review has compiled a guide entitled "UCIA: Universal Citation in International Arbitration" which aims to standardise document and exhibit cross-referencing in international arbitration, and may be a useful reference when preparing pleadings, evidence and bundles.

3.6 Filing

(a) Hard copy

Although electronic filing of parties' submissions and communications is increasingly used, many tribunals will want to receive longer documents, such as the pleadings, the hearing bundles and evidence, in hard copy as well as electronically. This is partly because many arbitrators are more comfortable working on paper copies and it can be expensive and time consuming for the arbitrator to print and organise long submissions from various electronic documents. Furthermore, law firms are ordinarily better equipped and have the resources to assemble hearing bundles much more efficiently than a sole tribunal member, who may or may not be technically proficient and who may or may not have an office, a photocopier or an assistant.

> **TIP** It is wise to take direction from (or to ask) each individual tribunal member as to how the documents should be filed. Some will want documents in A4-size bundles (perhaps because they find larger print easier to read); others may want double-sided A5-size bundles (because they find them more convenient to carry and store). Some tribunals will only want to receive a hard copy of the final hearing bundle and are content to receive all prior versions of the pleadings and submissions in electronic form. Many arbitrators have limited space for storing multiple hard-copy bundles or voluminous documentary materials and do not want their rooms to be filled with multiple copies of the same documents during an arbitration. Another reason could be that busy arbitrators are often travelling, and carrying large and heavy documents is not practical.

(b) Electronic media/DVD/USB/email

Tribunals increasingly correspond with the parties by email. As internet download speeds have increased and data storage has become cheaper, email systems are now capable of sending, receiving and storing very large volumes of information. There are, however, a few matters to remember that will make matters easier for a tribunal.

The first is to ask the arbitrators (or secretary to the tribunal) how the arbitrator would like to receive correspondence and pleadings. Some email systems have limits (usually 10 megabytes (MB) or 20MB) on the size of email attachments. It is important to observe these limits to avoid failures in document delivery.

It is also a good idea to ask the tribunal in which format it would like the documents to be filed. While many law firms automatically file documents as portable document format (PDF) files due to the perception that these cannot be altered once sent, or in order to avoid inadvertently granting access to previous drafts of a document through metadata, the tribunal may in fact want to receive documents in Microsoft Word (or similar word processing format) that is easier to work with electronically. Many tribunals will want to quote submissions directly from the parties in the award, and it is much easier to copy and paste from a Word document than it is from a PDF. Further, Word documents are always text searchable, whereas documents scanned on a photocopier to a PDF are not. If PDFs are filed, tribunals increasingly request that these are text searchable, as submissions or decisions that are text searchable reduce the tribunal's time in locating various parts of submission or authorities when it comes to drafting the award. Additionally, where the native format of a document is outside of the usual Word or PDF written form (ie, spreadsheet, audio or video), an easily accessible format and reliable method of transmitting such documents will need to be considered in advance of any procedural deadlines. Conferring with your IT department regarding an appropriate format for electronic materials can be helpful to avoid situations where counsel or tribunal members cannot access the material.

Where the volume of documents is very large, it may be appropriate to file them on a portable hard drive, DVD, USB stick or equivalent. Similarly, a cloud-based online system (eg, Dropbox or ShareFile) can be a useful platform for documents to be uploaded to and accessed by counsel and the tribunal. Many law firms and private businesses have software and hardware available to create electronic document 'bibles' that enable many documents to be organised and accessed from electronic storage more efficiently than can be achieved in paper format. Some tribunals may request cross-references to evidence, exhibits and authorities to be hyperlinked within PDF versions of pleadings. Again, it is important to discuss with the tribunal what it requires and to ensure that the tribunal is comfortable with receiving the documents in the manner proposed and can use whatever system is suggested. There is no use filing documents in a sophisticated electronic manner if the tribunal cannot read or access them with standard equipment and facilities.

3.7 Need for oral hearing or 'on the papers'

Whether it is appropriate to call an oral hearing or whether an issue can be decided by considering the written submissions of the parties without the need for oral submissions depends to a large degree on what the parties want and the complexity of the issues at stake. If the parties both agree that an oral hearing is required, the tribunal will usually respect that decision and set an appropriate hearing date as soon as is practicable. This hearing will allow the parties to make full submissions to the tribunal and to answer any questions that the tribunal may have. The tribunal may give and receive feedback during the hearing itself, which may facilitate the resolution of particular issues between the parties and thus avoid the need for the tribunal to determine them. It is not uncommon at an oral hearing for the parties to realise that the tribunal is more concerned with some issues than others and to refocus their case accordingly as the arbitration progresses.

On the other hand, it is significantly more expensive (at least in the short term) to hold an oral hearing than it is to determine an issue 'on the papers'. The arbitrators and lawyers will have to travel to the hearing venue, hotel rooms may need to be booked, transcription and/or translation services may need to be provided, and the hearing may last several days (depending on the complexity of issues involved and the number of witnesses/experts to be cross-examined). For this reason, where the issue at stake is relatively straightforward, it may be appropriate to allow the tribunal to consider the parties' written submissions only and ask the tribunal to issue its decision in writing. The disadvantage is that the tribunal loses the benefit of oral submissions and explanations from the parties' representatives. It will therefore be more difficult for it to assess the relative strengths and weaknesses of the parties' respective cases.

TIP If a dispute is to be decided 'on the papers' only, it is a good idea to include a phase in the procedure, once all written submissions have been filed, for the tribunal to put questions in writing and invite (brief) responses to them.

For the above reasons, procedural or discovery issues are often (but not always) resolved 'on the papers', while the final hearing will almost always be an oral in-person hearing. It is unusual in international arbitration for a tribunal to issue an award without examining the parties, even where the respondent does not file a response to the Request for Arbitration or any form of defence, or where the respondent chooses not to appear. This is due to the perception that the tribunal's award will be seen as a considered opinion and may reduce the risk of challenge at the enforcement phase.

3.8 Hearing length

Estimating the length of a hearing is not an exact science. It will generally depend upon the nature and number of the issues to be decided, the volume of evidence and the number of parties and witnesses (factual and expert) involved, how contentious the witness evidence is and the advocates' skill in examining and presenting the case. It is also important to factor in the additional time required in the event that a witness requires the assistance of an interpreter when giving oral evidence. A hearing will typically proceed in the basic order as shown on the following page.

When estimating hearing times, it is necessary to build in time for all stages of the hearing, including time for breaks for the tribunal, counsel and any translators and transcribers; usually an adjournment for lunch; and mid-morning and mid-afternoon short adjournments. Although there is no need for exact parity between the time allocated to each party, the tribunal will want to ensure that each party has a fair opportunity to present its case. Failure to do so may provide grounds for challenging the arbitral award. Often, therefore, parties will be allocated an equal number of days or hours, unless there is a large disparity between the number of factual witnesses/experts to be cross-examined by each side. The tribunal will also be concerned that the allocated number of days for the hearing is sufficient to elicit and test all of the evidence and submissions.

A typical international arbitration hearing will run from 10:00am until 5:00pm each day. Taking into account breaks and minor interruptions, there is usually between five and six hours of hearing time per day available for the parties to present their respective cases. Hearing time is expensive and should

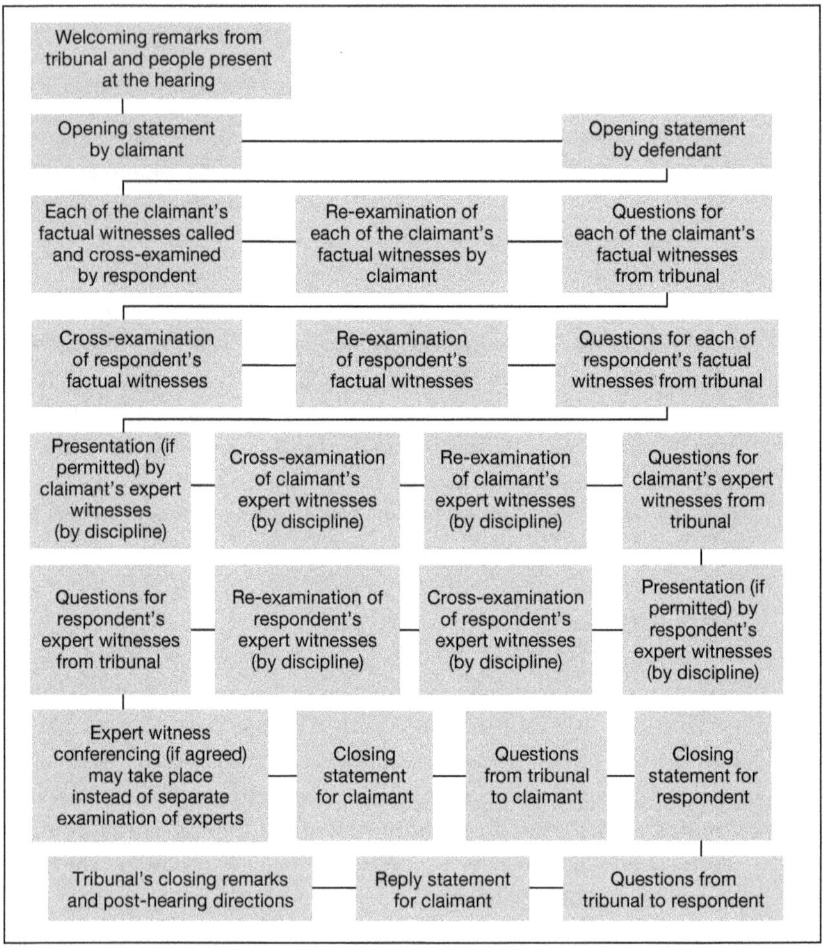

be used as efficiently as possible to present the parties' cases and help the tribunal to resolve the issues in dispute. Many tribunals will be willing to start earlier and/or finish later on a particular day in order to complete the examination of a particular witness or expert, or if it would help the hearing end sooner and thus avoid the cost of a subsequent hearing day.

TIP Allocate responsibility to a team member to keep a record of the time spent by each party during the hearing. This record can be shared with the other party/parties to ensure that they are aware of the time spent by each party and agree with the calculation. This can avoid debate towards the end of the allocated hearing period and can be useful in opposing any pre- or post-award challenge as to an alleged lack of fair opportunity to present a party's case.

In most international arbitrations, factual witness evidence in chief is provided in advance by way of written witness statements and forms part of the hearing bundle. If a particular witness's evidence is not in dispute, the parties may elect not to call that witness. That witness will not appear at the hearing unless the tribunal seeks to examine them. Hearing time is therefore used for cross-examining the witnesses by the advocate acting for the counterparty rather than being spent on leading the witness evidence (ie, evidence in chief).

When a witness is called, the tribunal will ordinarily invite the witness to confirm the correctness of the witness statement before allowing cross-examination to proceed. The tribunal will provide an opportunity to the party calling the witness to re-examine the witness on any issues that arose from cross-examination. This is usually followed by any questions to that witness from the tribunal.

Following the presentation and examination of factual witnesses, any expert witnesses will normally be called and examined. This often happens in the same way as for factual witnesses, although increasingly experts may give a short presentation on their report before cross-examination begins, and thus time will need to be factored in for this. An alternative method of examining experts known as expert conferencing (or 'hot-tubbing') is also becoming more popular, where experts are examined simultaneously. This can reduce the time needed for expert evidence at the hearing.

Cross-reference Expert conferencing is discussed in more detail in Chapter 12.

At the beginning of an arbitration proceeding it may be difficult to judge which witnesses are required and how significant various issues may become. It is important for each side to communicate and reasonably discuss the time required to examine witnesses and for the hearing itself as the arbitration continues. A firm hearing date and duration should be fixed well in advance so that the appropriate time can be entered in everyone's diaries (including the witnesses), and venues can be booked and hotel and travel arrangements made. The parties should also keep the tribunal informed on these issues and seek its guidance or decision if in doubt or where the parties cannot agree.

TIP If post-hearing briefs are to be provided, there may be no need for closing statements. To assist the tribunal, the parties should seek to agree, before the end of the hearing, whether they want to give oral closing statements or only file written briefs.

4. Amendments to the procedural timetable

4.1 Seeking agreement of the counterparty

As with any other issue that might arise between the parties, it is best practice to seek agreement to any proposed amendment to the procedural timetable from the counterparty first. If agreement is reached, the party requesting the amendment should then write to the tribunal to seek a formal amendment, explaining that it has been agreed between the parties. In any event, a tribunal's first step on receiving any such request will be to seek the views of the counterparty. There is thus no point in attempting to seek amendments without first establishing the position of the counterparty. It is almost always cheaper and more efficient for all parties involved to proceed in this manner.

A tribunal will ordinarily grant amendments where the parties agree, although it will be concerned that the timetable does not slip too far and endanger the hearing date. For example, a tribunal is unlikely to have difficulty granting a claimant an extra week to file its statement of claim, and will ordinarily also grant the respondent an extra week to file the defence. Opposing such an amendment, unless there is very good reason for doing so, will waste the parties' money and tribunal's time (as a more substantial application to the tribunal is required and a formal decision or direction must be delivered). However, tribunals will be reluctant to move hearing dates that have been set down for a long period without sufficiently good reasons for doing so. This is due to the logistical and timetabling issues that moving a hearing creates among international parties and tribunal members. Many arbitrators will also charge significant cancellation fees if a hearing is abandoned close to the hearing date. Holiday plans or commitments to other matters are usually not accepted as good reasons for moving hearing dates. Illness of key witnesses or other matters beyond the parties' control may, however, be acceptable reasons.

4.2 Where the counterparty does not agree

If the counterparty does not agree to any proposed amendment to the timetable, it is appropriate to apply to the tribunal instead. The application should be in writing and clearly state why the amendment is being sought and the applicant's views on how the tribunal ought to deal with the application. Any application to the tribunal should include a statement of the relief or orders sought, and usually also include the applicant's position on costs. Any documents relevant to the tribunal's decision should be included, and the application must be copied to the counterparty. The tribunal will then give the counterparty an opportunity to file a response, following which the tribunal will consider the parties' positions and arguments and make an order.

Appendix: Draft Procedural Order No. 1

[NAME OF ARBITRAL INSTITUTION]

CASE NO.

[NAME OF CLAIMANT(S)]
Claimant(s)

- v -

[NAME OF RESPONDENT(S)]
Respondent(s)

DRAFT PROCEDURAL ORDER NO. 1

Having consulted with the parties, the Arbitral Tribunal ("the Tribunal") makes the following Order:

A. General

1. This arbitration shall be conducted in accordance with the [NAME OF RULES], the language of the arbitration shall be [LANGUAGE], and the seat of arbitration shall be [SEAT]. The seat of arbitration does not preclude the Tribunal from meeting the parties, their representatives or witnesses at some other place, or communicating by video link or conference call, if considered appropriate by the Tribunal.
2. [The Chair of the Tribunal shall have the power to make procedural decisions alone when required in the interest of expediency.]

B. Timetable

3. By [DATE], the Claimant will submit its Statement of Case setting out in full the factual and legal arguments in support of its claims and relief sought, together with [any witness statements, expert reports and[1]] copies of the documents upon which it wishes to rely.
4. By [DATE], the Respondent will submit its Statement of Defence [and Counterclaim] setting out the factual and legal arguments in support of its

1 Wording in square brackets to be included (and the wording in paras 4–6) if proceeding on the basis of 'memorial' pleadings. If so, then paras 11–15 should be removed. If witness statements and expert reports are to be exchanged post-pleadings, however, then do not include this wording here (or in paras 4–6) and do include paras 11–15. Alternatively, witness statements may be included with pleadings, but expert reports exchanged separately, in which case both sets of directions will require amending accordingly.

defences and counterclaims, if any, together with [any witness statements, expert reports and] copies of the documents upon which it wishes to rely.

5. By [DATE], the Claimant will submit its Statement of Reply [and Defence to Counterclaim], together with [any rebuttal witness statements, rebuttal expert reports and] copies of the documents upon which it wishes to rely.
6. [By [DATE], the Respondent will submit its Statement of [Rejoinder/ Reply to Defence to Counterclaim], together with [any rebuttal witness statements, rebuttal expert reports and] copies of the documents upon which it wishes to rely.]
7. By [DATE], either party may submit a Request to Produce to the other party (but not to the Tribunal) in accordance with Article 3.3 of the IBA Rules on the Taking of Evidence in International Arbitration (2010) ("the IBA Rules") in respect of any documents, exhibits or other evidence in the possession or custody or under the control of the other party. Any Requests to Produce are to be made in the form of a Redfern Schedule.
8. By [DATE], each party shall produce to the other the requested documents or submit a reasoned objection (in accordance with Article 3.5 of the IBA Rules) to the requesting party.
9. To the extent any objections to production are raised, each party may submit to the Tribunal a Redfern Schedule setting out the outstanding document requests, the objections to production and the requesting party's response to such objections by [DATE].
10. The Tribunal shall rule on any outstanding Requests to Produce by [DATE] and all documents ordered to be produced shall be exchanged within [one week] of such ruling.

[11. The parties shall exchange witness statements by [DATE].][2]

[12. By [DATE], the parties shall disclose the number of expert reports that they intend to submit (if any) and specify their subject matter.]

[13. The parties shall exchange rebuttal witness statements (if any), by [DATE].]

[14. The parties shall exchange expert reports (if any), by [DATE].]

[15. The parties shall exchange rebuttal expert reports (if any), by [DATE].]

16. By [DATE], the parties shall identify all witnesses of fact and experts whom they wish to call at the Oral Hearing and those whom they wish to cross-examine.
17. By [DATE], the parties shall agree and deliver to the Tribunal agreed paginated bundles in [A4/A5], [single-sided/double-sided] format for use at the Oral Hearing.
18. A Pre-Hearing Conference shall be held as directed by the Tribunal.
19. Skeleton Arguments for the Oral Hearing, accompanied by full copies of

2 Paragraphs 11–15 to be included if pleadings are not filed in the 'memorial' style, and evidence is exchanged subsequent to pleadings. See footnote 1.

any legal authorities relied on, shall be exchanged and submitted to the Tribunal by [DATE].

20. An Oral Hearing will be held in [NAME OF CITY] at a venue to be agreed or fixed by the Tribunal, and will commence on [DATE], with [NUMBER OF DAYS] days in total reserved. The Tribunal shall issue such further procedural directions prior to the Oral Hearing as are appropriate.
21. The parties shall agree and submit to the Tribunal a timetable for the Oral Hearing not later than two clear days before the start of the Oral Hearing, including an estimate of its length, the order in which witnesses are to be heard and the likely length of the examination of each witness. Failing agreement, the Tribunal shall determine the appropriate timetable on the basis that each party will be given half of the time available.
22. The Tribunal reserves the possibility of requesting post-hearing submissions in writing from the parties, to be served on a date to be determined.

C. Rules of Evidence

23. [The parties and the Tribunal may use the IBA Rules as an additional guideline, always subject to changes considered appropriate in this case by the Tribunal.]
24. [Any issues with regard to the admissibility, relevance, weight or materiality of the evidence offered by a party or a witness shall be determined by the Tribunal.]

D. Documentary Evidence

25. All documents on which a party wishes to rely to prove its case shall be submitted as far as reasonably possible with the written Statements described in paragraphs 3 to 5 above.
26. Each exhibit submitted by the Claimant shall commence with the prefix 'C' followed by the applicable number (ie, C-1, C-2, etc). Each exhibit submitted by the Respondent shall commence with the prefix 'R-' followed by the applicable number (ie, R-1, R-2, etc). Reference to legal authorities shall be made by using the prefix 'CLA-' for the Claimant and 'RLA-' for the Respondent followed by the number of the exhibit (ie, CLA-1, CLA-2, etc).
27. If a party wishes to rely on a document written in a language other than English, that party is to produce both the original document and an accurate translation of either the whole document or of such part of the document on which the party wishes to rely. If the opposing party wishes to rely on a further part of such a document not already translated, it is to produce an accurate translation of such further part with its pleading.
28. Without prejudice to any other powers that the Tribunal may have, including the power to make peremptory orders, in the case of failure to comply with any order by the Tribunal to produce a document, the

Tribunal may take such non-compliance into consideration and draw its own conclusions.

E. Witness Evidence

29. Unless the Tribunal otherwise orders, witnesses shall provide their evidence in chief by means of a signed written witness statement submitted [together with the written submissions referred to at paragraphs 3 to 6 above]/[in accordance with the timetable set out at paragraphs 11 and 13 above].
30. Each witness statement shall:
    30.1 contain the name and address of the witness, his or her relationship to any of the Parties (past or present and in whatever capacity, if any) and a description of his or her background, qualifications and/or relevant experience;
    30.2 contain an affirmation of the whole truth of the Statement; and
    30.3 be signed by the witness and give the date and place of signature.
31. Witnesses who have provided signed written witness statements shall be made available for examination upon the request of the opposing party or upon the Tribunal's request. Oral examination may be requested of any witness. The Tribunal may question witnesses at any time, before, during and after examination by counsel for the parties, subject to the parties' right to any further re-examination thereafter.
32. The Tribunal shall at all times have complete control over the proceedings in relation to the presentation of evidence, including the right to limit or deny the right of a party to examine or re-examine any witness.
33. If the Tribunal orders a party to produce a witness and the witness fails to attend the Oral Hearing without good cause, the Tribunal may place such weight on the written testimony (or exclude the same altogether) as it considers appropriate in the circumstances of the case.
34. If a witness wishes to give oral evidence in a language other than English, the party relying on the evidence shall arrange for a suitably qualified interpreter to be present at the Oral Hearing to translate the evidence into English. The cost of any such interpreter is to be borne in the first instance by the party requiring an interpreter, subject to the Tribunal's award on costs.

F. Expert Evidence

35. The parties may submit expert opinions on [ISSUE/DISCIPLINE] and offer the testimony of expert witnesses, such reports to be submitted [together with the written submissions referred to at paragraphs 3 to 6 above]/[in accordance with the timetable set out at paragraphs 12, 14 and 15 above].
36. Should the parties wish to present expert testimony, the same procedure shall apply as for factual witnesses.
37. [The Tribunal may appoint one or more experts on its own initiative, or at

the request of a party. Before appointing an expert, the Tribunal shall allow the parties to be heard on the issue and shall cooperate with the parties in respect of defining the expert's mission and of drafting the questions to the expert.]

38. [Any expert appointed by the Tribunal shall in principle submit a written report and, at the request of one of the parties or the Tribunal, may be asked to appear at a hearing to be heard personally.]
39. [The costs of any expert appointed by the Tribunal shall be incurred equally by the parties, subject to the Tribunal's decision on costs in the award, and paid in advance.]

G. Communications

40. Copies of all written communications between the parties and the Tribunal, including the written pleadings described in paragraphs 3 to 6 above, may be transmitted by email to the following email addresses: [INSERT EMAIL ADDRESSES].
41. All communications of more than [10] pages and/or those attaching a large number of exhibits, including all pleadings and applications, shall also be sent in hard copy by courier to the other party, the Tribunal and the [NAME OF INSTITUTION].
42. Any amendments or changes or additions to the names, descriptions and contact details of the parties, or their representatives, must immediately be advised to the Tribunal and the [NAME OF INSTITUTION]. Unless and until such advice is given, communications sent in accordance with the contact details set out above will be effective and valid.
43. All filings shall be deemed timely if sent by a party by [18:00] [LOCATION] time on the relevant date.
44. Submissions, exhibits and documents provided electronically shall be in searchable PDF format. Submissions shall include a table of contents, and shall have numbered paragraphs and pages.
45. The Tribunal is to be sent only those communications (or copies) which it is relevant for it to see. Any communication between a party and the Tribunal and/or the [NAME OF INSTITUTION] is always to be copied to the other party and marked to that effect.
46. These communication obligations do not apply to any communications between the parties that are unrelated to this arbitration or that are intended to be confidential as between the parties, for example, without prejudice attempts to settle the dispute.

H. Confidentiality

47. The parties agree to keep confidential all evidence, submissions, orders and awards in this arbitration, including all materials created for the purposes

of this arbitration and all documents produced in this arbitration not otherwise in the public domain, as well as the existence of this arbitration, and the parties shall ensure that they, as well as any person instructed by the parties, protect the confidentiality of these proceedings.

I. Transcripts

48. A verbatim record of the hearing shall be transcribed by LiveNote or a similar real-time transcription system and copies of the transcript provided to each party, the Tribunal and the [NAME OF INSTITUTION]. The costs shall be incurred equally by the parties, subject to the Tribunal's decision on costs in the award.

J. Costs

49. Costs of the case management hearing on [DATE] are to be costs in the arbitration.

K. Liberty to apply

50. The parties shall each be at liberty to apply to the Tribunal for further directions.

Made by Order of the Tribunal and signed on behalf of the Tribunal on [Date].

[NAME OF ARBITRATOR] [NAME OF ARBITRATOR] [NAME OF ARBITRATOR]

10. Interlocutory applications and provisional measures

1. Interim, conservatory or provisional measures

Interim, provisional or conservatory measures (these terms are often used interchangeably) are orders given by a judge or tribunal after the dispute has arisen, but before the final award is rendered. As the names suggest, they are temporary orders put in place to protect one or other of the parties' rights while other substantive issues are resolved. Without such relief, the parties' claims may be frustrated.

A common problem is a respondent intending or attempting to move or dissipate its assets before an award against it can be made and/or enforced. In this case, the claimant may establish its claims, but there may no longer be assets available against which the award can be satisfied. This problem may also arise when a company transfers to a third party all of the shares in the subsidiary that owns the assets. A similar problem can arise when a party removes, hides or destroys evidence.

In other cases, a claim for damages or payment may not be enough to compensate the claimant. The publication of defamatory statements about the counterparty, for example, or the illegal exploitation of intellectual property (IP) rights may cause irreparable harm or prejudice unless the conduct ceases or is prevented in the first place.

On the other hand, when a claimant brings a claim against a respondent, the respondent is likely to incur significant costs in defending the claim. If the respondent's defence is successful, but the claimant does not have sufficient assets to meet any adverse costs award, the respondent will be left out of pocket. This can be of particular concern in arbitration, as tribunals have historically been unwilling to determine a case summarily or to dismiss a frivolous claim early on, though several institutions have now amended their rules to include provisions for summary procedures (see section 5 below).

Each of the above results is unjust. In cases such as these, international tribunals and courts may be prepared to order interim or conservatory measures if they are satisfied that it is just to do so. Different measures used to counteract these circumstances are outlined below. However, interim measures may affect the relative positions of the parties before they have had a chance to present their respective cases fully. The court or tribunal will therefore exercise these powers cautiously.

2. Court or tribunal?

The right to obtain interim measures from the tribunal or court (or both) will depend on the law at the seat of the arbitration or in the place where the assets are located, the arbitral rules chosen by the parties, and/or any other express agreement that empowers the tribunal to make interim or provisional orders.

When a party makes an interlocutory application, it must first consider whether to do so to the court at the seat of the arbitration or in the jurisdiction where the counterparty's assets are located (eg, in the case of a freezing order), or whether to make the application to the tribunal. This decision will depend on the stage that has been reached in the arbitration, the nature of the application, the relevant procedural rules, the arbitral law at the seat of the arbitration, the party against which the order is sought and where the assets subject to the proposed order may be located.

TIP Before applying to the tribunal for interim relief, always check its powers to make provisional or interim measures under the applicable arbitration law, arbitral rules and any agreement between the parties. In some jurisdictions, the arbitral tribunal has no such powers. In others, an application for interim relief must be made to the tribunal first before a court will consider such an application.

Historically, a party seeking urgent interim measures prior to the constitution of the arbitral tribunal had no option but to turn to national courts. However, numerous arbitral institutions have now introduced emergency arbitrator provisions in their rules, leaving parties to decide whether to go to national courts or instead request the appointment of an emergency arbitrator (see section 4.3 below).

Where the seat is in a country with a well-developed legal system and arbitration laws and practice – for example, England and Wales, France, the United States, Switzerland, Sweden or Singapore – any applications against the counterparty should be made first to the tribunal. However, it is important to check what arbitration rules the parties have agreed to apply, as well as the relevant arbitration law and rules of civil procedure at the seat: in some jurisdictions, the tribunal has no power to order interim or provisional measures.

In other jurisdictions, a court is unlikely to award interim or provisional measures unless the party seeking such measures has first applied to the tribunal. Exceptions are if the parties have agreed that such application can be made to the court, the tribunal has agreed this, it is necessary for the application to be made *ex parte* or the need is urgent. Under some institutions' rules, a party may only apply to a court, rather than the tribunal, in 'appropriate circumstances'[1] or 'exceptional circumstances'[2] and the tribunal's permission should be sought. A court may decline jurisdiction where the application appears to be in breach of the arbitral rules agreed by the parties. Depending on when in the arbitration proceeding the application is made, the tribunal is often better able to assess the merits of the application and the need for the orders sought in the context of the ongoing arbitration than the domestic court, and will better understand the issues at stake.

Applications to the tribunal rather than the court will also keep the issues between the parties confidential. In many domestic legal systems, court proceedings are generally open to the public and cases reported. Filing an application in court may therefore mean losing the confidentiality of the dispute. However, some national courts have special procedural rules to protect the confidentiality of arbitral proceedings in such circumstances, so it is a good idea to check whether applications for confidentiality can be made at the same time as the substantive application.

The arbitral tribunal does not have jurisdiction over any person or entity that is not a party to the arbitration proceeding. It cannot make enforceable orders for provisional measures against a non-party. Any applications for relief against non-parties must therefore be made to a court of competent jurisdiction.

The tribunal itself has no power directly to enforce the orders it makes. Arbitrators are not bailiffs or police officers. Enforcement must always be done through domestic courts in support of the arbitral process. However, the tribunal can make an enforceable award of additional costs against a recalcitrant party that does not willingly comply with its orders. In some jurisdictions, such as England and Wales, such interim orders on costs can be converted into a court judgment with relative ease.

TIP Before deciding whether to make an application, you should consider where you may want to enforce it. If the courts in the relevant jurisdiction are unlikely to enforce a freezing order made by an arbitral tribunal, for example, it may be necessary to apply directly to that court.

3. Types of application

3.1 Interim performance orders or orders for injunctive relief/freezing orders

Applications for interim or injunctive relief usually come in two forms: either

1 2012 International Chamber of Commerce (ICC) Rules, Article 28.2.
2 2014 London Court of International Arbitration (LCIA) Rules, Article 25.3.

telling a party that it must do something or telling a party that it must not do something. For example, a tribunal may order that a party which is in breach of contract continue to perform that contract while the arbitration proceeds, to avoid ongoing damage. This might apply to a construction project, for example, which would otherwise stall. Indeed, in such a situation it may be wise to specify in the initial arbitration clause that the parties will continue to perform the contract pending the arbitration.

In another example, an injunction may order a party not to transfer or deal with any assets which are the subject matter of the dispute or up to the value of the amount in dispute.

Interim injunctions are often granted in circumstances in which one party would suffer irreparable harm for which damages would not provide an adequate remedy.

3.2 Preservation of evidence

Orders to preserve evidence may be necessary where there is a risk that necessary evidence will be lost before the tribunal (or a third-party expert) has had a chance to consider it. This may be the case, for example, where goods are perishable and the issue is whether the goods were fit for purpose on delivery. In such a case a tribunal may order that the goods be placed in special storage to preserve their condition until the issues can be resolved.

3.3 Security for costs

An order for security for costs is intended to protect a respondent (or claimant, where a counterclaim is brought by the respondent) from the situation where it has had to incur significant costs in defending the legal proceedings brought against it but has little chance of recovering those costs from the opponent (eg, due to that latter party's impecuniosity). If security is ordered but not provided, the claim (or counterclaim) will often be dismissed.

That said, the claimant might find itself in a position of doubtful solvency precisely because the defendant has not paid moneys due to it. This might be the very subject of its claim. On any application for security for costs, therefore, the court or tribunal will need to satisfy itself that the defendant is not using the application to stifle the claimants' right to bring its claims.

The court or tribunal will attempt to determine what is fair and just between the parties before it orders security for costs. In doing so it will assess:

- the *prima facie* merits of the claimant's claims and respondent's defences (but without pre-judging the dispute);
- whether the claimant's financial situation was caused by the defendant's actions;
- any delay in bringing the application for security for costs;
- the ability of the parties to raise the security; and

- the effect of the order on the claimant's ability to continue the arbitration.

3.4 Anti-suit injunctions

Another common interlocutory application is for an *in personam* order (ie, against the particular party, rather than an *in rem* order against particular property) to restrain a party from commencing or continuing with concurrent proceedings in another forum. This may be needed:

- to prevent unnecessary additional expense and delay;
- to prevent abuse of process;
- to ensure that the issues in dispute between the parties are consolidated and determined in the most suitable forum; and/or
- to avoid the undesirable result of different courts or tribunals reaching different conclusions on the same issues.

This order is commonly referred to as an 'anti-suit injunction'.

4. Making the application

Making interlocutory applications in an international arbitration often involves a similar process to that described in Chapter 11 regarding the main hearing. Many of the issues that need to be considered when making the application and drafting the application documents will be the same, for example:

- when and whether documentary, witness and/or expert evidence are to be filed;
- the preparation of appropriate bundles to include only those materials relevant to the application; and
- whether the application should be determined at an in-person hearing or on paper.

An interlocutory application is like a mini-arbitration within the main proceeding. When determining the appropriate manner for dealing with the application, it is necessary to consider the timing of the application, its effect on the ongoing conduct of the arbitration, the procedural steps that need to be agreed or ordered by the tribunal to ensure that the parties have a fair opportunity to present their respective positions, the costs of bringing the application and the enforceability of the orders sought.

There are, however, some important differences that should be considered before making or responding to an interlocutory application.

TIP If making the application to the local court, be sure to check the procedural rules regarding how such applications must be made. Local lawyers may be needed.

> **TIP** Making an application to the local court will not necessarily suspend the arbitration (unless the parties and tribunal agree that it should, or the court orders such a suspension).

4.1 Content of the application

Applications for interlocutory relief normally rest on discrete legal grounds. These vary depending on the type of application made. Although the main proceeding is necessarily important factual background, the issues and points of law that the tribunal must decide on an interim application are often separate from and may even be entirely unrelated to the legal claims or defences made in the substantive proceeding. For example, an application for a freezing order or security for costs will concern primarily the financial position of the relevant party and the question of whether assets will be available at the end of the proceedings – such issues are unlikely to be relevant to determining the merits of the arbitration.

For this reason, it is often sensible to prepare separate interlocutory hearing bundles that include only the legal and factual materials that are relevant to the parties' submissions in the application and which the tribunal needs to determine the particular interlocutory issue.

As with any application to any court or any tribunal, the decision maker is interested in:

- the relief being sought;
- the legal grounds for seeking that relief;
- the factual basis upon which the application is made;
- whether the decision maker has the power to grant that relief; and
- why the decision maker should grant the relief.

An application that misses any of these points is unlikely to be successful.

In addition, where interim measures are sought, the tribunal will consider:

- the risk of harm to the applicant if relief is not granted;
- whether any such harm can be adequately remedied by damages;
- the risk of harm to the respondent should the relief be granted; and
- whether the applicant should have to provide security to the respondent in case the relief turns out to be unnecessary and causes loss.

4.2 Determining the procedure for the application

Most interlocutory applications involve considerable time pressure and urgency to secure an order against a counterparty or its assets. This may be because the applicant is continuing to suffer losses from the other party's ongoing conduct (eg, one party may be continuing to sell products in breach of a licence agreement or making disparaging statements in the media). It may be because there is a significant risk that the counterparty will transfer its assets in the immediate future to a third-party entity (usually another company owned or controlled by the counterparty) that is not party to the proceedings or arbitration agreement. Or it may be because property or evidence is likely to be destroyed.

In such cases, the parties will have diametrically opposed views on the procedural timetable required. The applicant, for example, will want a short timetable that results in an order that will prevent the loss and/or preserve the status quo as soon as possible. It may also want to gain a tactical advantage over the respondent – if it has spent considerable time preparing a full application, the applicant may then request a very short timetable in order to restrict the time available for the respondent to prepare and file its response.

The respondent, on the other hand, will want to delay the application to ensure that it has enough time to respond to the application or avoid breach of contract with third parties, or, less honourably, complete the removal of its assets before the order is made.

Depending on the particular issue at stake, factors such as these may make it difficult to agree on an interlocutory procedural timetable. If the tribunal has already been constituted, the applicant should seek an order from it for procedural directions, setting out its proposal and full reasons. A respondent wishing to defend any interim application will usually also write to the tribunal to set out its position and realistic proposals regarding the timing for filing its response and how the issue should be resolved. In a more complex dispute, with multiple issues at stake, a tribunal may call for, or a party may request, a telephone conference or even an in-person hearing to resolve such procedural issues.

In most cases the tribunal will want (and will often have a duty) to ensure that both parties have sufficient time to present their views. The tribunal is less interested in how much time a party wants to respond to an application than in how much time it needs to do so. Genuine inability or insufficient time to take proper instructions from a client, which may reside in a different jurisdiction or speak a different language, may be a good reason to request a longer time period. Lawyers' holiday plans, however, are rarely a sufficient or adequate reason.

4.3 Emergency arbitrator provisions

A particular problem in international arbitration arises where interim relief is needed before the tribunal has been constituted. This is especially true if the relevant courts are not efficient or arbitration friendly. It inevitably takes some time for the parties to agree on the appointment of the arbitrators or for an arbitral institution or court to constitute the tribunal.

To deal with this problem, various arbitral institutions[3] include rules for the appointment of an 'emergency arbitrator'. These usually include provision for an expedited procedural timetable to ensure that the emergency arbitrator is appointed and orders are made within a very short period of time, while maintaining considerations of natural justice (eg, not permitting an emergency arbitrator to make an order *ex parte*). Interim orders made by an emergency arbitrator often cease to be effective if a tribunal is not appointed to hear the dispute within a short period. Once a regular tribunal has been formed, any further applications relating to interim measures must be made to that tribunal.

In 2012, the ICC introduced its emergency arbitrator provisions. Under these rules, and for a fee of US$40,000, the ICC will appoint an emergency arbitrator who has the power to order interim relief and make orders for costs. The emergency arbitrator is separate from the tribunal that will be constituted for the main dispute, and his or her decision will not bind future tribunals or prevent the parties from applying to a relevant court. The emergency arbitrator provisions are intended merely to allow relief to be obtained to protect a party's position until the main tribunal can be properly constituted. Once the tribunal is constituted, either party may apply to maintain, vary or discharge the emergency arbitrator's order.

The availability of interim relief from an emergency arbitrator may be used as an argument against an application to a national court for such relief. In England and Wales, it appears from the case of *Gerald Metals SA v Timis & Ors*[4] that a party will be prevented from applying to the English court under Section 44(3) of the Arbitration Act 1996 for interim relief where that party could make an application for the appointment of an emergency arbitrator. The court held that it can only act to the extent that the arbitral tribunal has no power or is unable for the time being to act effectively. The LCIA had already refused to appoint an emergency arbitrator to hear an application for a freezing order in the case.

Cross-reference For further discussion of this issue in the context of commencing an arbitration, see Chapter 6.

Interim measures ordered by an emergency arbitrator may not be enforced by national courts in all jurisdictions. While some jurisdictions, including Singapore and Hong Kong, have amended their laws to ensure the enforceability of such orders, in other states such orders may not be enforceable as they are not considered a binding award.

3 Institutions that have introduced emergency arbitrator provisions include the International Centre for Dispute Resolution (ICDR) in 2006, the Stockholm Chamber of Commerce (SCC) in 2010, the Singapore International Arbitration Centre (SIAC) in 2010, the ICC in 2012, the Hong Kong International Arbitration Centre (HKIAC) in 2013 and the LCIA in 2014.

4 [2016] EWHC 2327 (Ch).

TIP Check whether any emergency arbitrator provisions in the relevant institutional rules apply to your arbitration: some are retrospective,[5] but most will only apply to arbitration agreements concluded since the emergency arbitrator provisions were introduced.

TIP Check whether the arbitration agreement expressly disapplies any emergency arbitrator provisions in the relevant institutional rules.

4.4 *Ex parte* applications

It is sometimes necessary to seek an order urgently without alerting the other party to this fact. An example is where the applicant believes there is a high risk of assets being dissipated, and that the counterparty may remove those assets as soon as it becomes aware that an application to freeze them is being made. In this case, the applicant may consider it appropriate to apply *ex parte* (ie, without notice) to the court that has jurisdiction over the assets.

Unlike an arbitral tribunal, a court may be able to make such an *ex parte* order, depending on the civil procedure rules in its jurisdiction. However, because *ex parte* orders do not allow the counterparty to respond, courts will ordinarily require the applicant to provide a full and frank explanation of the facts and basis for the claim (including any opposition that the applicant believes might have been made). They may sometimes require the applicant to undertake to pay the counterparty's damages in the event that the relevant order was unfounded and caused loss.

TIP When considering making an application to court, it is important to remember that this may result in a loss of confidentiality about the existence or nature of the arbitration.

Arbitral tribunals almost never hear *ex parte* applications or make *ex parte* orders. One of the clearest grounds available for resisting the enforcement of an award, or for upholding an application to have an award set aside at the seat of the arbitration, is when a party to the arbitration agreement has not been given the opportunity to present its case.

By definition, an *ex parte* application is made in order to obtain an order without the counterparty being aware of the application. Were such an *ex parte* order made by an arbitral tribunal, it is likely that it would be immediately challenged and set aside by the counterparty, undermining the enforceability of any future award.

5 Eg, the SCC Rules in force as of 1 January 2017, which include an emergency arbitrator provision, apply to all SCC arbitrations, regardless of when the arbitration agreement was entered into.

5. Default and summary procedures

The availability of summary judgment as a way to dispose of meritless claims or defences by national courts has traditionally been a notable difference between court litigation and arbitration. Arbitration has historically required a 'full merits' hearing to ensure a fair resolution of the dispute between the parties, though there are examples of the exercise by tribunals of case management powers to use a more summary procedure, and of such decisions being upheld when challenged.[6] However, the widely recognised need to increase the efficiency and reduce the costs of arbitral proceedings has led to moves by some institutions to introduce express summary procedures.

Since 1 August 2016 the SIAC Rules,[7] and since 1 January 2017 the SCC Rules,[8] have included provisions for the summary disposal of claims or defences which are manifestly without merit. Neither set of rules provide for a particular form of summary procedure, but both emphasise that tribunals must hear and decide applications for summary determination expeditiously. Other, smaller, institutions have revised their rules since, introducing similar provisions.[9] Neither the LCIA nor the ICC have introduced such express rules, but in October 2017 the ICC updated its practice note on the conduct of arbitration, stating that the "expeditious determination of manifestly unmeritorious claims or defences" is allowed within the tribunal's broad case management powers. The LCIA Rules contain similarly broad case management powers and a duty on the tribunal to adopt procedures suitable to the circumstances of the arbitration and avoid unnecessary delay and expense, meaning that a tribunal could decide to determine certain issues, or the whole claim, on a summary basis where one party's position is meritless.

In practice, many tribunals may feel uncomfortable about disposing of a case on a summary basis, fearing a challenge to the award or to its enforcement on the grounds of a failure to observe due process. The threshold at which a tribunal may decide that a party's position is manifestly without merit may be higher than in some national courts where a well-established process for summary decisions exists.

TIP If your opponent in arbitral proceedings appears to have no valid arguments and may merely be attempting to drag out the arbitration, consider whether an application to the tribunal for an expedited determination is appropriate, but consider any relevant institutional rules and the attitudes of the national courts in any jurisdiction where an award may need to be enforced.

---

6 For example, *Travis Coal v Essar Global* [2014] EWHC 2510 (Comm).

7 Rule 29.

8 Article 39.

9 The Moscow based International Commercial Arbitration Court (ICAC) at the Chamber of Commerce and Industry of the Russian Federation (RF CCI) and the Vietnam International Arbitration Centre (VIAC) both did so on 1 January 2017.

11. Developing the case

1. Written submissions

1.1 Purpose

In common law courts, the pleadings tend to be a series of statements of material facts that establish the cause of action and relief sought. The evidence and legal submissions usually follow later. In contrast, civil law legal systems often require most of the evidence to be submitted at the same time as the pleadings. In international arbitration it is common for pleadings to contain full submissions of fact and law which aim to tie together the facts and the relevant law in order to convince the tribunal to grant the relief sought by the claimant or the respondent, rather than to file 'common law-style' court pleadings. The pleadings will usually also be supported by all documentary evidence available that the party relies on. Often witness statements and expert evidence (if any) are also filed together with the pleadings, although this can depend on the particular dispute, and the legal background of the tribunal, counsel and parties who may be more used to filing such evidence subsequently. However, the parties and tribunal are free to agree on all of these matters (as discussed in Chapter 9).

Written submissions and evidence are generally followed by oral submissions and witness and expert testimony at an oral hearing. In some arbitrations, however, a tribunal may, where appropriate, decide to forego oral submissions entirely and determine the dispute on written submissions alone. In such cases, it is important to ensure that the written submissions are complete in every respect.

> **TIP** The legal background and culture of the tribunal can influence the style of procedure it adopts. If you would prefer a particular style, you should bear this in mind when selecting the tribunal.

It is important to consider at the outset of the arbitration whether it is more beneficial to plead all facts and the law upfront in the Statement of Claim or Statement of Defence, or whether it is better to hold back some facts and arguments for the Statement of Reply or Statement of Rejoinder.

It may be advantageous for the claimant to plead all matters early. This enables it to 'own the facts', forcing the respondent to answer allegations already before the tribunal. A full Statement of Claim gives the tribunal an overview of the case from the claimant's perspective. It is also likely to elicit a more fully pleaded defence from the respondent. This approach also enables the parties to identify the issues and merits of their respective positions at an early stage in the proceeding. It may also help to facilitate an early settlement. The burden of proving a case lies with the claimant, and a full pleading supported by evidence will go a long way to discharging this.

However, pleading a case fully at the outset can be a costly and expensive process. Whether it is appropriate will depend on the nature of the case and the respondent's anticipated response. There may be no point in investing the time, effort and expense of preparing a fully substantiated Statement of Claim if the respondent has no defence to the legal claims. Tactically, it may also benefit the claimant to hold back some facts for its Statement of Reply, once it has had an opportunity to review the Statement of Defence submitted by the respondent. Although a Statement of Reply should not raise new issues, a claimant may be able to put the facts to better use once it knows the nature of the defences raised. This is particularly so where there are three pleadings, rather than four, as the claimant will have the last word (as far as the pleadings are concerned) on the matters raised.

The respondent, on the other hand, is required to answer the claimant's case as pleaded. It is not required to bring additional issues unless it seeks to lodge a counterclaim. Many cases fail because the claimant cannot bring sufficient evidence to prove its case. For this reason, it may be in the respondent's interest not to plead all of the facts until the claimant has raised an issue that requires an answer. Discovery powers in international arbitration are often not as extensive as in typical North American or other common law jurisdictions, and thus, the respondent may not wish to give the claimant ideas for further lines of inquiry, but instead submit the minimum information required to answer the claims.

Another issue to consider is whether the pleadings should include a full pleading of the law or whether the tribunal is entitled to investigate the law itself. The Latin maxim *iure novit curia* ('the court knows the law') is adopted by several Roman/Germanic civil law legal systems. In practice, this means that the parties to a legal dispute do not need to plead or prove the law that applies to their case. Many civil law courts have inquisitorial powers and investigate both the law and factual matters. In English common law systems, however, the parties must generally plead the law applicable to their case and bring all facts before the court. These courts will not go beyond what is presented by the parties.

Some courts (eg, those in the US) adopt a mixed approach where the parties plead the law and the facts on which they rely, while the court may, in addition, undertake its own inquiries into the law. A mixed approach is often adopted in international arbitration. Since both the parties and the tribunal members may come from different legal backgrounds, and the applicable substantive law may be foreign to at least some of the tribunal members, it is often necessary to educate the tribunal about the law that is applicable to the issues. Legal experts are often appointed to assist with this, although unlike national court systems, the parties' counsel are free to plead the laws of any jurisdiction. It is common for a party who intends to rely upon a specific legal argument to appoint a co-arbitrator who is qualified in the relevant law and who can bring in jurisdiction-specific legal knowledge to the tribunal's deliberations.

1.2 Drafting pleadings: initial considerations

(a) Factual chronology

The first step when drafting any pleadings is to establish a comprehensive view of the facts of the case from the relevant party's perspective. In this way it is possible to identify which facts you wish to plead. An effective method is to compile a chronology of dates and events. It is helpful to keep this as a running document, and to update it once further evidence is available or when the other side submits its pleadings. The chronology should include dates, a description of the event, the source of information, relevant persons, document references and so on, in order that each event can be fully examined at a later date if required.

(b) Case theory/ongoing review

Developing a case theory is fundamental to the pleading of any dispute. This will highlight, for example, the strengths and weaknesses of the case, where additional evidence is required or where further development of the legal argument is necessary. The case theory becomes the roadmap for managing the dispute. It provides the framework within which strategic planning can be conducted and major decisions taken. In essence, counsel's job in any international arbitration is to analyse and sort the facts, simplify these into the salient points, organise them, analyse the legal principles, identify which legal arguments to run and which to avoid, and finally apply the law to the facts so as to convince the tribunal to decide in that party's favour. The main objective of the case theory is to provide the tribunal with a coherent, logical and consistent picture of the dispute from that party's perspective, in a manner that will help it to make a legally correct, just and fair choice in favour of that party.

A case theory should be a live document, regularly reviewed and analysed. This is particularly important when different pleadings are filed or major new evidence comes to light. Effective case theories often address the following issues:

- the factual narrative;
- the key facts to stress to the tribunal;
- the parties' motives and reasons;
- a clear argument on the legal issues in dispute;
- recognition of the weaknesses in the case and suggestions for overcoming them;
- a review of the other side's case, including strengths and weaknesses; and
- an explanation of why the party is the 'good guy' in the dispute and not at fault, which is a message that needs to be communicated to the tribunal.

TIP It can be helpful, particularly in complex cases, to draw up a table of the allegations/issues to prove (or overcome if the respondent) and identify for each one the evidence available. This can highlight where there are any evidential gaps, and particularly where further documentary evidence may need to be searched for.

(c) Document management

International arbitration cases are often highly technical and complex. They may span different countries, entities, industries and subject matters. They also often involve a large volume of documents. This is no different from complex commercial litigation, and document management strategies should be approached in the same way. Clearly, a sensible and up-to-date system should be put in place from the start, and updated regularly whenever new documents become available. In particular, documents produced from the other side's pleadings and from the document production process should be included as they are obtained, and possibly with reference to the source of the document.

The system to be used depends entirely on the nature of the dispute. It may be best to adopt a simple chronological run of documents, or to order documents according to type (eg, correspondence between X and Y, financial statements, technical reports, board minutes) or to use another suitable system. Ideally, the referencing used in the document management system should be synchronised with that used in the factual chronology and case theory.

1.3 Statement of Claim

(a) Key requirements

The Statement of Claim (which may also be known as the Statement of Case or the (First) Memorial) is the foundation document of a claimant's case. In international arbitration it is often what sets out the claimant's argument on why the tribunal has jurisdiction to hear the dispute, its position regarding the facts surrounding the dispute, its legal arguments and the application of the law to the facts, and (if quantum is not bifurcated) the claimant's justification for the amount of its claim. The Statement of Claim generally exhibits documentary evidence relied on by the claimant, and may also include witness statements and experts' reports. It will often delimit the scope of the overall dispute. It is therefore important to ensure that all (potential) legal claims and requested relief are included, or are expressed in language that allows them to be specified later.

Having provided details of the parties in dispute, their counsel and other entities involved, the claimant ordinarily first sets out the basis of the tribunal's jurisdiction. In commercial arbitrations, this will generally be based on an arbitration clause between the parties (see Chapters 3 and 6). It is usually enough for the claimant to quote this and explain briefly why the dispute at hand falls within the scope of that clause.

TIP If the respondent has already indicated that it intends to challenge the tribunal's jurisdiction, the claimant may want to include details of the legal and factual reasoning supporting its case on jurisdiction in the Statement of Claim.

The claimant usually also presents its arguments on the substantive law(s) applicable to the dispute, or, if relevant, a simple statement about the parties' prior agreement on this (whether in the underlying contract or otherwise).

A Statement of Claim is then generally divided into three sections:

- the facts;
- the law; and
- the claim for damages (or other relief).

Long submissions should also include a summary at the start.

There are a number of ways to present the facts, but often the most effective manner is simply in chronological order, with cross-references to the relevant documentary exhibits. This allows the relevant documents to speak for themselves. It also shows that the facts presented by the claimant are a true record of the circumstances or relationship at the time between the parties. Another way to present the facts is to group different issues thematically. This is effective for a complex factual matrix or for wide-ranging claims, but it requires careful signposting to explain why different facts are relevant to different topics and how the topics intersect chronologically.

Similarly, there is no standard format for presenting the legal section. This depends significantly on the points of law being pleaded and how these relate to the facts in dispute. It may be helpful for thematic factual sections to be designed to match thematic legal sections. Inversely, legal pleadings may need to be designed separately from chronological factual sections and to cross-refer to the relevant facts. The key to effective legal pleading is logical structure, clarity and brevity. Disparate legal issues should be tied together through the use of linking paragraphs and cross-references.

Unless the tribunal has ordered the separation of liability and quantum, the quantum section will be included in the Statement of Claim, setting out the amount of loss or damages claimed. There is generally some crossover between the legal and the quantum sections with respect to arguments of causation or legal methods to determine damages. If so, legal points on the right to recover damages should be presented first, followed by the financial discussion of the value of the damages claimed. While it is common to submit a report from a damages expert in larger or complex claims, this is not standard for all arbitrations. Tribunals generally expect counsel to plead the financial elements of a claimant's claim as well as the factual and legal cases. The most effective damages pleadings are those that reduce complex financial calculations to logical or common-sense stages, guiding the tribunal through the calculations and providing explanations where necessary.

The final section of a Statement of Claim is generally the 'prayer for relief'. This is where the claimant sets out clearly, in bullet-point form, the orders that it requests the tribunal to make. To the extent that there is an operative section of the Statement of Claim, this is it. The requests may include orders for jurisdiction (if relevant), liability, causation and quantum or damages. It will also set out any other relief that may be sought, such as an injunction, specific performance or some form of declaratory relief. Also, usually included are requests for interest on any final amount awarded (both interest running to the date of the award, and any post-award interest to accrue until payment is received), plus legal and procedural/arbitration costs.

TIP Detailed submissions regarding legal and procedural/arbitration costs are often made after the conclusion of the main substantive hearing (either in a post-hearing brief or in separate costs submissions). They are not included in the parties' pleadings.

Cross-reference More on costs submissions can be found in Chapter 13.

The claimant generally has first-mover advantage, and the Statement of Claim sets the boundaries within which the dispute will generally be heard. However, the claimant is also at a disadvantage in that it may not know all of the respondent's defences. It will need to anticipate the weaknesses of its case and account for these. If it does not, the respondent can rebut these in its Statement of Defence, and the claimant will have only one more opportunity (the Statement of Reply) to explain its position.

(b) *Presentation*

The key to an effective Statement of Claim, or indeed any written submission, is to present a convincing and complete picture of the dispute in a logical and coherent manner. The easiest way to do this is to ensure that the pleading starts with an introductory section explaining what will be addressed in the Statement of Claim and how these issues fit into the overall structure of the claim, and ends with a conclusion section reminding the tribunal what was addressed and why it was relevant.

Each chapter and subsection of the pleading should also have a brief introduction explaining what is coming, and a brief conclusion linking it to the bigger picture, stating why it is relevant and how it fits into the overall case analysis.

In other words, tell the tribunal what you are going to say, say it, then tell the tribunal what you have said and why it should be remembered.

It is useful to adopt consistent phrasing or terminology that will help the claimant's case. For example, if the claimant's case is that the respondent has wrongfully terminated a contract by sending a letter, instead of naming that letter by its date and parties each time, the claimant could define it as the 'Wrongful Termination Letter' and repeat this phrase throughout its pleadings. This not only highlights the importance of the letter (as distinct from other correspondence), but also reinforces the claimant's position that the termination of the contract was wrongful.

Signposting within a pleading is a simple way to link different sections and ensure that the overall picture is presented clearly. Statements such as "The claimant now turns to discuss X in order to explain why Y occurred", "A above is important because it establishes B" and "We explained above how J relates to K. This is relevant to L for the following reasons", and similar signposts are helpful, and need not be limited to introductions and conclusions.

While tribunals generally have extensive arbitral experience, it is not unusual for an arbitrator to have little experience in the particular subject matter. A detailed summary of specialist issues may therefore be beneficial. Again, it is useful to tie this into the overall picture of the claim. It is safe to assume that trade-specific issues or concepts will require explanation, unless the arbitrators are all experts in the field.

The Statement of Claim is generally supported by documentary evidence, and potentially with witness statements (and possibly also expert reports if the tribunal has ordered these to be produced at the same time.

TIP Witness statements are generally either:

- served by each party with its Statement of Claim or Statement of Defence;
- simultaneously exchanged after the Statement of Defence; or
- simultaneously exchanged after the Statement of Reply/Statement of Rejoinder.

Cross-reference See further on this in Chapter 9.

It is helpful to quote from evidence and documents as much as possible for the factual section, both to avoid misrepresenting statements or facts and to support one's case by referring to statements that can be separately evidenced. This applies similarly to legal argument – quoting brief sections of law or jurisprudence can be more effective than rephrasing a legal principle.

TIP Contemporaneous documentation is considered the most reliable source of evidence (other than in rare cases where documents are claimed to have been manufactured or tampered with fraudulently), and should be given priority over witness evidence wherever possible.

Footnotes are recommended, although they should be used sparingly for long sections of text. They are best used for making cross-references to documents, pleadings or cases, and for noting less relevant or oblique issues.

TIP The Global Arbitration Review publication "UCIA – Universal Citation in International Arbitration" is a helpful guide on best practice for citing and cross-referring to exhibits and authorities in an effective and consistent manner. The UCIA is available at: www.globalarbitration review.com/ category/ucia.

1.4 Statement of Defence

(a) Key requirements

The Statement of Defence (or Counter Memorial or Respondent's First Memorial) is the respondent's first opportunity to present its defence. It has two main functions: to rebut the claimant's allegations and to present the tribunal with an alternative explanation of the facts and/or law that may persuade the tribunal to find for the respondent. Best practice states that a tribunal may be more inclined to find for respondents that have presented a credible alternative picture. When the respondent believes that the claimant has no case to answer, it may wish simply to negate the claimant's case without providing an alternative view. However, this may leave the tribunal without a second-choice explanation if it chooses to find against the claimant.

Although the claimant, as first mover, is able to set the parameters of the case, it is the claimant's case to lose. All the respondent needs to do is remove a single pillar supporting the claimant's case – it rarely needs to disprove every element. The key action for a Statement of Defence is therefore to highlight the weaknesses of the claimant's case: on jurisdiction (if relevant) and on the facts, the law, the quantum and/or the relief. These elements are separate and an effective Statement of Defence will address each one individually. While the claimant must meet the burden of proof for all of these issues, the respondent generally needs to defeat only one. That said, the burden of proof is usually reversed in relation to jurisdiction, as the tribunal will assume it has jurisdiction (especially in the face of an arbitration agreement) unless the respondent can persuade it otherwise.

Nevertheless, respondents generally attack all elements of the claimant's claim, often with a number of different strategies per element. This creates hurdles for the claimant to overcome in its Statement of Reply. A respondent may, for example, contest the claimant's facts of a particular scenario, arguing that these facts do not meet the claimant's case, but instead support the respondent. The claimant's case is thus not made out because it has not established liability. Furthermore, it may be that the claimant's quantum claim is also not made out because its calculations are flawed, for example. Alternatively, the parties may agree on the facts in dispute, but provide alternative legal analyses or even, where a respondent has admitted liability, argue only on the quantum. Respondents also rephrase or represent the claimant's case in a way that suits their argument. Showing the tribunal that the respondent has its own credible version of events places the claimant on the defensive, as it has to re-establish the picture that it tried to create first.

An occasional tactic is to obfuscate or confuse matters, instead of responding to the case in an analytical manner. This makes it more difficult for the tribunal to understand the claimant's case. This might be done, for example, by purposely conflating different issues, by addressing many topics within one paragraph, or by not adhering to a pre-defined structure for the pleading. This is generally not advised: it may succeed only in making the respondent's case more difficult to follow (thus leading the tribunal to prefer that of the claimant), and tribunals certainly prefer defence submissions that make analytical review more straightforward. However, it can be effective to cast doubt on the claimant's case. Of course, the counter-view is that respondents only draft in this manner when they have nothing positive to say in their defence.

(b) Presentation

Many of the general written advocacy points noted above for the Statement of Claim – drafting, presentation of a case, use of signposting and introduction/conclusion/summary paragraphs, and so on – apply equally to the Statement of Defence, as well as to the Statement of Reply and Statement of Rejoinder (discussed below).

Although the structure of the Statement of Defence is, to some extent, dependent on the respondent's facts and legal analysis, it will generally address all sections of the Statement of Claim.

If the respondent is contesting the tribunal's jurisdiction, this is generally presented at the start of the Statement of Defence. However, jurisdictional arguments may be intertwined with the facts of the case. Thus, the respondent may need to present its version of facts before arguing its jurisdiction case on the law. The respondent's version of the facts is usually followed by the respondent's legal case, and by quantum/relief counterarguments. The Statement of Defence ends with the respondent's prayer for relief – usually the respondent requests the tribunal to dismiss all claims and award costs to the respondent.

If a counterclaim is brought, this will often be set out in a separate section, although with reference to the relevant facts as discussed in the main body of the Statement of Defence. The structure and purpose of the counterclaim will be similar to those required in the claimant's Statement of Claim since, as counterclaimant, the respondent bears the burden of proving its case.

The most effective defence pleadings summarise the claimant's position and then explain why this is wrong, on either the facts or the law. This can be done most simply by using the format of: "The claimant alleges that X occurred. This is incorrect, and the facts of Z show instead that Y occurred." Similarly, on the law, it is common to adopt the approach of: "The claimant argues that A applies in the circumstances, but this case is distinguished because of B/but this does not support the claimant's argument because a close reading of the case will show C instead."

Arbitration practice is different from general court practice in that there are no procedural requirements for a respondent to address every item of a Statement of Claim. In contrast, courts in many jurisdictions require the respondent to rebut, or at least address, each item in the claimant's pleading. If it does not, the respondent is deemed to have accepted the claimant's point on that item. The less rigorous requirements for arbitration pleadings give drafters more flexibility in structuring their Statement of Defence. Unlike many courts' proceedings, the respondent need not work through the claim line by line, stating its position on each point. This allows it to depart from the structure of the claimant's pleading and approach the subject from a different perspective. Nevertheless, it is generally advisable to help the tribunal by retaining the claimant's structure, unless to do so would not portray the respondent in a positive light. The claimant may state its facts in a chronological sequence, for example, while it may be more appropriate for the respondent to present its position using a thematic structure. This is more difficult to do if required to adopt a court's more rigorous line-by-line format.

TIP

In court practice, it is common to respond to points in the claimant's pleading by way of cross-reference. For example: "The allegation in para X is denied, because...." It is often more helpful for a tribunal, however, for the Statement of Defence to summarise those allegations which can then be credibly rebutted. For example, "At para X the claimant alleges that...; this is wrong because...". This saves the tribunal the trouble of switching between the pleadings in order to follow the Statement of Defence.

As with the Statement of Claim, the Statement of Defence is generally accompanied by documentary evidence, as well as witness statements (and possibly also expert reports) if the tribunal has ordered for them to be produced at the same time.

1.5 Statement of Reply

The sequence of parties' responses continues with the Statement of Reply. This is the claimant's second opportunity to state its case and to address the defences raised by the respondent. Just as the Statement of Defence was the respondent's opportunity to frame the issues in dispute in a particular manner, the Statement of Reply is the claimant's chance to return the dispute to its preferred agenda and to show the tribunal that the respondent's defences have no merit, or even that the respondent has no realistic defences at all.

Because the Statement of Defence addressed the respondent's stronger points of argument, it is generally accepted that these will be the issues over which the parties will now argue. In other words, if the Statement of Defence concedes or ignores an issue raised in the Statement of Claim, there is often little need to address this point in detail in the Statement of Reply. For this reason, a Statement of Reply is often structured to respond to the points in the Statement of Defence, and thus is expected to be a shorter document than the Statement of Claim (although this may not always be the case).

The Statement of Reply may note an issue that it wishes to rebut and should explain why it merits a rebuttal. For example, the Statement of Reply may state: "The respondent's defence to X is to claim that Y occurred. This, however, is not the true picture, because the respondent chooses not to address Z"; or "The respondent has mischaracterised A by ignoring B. The true picture is different, because C." Similarly, for the legal sections, a brief summary statement of the argument being rebutted should accompany any detailed rebuttal.

The Statement of Reply is often also the claimant's final opportunity to submit pleadings. Best practice suggests that its final section should summarise the claimant's complete case, and include an explanation of why the respondent's defences are invalid and why the claimant's case is strong.

TIP Claimants occasionally omit important arguments or facts from the Statement of Claim in order to present these in the Statement of Reply. This happens particularly where there is to be a Statement of Rejoinder. A careful respondent will prevent this by ensuring that the tribunal's procedural orders stipulate that no new evidence or arguments may be introduced by the claimant in the Statement of Reply unless they are responding to issues that have been raised in the Statement of Defence.

1.6 Statement of Rejoinder

The common law style of pleadings ends at the Statement of Reply, without any rejoinder. However, a Statement of Rejoinder is regularly included in international arbitration proceedings in order to give both sides an equal number of pleadings.

If it is included, the Statement of Rejoinder is the respondent's final opportunity to present its defence. It is also the final pleading to be submitted to the tribunal, giving the respondent a unique chance to have the final word. It is able to summarise the entire dispute in a favourable manner, highlighting its defences and how the claimant's case does not stand scrutiny.

As with the Statement of Reply, the Statement of Rejoinder should address and rebut the points of the claimant's Statement of Reply. All of the points noted above regarding the Statement of Reply apply to the Statement of Rejoinder.

> **TIP** The respondent should ensure that the procedural order allows for a Statement of Rejoinder in order to ensure equality of pleadings.

2. Evidence

2.1 Evidence generally

As discussed in Chapter 9, the tribunal can conduct the proceedings as it sees fit. While there are no express rules regarding the taking and submission of evidence, tribunals often look to the Rules on Taking of Evidence in International Arbitration 2010 produced by the International Bar Association (IBA) Rules. Tribunals often adopt these rules as guidance, although less often as concrete rules of procedure. The rules were issued as "a resource to parties and to arbitrators to provide an efficient, economical and fair process for the taking of evidence in international arbitration". They provide mechanisms for documentary evidence, factual witnesses, party-appointed experts, tribunal-appointed experts, evidential issues arising during hearings and guidance for the admissibility and assessment of evidence.

While this chapter does not discuss the individual provisions of the IBA Rules – these are generally quite clear – it does explain how the principles should be adopted for use when gathering evidence.

2.2 Witness evidence

(a) *Civil law versus common law approach*

The different approaches to evidence in common law and civil law jurisdictions may affect how witness evidence is employed in international arbitration proceedings. One key difference is that contact with witnesses before the hearing is accepted practice in common law jurisdictions, but not in some civil law jurisdictions. In common law jurisdictions, for example, counsel are accustomed to interviewing witnesses before any hearing and taking a statement from them (although they cannot attempt to influence a witness or tamper with their evidence). In civil law jurisdictions, counsel may be prevented from even contacting witnesses before the hearing and there may also be limits on who can give witness evidence (for example, a party's employees may be excluded). International arbitration proceedings will generally adopt a mix of the features of both systems, and indeed it is standard practice for witnesses to be interviewed by counsel before a hearing, for no limits to be placed on who may be called as a witness, and for written witness statements to be produced (see further below).

(b) Rules and law governing witness evidence

The main arbitral institutions give quite broad guidance on the use of witness evidence. The 2014 London Court of International Arbitration (LCIA) Rules, for example, give tribunals broad discretion to control the use of witness evidence. They state that the tribunal:

- may require a party seeking to rely on the evidence of a particular witness to explain the relevance of that evidence (Article 20.1);
- may limit or refuse the appearance of a witness (Article 20.3); and
- controls the questioning of witnesses (Article 20.8).

The 2017 International Chamber of Commerce (ICC) Rules do not require the tribunal to agree to the hearing of witness evidence – Article 25.3 merely provides that the tribunal "may decide to hear witnesses". Similar to the LCIA Rules, the 2017 Stockholm Chamber of Commerce (SCC) Rules permits the tribunal to order the parties to identify each witness intended to be called and to explain the relevance of that evidence (Article 33.1).

The 2016 Singapore International Arbitration Centre (SIAC) Rules provide that the Tribunal may require the parties to give notice of the identity of any witnesses they intend to produce and that the Tribunal may allow, refuse or limit the appearance of witnesses to give oral evidence at any hearing (see Rule 25).

Another useful source and reference is the IBA Rules. These are regarded as good general guidance for international arbitration proceedings as they seek to harmonise civil and common law norms. However, as discussed in Chapter 9, in response to concerns amongst those users, practitioners and arbitrators from the civil law tradition that the IBA Rules do not properly cater for the civil law approach, the Prague Rules on the Efficient Conduct of Proceedings in International Arbitration (Prague Rules) have been developed.

(c) *Witness statements*

Witness statements are common in international arbitration. They often stand as a witness's main written evidence document (known as 'evidence-in-chief'; see Chapter 12), and are generally accompanied by documentary evidence or exhibits.

Factual witness evidence is far more widespread in common law countries than civil law countries. As such, most international arbitrations adopt a hybrid approach that involves some factual evidence. However, as noted above, this is often given less weight than the contemporaneous documentation. The IBA Rules give useful guidance on the use of witness evidence. Some of the key provisions include the following:

- Any person can be a witness, including a party or a party's employee. This is important as some legal codes do not give as much weight to the testimony of a party or its employees (Article 4.2).
- A party can interview its own witnesses and produce a witness statement (accompanied by a statement of truth rather than a sworn oath), which the other party may respond to with witness statements of its own (Article 4.4). Again, this is important as some civil law countries prevent parties from discussing the case with witnesses.
- Any person giving a witness statement should appear at the hearing unless the parties agree otherwise (Article 4.7).
- The tribunal may apply to the national courts of the seat of arbitration in order to compel a witness to give evidence and appear at the hearing, provided that the witness is subject to that court's jurisdiction (Article 4.9).

There is no provision in the IBA Rules for depositions or interrogations, but these are in any event rare in international arbitrations.

The witness statement should be a factual explanation of what the witness knows, or experienced or understood to be the situation at the time. It should be a statement only of the facts about which the witness is giving evidence and should not contain opinion or speculation on the part of the witness. It should not make arguments about the law or seek to point out deficiencies in the opposing party's positions. This is the job of counsel.

Unlike most national court proceedings, there are no formal requirements for a witness statement in international arbitration. However, the IBA Rules suggest that a witness statement is generally expected, at minimum, to include the following:

- full details of who the witness is and why he or she is giving the statement;
- a full and detailed description of the facts and the source of the witness's knowledge;

- a statement on the language and method of preparation of the witness statement;
- an affirmation that the statement is true to the best of the witness's knowledge; and
- the witness's signature.

It should also contain an introductory section explaining the witness's background, current position and involvement with the issues in dispute.

TIP It is a good idea for the tribunal to set out in its first procedural order any requirements as to witness evidence, whether by reference to the IBA Rules or otherwise. This will ensure that both parties approach witness evidence in the same way and so avoid unnecessary later arguments as to the weight that should be placed on the evidence solely by reason of the form of the statement.

Cross-reference See Chapter 9 for more on setting the procedure.

Tribunals often regard witness statements that are corroborated by contemporaneous or written evidence as convincing. Similarly, statements that are contradicted by documentary evidence may be disregarded or given less weight. It is therefore important to assess the witness's supporting or contradicting evidence, and those points that the witness wants to address or avoid in his or her statement.

(d) Choice of witnesses

Clearly, a witness's evidence will be more effective, cogent and convincing if they have direct knowledge of a particular situation. Furthermore, it is beneficial if the witness has relevant experience that helps them understand the situation at the time, and later explain it to the tribunal. Evidence from witnesses reporting on facts second-hand is less persuasive and thus, if it is necessary at all, should be supported with documentary evidence wherever possible.

Cross-examination is often a major consideration when choosing witnesses. Cross-examination may be an uncomfortable process and is beyond the control of the party's counsel. Opposing counsel can try to discredit a witness in a number of ways, and not all witnesses can deal with the adversarial nature of this process. Therefore, it is important to consider whether a witness's testimony and character will withstand cross-examination. If not, the witness may be led to make statements that discredit their testimony or otherwise contradict the party's position. This may damage a party's case more than if the witness had not appeared at all.

For this reason, the best witnesses are often people who present themselves as clear, focused and considered. Parties may want to avoid witnesses who are overly loquacious (they may give away too much information), who are taciturn and withdrawn (they may say nothing and appear obstructive), or who are liable to be provoked during cross-examination into argument or outbursts. Witnesses who are too connected to the facts emotionally may also appear to bear a grudge or be self-serving if they cannot control their emotional involvement. Any of these factors can negatively affect the cogency and credibility of a witness's evidence.

If there is only one witness who can address a particular point, and counsel believes that they may not deal with cross-examination effectively, it is even more important to limit the witness's statement to only the most necessary points. This may help to limit the scope of cross-examination, which ordinarily can address only the points made in a witness statement.

Cross-reference See more on cross-examination in Chapter 12).

If a witness has trouble recalling facts, events or dates from a few years ago, it is often helpful to use diaries, phone records, travel arrangements and so on to help them to recollect events in the correct order. If this is set out in detail in the witness statement, the witness may be more confident about their recollection during cross-examination.

TIP Thoroughly investigate potential witnesses to identify early any potential credibility issues which may be exposed in cross-examination. Such issues should be identified during document review; however, general searches should also be carried out. If problematic documents exist within the document production set yet submission of a statement by that witness is critical, consider addressing the issue in the witness statement to take the impact out of any cross-examination on the issue.

2.3 Experts

(a) Role of experts

It is common in international arbitration for parties to submit expert testimony. This is most often provided on technical issues (such as engineering, manufacturing, industry practice, etc), financial issues (such as assessing the level of damages that a party has suffered or might suffer, or opining on accounting or regulatory compliance) or legal topics (such as issues of foreign law).

An expert witness may not always be necessary, however. Before instructing anyone, it is important to think carefully about whether expert evidence is needed. The tribunal will not want to be bothered with additional evidence that is not material to the case. The 2018 (second edition) of the ICC report on controlling time and costs in arbitration suggests that it should be presumed that expert evidence is not required unless it is needed to inform the tribunal on key issues in the dispute.

The expert's primary duty is to assist the tribunal. This should override any obligation that they may have towards the party appointing them or paying their fees. The expert should not be seen to act as an advocate for that party. It is generally accepted, however, that a party-appointed expert would not have been instructed if they might have provided testimony that would compromise their appointing party's case. An experienced expert is adept at remaining neutral with regard to their opinion while ensuring that any testimony does not disadvantage the appointing party.

In order to overcome potential concerns regarding party-appointed experts' possible (even if unconscious) bias towards their appointing party, the tribunal is also often empowered to appoint its own experts, as in Article 25(4) of the 2017 ICC Rules, for example (similar provisions can be found in the LCIA Rules Article 21, SIAC Rule 26 and Conflict Prevention and Resolution (CPR) Rule 12.3). This is a common practice in civil law courts. While less common in international arbitration than party-appointed experts, this does have the considerable advantage of reducing costs for all parties and the tribunal is likely to be confident that the expert is impartial. However, such appointments remove control from the parties, who may not agree with a particular expert's appointment, or indeed with the opinion provided. It is a good idea for the parties and the tribunal to agree on party or tribunal appointment in the first procedural order.

Cross-reference See Chapter 9 and discussion below concerning the 'Sachs Protocol').

The IBA Rules again provide guidance on the use of experts (whether appointed by the parties or the tribunal) and the contents of their reports. In particular, they state that an expert must be independent of the parties, the reports should be directed to specified issues that are in dispute and the experts should appear at the hearing to answer questions if requested to do so by either party (Article 5). The tribunal may also, after consulting the parties, appoint an expert of its own volition on specific Terms of Reference (Article 6). Where this is the case, the IBA Rules give the expert the same powers as the tribunal to request documents from the parties or access certain sites or equipment for inspection (Article 6.3).

(b) Selecting experts

If expert evidence is required, it is extremely important to select the most appropriate candidate with the relevant experience and expertise. It is also worth considering whether the expert has served as a witness before, as it is helpful if they have had prior experience of drafting reports for legal proceedings and of giving oral evidence. The latter is particularly important: giving evidence at an oral hearing can be quite daunting and it is vital that the expert gives their opinion confidently and credibly. In any event, you should ensure that the expert is fully prepared and aware of how and where proceedings will take place (see also Chapter 12).

With regard to party-appointed experts, parties are generally free to appoint whomever they want, subject to conflicts. Direct experience and expertise in the relevant issue in dispute, as well as suitability to perform under cross-examination (as discussed above), are often the main selection criteria. It is easy for an opposing counsel to highlight to the tribunal that a party's expert does not, in fact, have sufficient or relevant experience or expertise in the field that they purport to have. This can be extremely specific: for example, when opining on a contract for the sale of natural resources, even if an expert has general experience in the trade of the material globally, there may be local factors that require specific experience in a small area. Similarly, a foreign legal expert could be compromised during cross-examination if their expertise is mostly related, for example, to a niche area of law such as trusts when the dispute focuses on general contractual principles.

You should seek to instruct an expert as soon as possible, particularly if the area in question is quite niche and the number of good-quality experts available may be scarce. This will ensure that the opposing party does not instruct your preferred expert first and/or will create a conflict of interest to ensure that the other side cannot instruct them, even if you end up not proceeding with that expert.

A hybrid party/tribunal appointment of experts, named the 'Sachs protocol', is an alternative method of expert appointment. Under this protocol, each party nominates a list of an agreed number of experts, from which the tribunal chooses one from each. These two experts are then appointed by and report to the tribunal but are nevertheless acceptable to the parties. This approach can result in a greater perception of the impartiality and independence of the experts and may minimise the issues which can arise in connection with party-appointed experts such as the level of assistance and guidance given to an expert by counsel including cross-examination preparation.

(c) Rules and law governing expert evidence

The tribunal will issue directions on the form and timing of expert evidence in accordance with the applicable institutional rules and the law of the seat of the arbitration. The English Arbitration Act 1996, for example, provides that "It shall be for the tribunal to decide all procedural and evidential matters, subject to the right of the parties to agree any matter" (Section 33(1)).

The 2017 ICC Rules provide that "the arbitral tribunal may decide to hear experts appointed by the parties...in the presence of the parties, or in their absence provided they have been duly summoned" (Article 25(3)), and that "after having consulted the parties, [the tribunal] may appoint one or more experts, define their Terms of Reference and receive their reports. At the request of a party, the parties shall be given the opportunity to question at a hearing any such expert" (Article 25(4)).

Articles 20 and 21 of the 2014 LCIA Rules govern the provision of witness evidence, including that of experts. Under those rules, the tribunal may appoint an independent expert to report on specific issues, and may require the parties to provide that expert with relevant documents or other materials. The parties are entitled to examine the expert at a hearing. Similar provisions are set out in the 2013 United Nations Commission on International Trade Law (UNCITRAL) Rules (Articles 27, 28 and 29).

The IBA Rules also provide guidance on party-appointed experts (Article 5) and experts appointed by the tribunal (Article 6). These guidelines, which are frequently applied by arbitrators, offer useful direction as to the procedure for expert evidence. Common law systems generally allow an expert to be cross-examined on anything that falls within their expertise, while civil law systems generally restrict expert cross-examination to issues in the expert report (see Article 6 of the 2018 Prague Rules for an example of a civil law approach).

(d) Dealing with experts

While a tribunal has no express power to compel documents to be disclosed, it is always safe to ensure that any discussions between experts and the legal representatives who have appointed them take place under the cloak of privilege or confidentiality. It is not uncommon for a party to request that the instructions given to the opposing side's experts be produced in the arbitration, in order to investigate the neutrality of the expert's approach to the subject matter. Beyond that, any correspondence between the expert and the party/counsel will ordinarily be protected.

Care should always be taken with the instructions or questions that are put to an expert to enable them to draft their report. Clearly, these should all be relevant and appropriate, to reduce the risk of the expert's opinion being provided on questions that are irrelevant. It may also be helpful to include a wide 'catch-all' question to ensure that anything else which the expert considers to be relevant is not missed.

In order to ensure that no doubts can be cast on an expert's independence or impartiality, it is particularly important to ensure that their fees are not dependent in any way on the outcome of the proceedings, or linked to the amount that may be recovered.

The IBA Rules provide that an expert's report should contain:

- the full name and address of the expert;
- a statement of their past relationship with the parties and counsel;
- a description of the expert's background and experience;
- a description of the instructions received;
- a statement of independence;
- the expert's opinion;
- a statement on the language and manner of production of the report;
- an affirmation of the expert's genuine belief in the opinions expressed; and
- the expert's signature.

It is also good practice to include a confirmation that the expert understands that their primary duty is to the tribunal and an affirmation that their fee and remuneration do not depend upon the outcome of the proceedings.

Further guidance relating to the procedure and issues to consider with respect to the appointment and management of experts in international arbitration can be found in the following publications:

- Chartered Institute of Arbitrators (CIArb) Protocol for the Use of Party-appointed Experts: www.ciarb.org/guidelines-and-ethics/guidelines/arbitration-guidelines;
- LCIA 2018 note, "Experts in International Arbitration": www.lcia.org/News/experts-in-international-arbitration.aspx;
- IBA Guidelines on Party Representation in International Arbitration: www.ibanet.org/Publications/publications_IBA_guides_and_free_materials.aspx;
- ICC Techniques for Controlling Time and Costs in Arbitration: https://iccwbo.org/publication/icc-arbitration-commission-report-on-techniques-for-controlling-time-and-costs-in-arbitration/; and
- UNCITRAL Notes on Organizing Arbitral Proceedings (2016): www.uncitral.org/uncitral/en/uncitral_texts/arbitration/2016Notes_proceedings.html.

2.4 Documentary evidence

(a) Document production

Most common law litigation systems contain a procedure for the parties to request documents from each other, often supported by legal obligations imposed on counsel and on the parties' representatives. The US-style procedure of discovery can be all-encompassing, time consuming and costly; the English-law process of disclosure is generally less comprehensive, but is still a wide-ranging and potentially significant exercise. In contrast, in civil law systems document production tends to be limited to what each party intends to rely on.

There are often no general search obligations, and parties may have limited or even no opportunities to obtain documents from the other side. While it is open to the parties and the tribunal to adopt any disclosure/document production mechanisms (if any) that they consider most appropriate, it is common in international arbitration to adopt a document production system that sits between the two extremes such as the one provided for in the IBA Rules. Under this system, there is no general duty to search, and each party need only produce that on which it relies in the first instance. However, parties may submit substantiated document requests to each other that require reasonable searches for those documents to be carried out and for the relevant documents to be provided. If either party objects or fails to provide the requested documents, the requesting party may approach the tribunal for an order for document production. If the tribunal's order is not complied with, the requesting party may invite the tribunal to draw adverse inferences against the non-compliant party in respect of the document or issue at hand.

The key principle of the IBA Rules in this respect is that any 'Request to Produce' made of the other party must be either for documents that can be individually identified or for specific classes of documents. All documents requested must be relevant and material to the case. Although this may appear to create a streamlined procedure for document production, in practice – and particularly in large or complex disputes – such requests (as well as the document review processes that are required to satisfy them) can be long and costly. This can, in turn, lead the other party to raise objections which must be dealt with by the tribunal, further increasing costs and delays. In this regard, tribunals are becoming increasingly frustrated with parties who make numerous and wide-ranging requests (often not compliant with the IBA Rules) with little real thought as to why the documents requested are necessary or relevant. Indeed, making too many requests may not only alienate the tribunal, but could lead the tribunal to question whether the relevant party has sufficient evidence to support its case. In some cases, however, there may be tactical reasons for making a substantial number of requests, for example if the other side has control over all of the documents and it is necessary for a large number of those to be produced to ensure that the parties are on an equal footing, or if the cost and extent of any document searches may lead a party to consider early settlement. For these reasons, it is important to consider very carefully the document requests to be made, and in the context of what the requesting party is hoping to achieve.

The IBA Rules recognise the importance of electronic disclosure in international arbitration, although the rules do not provide guidance on dealing with the, often complex, technical issues that may arise in searching for electronically held documents.

It is common in international arbitration for the tribunal to specify that

'Requests to Produce' (whether in accordance with the IBA Rules or otherwise) be submitted in the form of a 'Redfern Schedule'. This sets out the following in table form:

- each of the requesting party's document requests;
- detailed justifications for the requests;
- the other party's objections to the request or information on the documents produced;
- the requesting party's responses to any objections; and
- the tribunal's order for document production (if any).

This information is set out in rows on the Redfern Schedule, providing the tribunal with a clear presentation of each document request and objections in one place, so that the tribunal may make an order if requested to do so.

TIP Redfern Schedules should not be used as an opportunity for a party to present submissions. Precise and deliberate requests are more likely to be viewed by the tribunal as valid.

The process of making document requests generally involves the simultaneous exchange of Redfern Schedules, then a later exchange of objections/produced documents, an application to the tribunal for an order for production including responses to any objections made, the tribunal's order (if any) and a final period for the parties to produce documents ordered. These steps are usually set out in the procedural timetable.

TIP Fill in the Redfern Schedule in a way that will be easiest for the arbitrators to follow, bearing in mind in particular that they may be reading it on a mobile device. For example, justifications and objections should be completed for each request, rather than cross-referring to the justification or objection made for another request in the schedule.

TIP A template Redfern Schedule is set out in the appendix to this chapter.

(b) Requesting documents

The IBA Rules require that documents requested fall into "narrow and specific" categories that are "reasonably believed to exist". The requesting party is therefore required to include details such as dates, names, subject matter and type of document. It thereby limits the request to specific known documents or categories in order to avoid wide-ranging speculative requests. Tribunals will usually refuse to grant orders for production where requests are too wide ranging, too burdensome to comply with, irrelevant, unspecified or otherwise insufficiently substantiated. Parties requesting documents should always ensure that their requests cannot be rejected for any of these reasons.

The IBA Rules also require a "statement as to how the documents requested are relevant to the case and material to its outcome" (Article 3(3)(b)). This is key. The stronger and more focused the justification for the request, the more likely that the tribunal is to order it to be disclosed. It is good practice to precisely explain why a document/category is relevant, which issue(s) in dispute it relates to, why the requesting party does not have this document and why it is believed to be in the "possession, custody or control" of the other party. This may require reference to the categories of the IBA Rules, including referencing the parties' pleadings and exhibited documents which are related to the documents requested. Be careful also with repeating verbatim the same justifications for multiple requests as this can give the impression to the tribunal that each individual request has not been properly considered.

When objecting to document requests, the general approach is to explain why the request is too wide ranging, irrelevant, privileged, unreasonably burdensome to comply with, technically or commercially confidential, politically or institutionally sensitive, disproportionate or otherwise unfair. This too may require reference to the IBA Rules. As above, it may be helpful to refer to the parties' pleadings or exhibited documents where appropriate.

It is common to request disclosure of electronic documents and emails. Institutions such as the ICC, the International Centre for Dispute Resolution (ICDR) and the CIArb, among others, have published protocols or guidelines to help parties deal with requests for electronic disclosure in international arbitration.

Cross-reference For more on disclosure of electronic documents, see Chapter 9.

TIP Examples of guidelines on requests for electronic disclosure include the IBA Rules on the Taking of Evidence in International Arbitration, the CIArb Protocol for E-disclosure in Arbitration and the ICDR Guidelines for Arbitrators Concerning Exchanges of Information. These can be found at the following addresses:

- www.ibanet.org/Publications/publications_IBA_guides_and_free_materials.aspx;
- www.ciarb.org/guidelines-and-ethics/guidelines/arbitration-guidelines; and
- www.adr.org/adr-resources.

(c) *Privilege and confidentiality*

There are no formal rules regarding questions of privilege and confidentiality in international arbitration. These issues are generally separate from the jurisdictions of national courts or bar associations which usually oversee them. This may create a source of conflict, since counsel are always subject to their own ethical rules and procedures, which may differ across jurisdictions. It is not uncommon for counsel in an arbitration to be subject to different privilege and confidentiality obligations, and the tribunal may then be required to resolve these.

In summary, in most common law jurisdictions, privilege applies to confidential documents or communications created by lawyers and/or for the purposes of legal advice and/or litigation or arbitration. Common law privilege generally attaches to the document itself, and is seen as an issue of substantive law. In contrast, in most civil law jurisdictions confidentiality exists as a professional or ethical duty imposed on a lawyer to keep his or her client's information confidential. This relates to the information, not the document, and is an issue of procedural law. There are also questions (with differing answers in different jurisdictions) as to whether in-house lawyers are subject to professional confidentiality or privilege obligations. It is the duty of the tribunal to resolve competing claims for privilege/confidentiality within this loose framework.

Tribunals have adopted a number of different approaches to resolving such questions. A tribunal may conduct a 'choice of law' analysis to determine the applicable privilege/confidentiality rules; it may choose to determine whether the question is a substantive or a procedural point and then apply the appropriate law; or it may consider the context and jurisdiction in which the document was created in order to guide its decision. Tribunals often adopt a sensible and pragmatic approach, weighing up the request against the privilege or confidentiality claim and the nature of the evidence. They generally try to ensure that counsel are not ordered to breach any professional or ethical obligations, and often resolve claims for privilege by assessing the conflicting rules and applying the provisions that provide the most protection for all concerned.

When queries arise as to whether a (pre-dispute) document giving legal advice is privileged, it is often most helpful to examine the law which the parties would have thought was relevant at the time the advice was being given. For example, if the (pre-dispute) advice relates to English contract law, then it may have been provided by English lawyers who would be subject to English laws regarding privilege. If, however, the document relates to advice regarding litigation or dispute management (rather than general legal advice provided before the dispute began), then it may be helpful to look to the privilege laws of the seat of arbitration.

Cross-reference For further information on privilege in international arbitration, see Chapter 5.

Appendix: Template Redfern Schedule

[NAME OF ARBITRAL INSTITUTION]

CASE NO.

[NAME OF CLAIMANT(S)] Claimant(s)

- v -

[NAME OF RESPONDENT(S)] Respondent(s)

[CLAIMANT'S/RESPONDENT'S] REQUESTS FOR DOCUMENT PRODUCTION

[Claimant's/Respondent's] Introductory Note:
This request is made pursuant to [Procedural Order No. 1] dated [DATE], that the parties submit Requests to Produce documents in the form of a "Redfern Schedule" and in accordance with Article 3 of the IBA Rules for the Taking of Evidence in International Commercial Arbitration. The [Claimant/Respondent] hereby declares that none of the documents requested below are in or under its possession and/or custody and/or control. The [Claimant/Respondent] further declares that it reasonably believes that all the documents requested below should be in the possession and/or custody and/or control of the [Respondent/Claimant].

For the avoidance of doubt, the requests set out below are limited to documents or specific categories of documents that are relevant and material to the outcome of this arbitration, in accordance with Article 3(3) of the IBA Rules of Taking of Evidence in International Arbitration.

For the avoidance of doubt, reference to "documents" and "correspondence" in the requests below is to any notes, memoranda, minutes, letters, faxes, emails, presentations or other documents or correspondence of whatever nature (including electronically stored documents) that have been produced or circulated by, provided to, or are otherwise within the possession, custody or control of, the [Respondent/Claimant].

The words "concerning", "evidencing", "relating", "referring" or "reflecting" mean in any way concerning, indicating, referring to, mentioning, reflecting, pertaining to, evidencing, involving, describing, discussing, responding to, supporting, contradicting, constituting in whole or in part, and being a draft, copy or summary of the whole or a part.

For the sake of clarity, the documents described below refer to any and all relevant documents, whether internally produced or otherwise, which have not already been filed in this case as part of the communications now on record.

[The defined terms employed below have been previously defined in [PLEADING REFERENCE]. To the extent possible, references are given to those areas where the key factual and/or legal issues in relation to each of the documents requested are covered.]

The [Claimant/Respondent] reserves the right to add to or amend these requests during the course of the Arbitration proceedings.

[NAME OF ARBITRAL INSTITUTION]

CASE NO. [xxxxxx]

[NAME OF CLAIMANT(S)]
Claimant(s)

- v -

[NAME OF RESPONDENT(S)]
Respondent(s)

[CLAIMANT'S/RESPONDENT'S] REQUESTS FOR DOCUMENT PRODUCTION

[Claimant's/Respondent's] Introductory Note:
This request is made pursuant to [Procedural Order No. 1] dated [DATE], that the parties submit Requests to Produce documents in the form of a "Redfern Schedule" and in accordance with Article 3 of the IBA Rules for the Taking of Evidence in International Commercial Arbitration. The [Claimant/Respondent] hereby declares that none of the documents requested below are in or under its possession and/or custody and/or control. The [Claimant/Respondent] further declares that it reasonably believes that all the documents requested below should be in the possession and/or custody and/or control of the [Respondent/Claimant].

For the avoidance of doubt, the requests set out below are limited to documents or specific categories of documents that are relevant and material to the outcome of this arbitration, in accordance with Article 3(3) of the IBA Rules of Taking of Evidence in International Arbitration.

For the avoidance of doubt, reference to "documents" and "correspondence" in the requests below is to any notes, memoranda, minutes, letters, faxes, emails, presentations or other documents or correspondence of whatever nature (including electronically stored documents) that have been produced or circulated by, provided to, or are otherwise within the possession, custody or control of, the [Respondent/Claimant].

The words "concerning", "evidencing", "relating", "referring" or "reflecting" mean in any way concerning, indicating, referring to, mentioning, reflecting, pertaining to, evidencing, involving, describing, discussing, responding to, supporting, contradicting, constituting in whole or in part, and being a draft, copy or summary of the whole or a part.

For the sake of clarity, the documents described below refer to any and all relevant documents, whether internally produced or otherwise, which have not already been filed in this case as part of the communications now on record.

[The defined terms employed below have been previously defined in [PLEADING REFERENCE]. To the extent possible, references are given to those areas where the key factual and/or legal issues in relation to each of the documents requested are covered.]

The [Claimant/Respondent] reserves the right to add to or amend these requests during the course of the Arbitration proceedings.

No.	Document(s) or Category of Documents Requested	Relevance/Materiality of Documents Requested (With Reference to Pleadings and/or Exhibits)	[Respondent's/ Claimant's] Comments of [DATE]	[Claimant's/ Respondent's] Reply Comments of [DATE]	Tribunal's Decision
1.	[DESCRIPTION OF DOCUMENT OR CATEGORY OF DOCUMENTS REQUESTED]	Reference(s) to pleadings and/or exhibits: [INSERT RELEVANT REFERENCES] Reason(s) for request: [INSERT JUSTIFICATION FOR WHY THIS DOCUMENT OR CATEGORY OF DOCUMENTS IS RELEVANT AND NECESSARY TO THE DETERMINATION OF THIS DISPUTE]	[COMMENTS TO BE INSERTED BY THE PARTY RECEIVING THE REQUEST, INCLUDING ANY OBJECTIONS TO PRODUCTION]	[REPLY COMMENTS TO BE INSERTED BY THE REQUESTING PARTY, IF REQUIRED]	[TRIBUNAL'S DECISION ON PRODUCTION TO BE INSERTED, IF REQUIRED]

12. The hearing

Unless the parties settle beforehand, most arbitrations end with an oral hearing before the tribunal. This is where witnesses and experts can be examined on their evidence, the parties can put forward their submissions orally and the tribunal can ask questions of the witnesses or counsel.

Arrangements for the hearing include both practical arrangements and the procedure to be followed. They may be set out at the outset of the arbitration in the first procedural order or, more commonly, dealt with shortly before the hearing by exchange of correspondence or a pre-hearing conference (usually by telephone).

1. Practical arrangements for the hearing

As a general rule, counsel for the claimant will take charge of the arrangements for the hearing. However, all parties must consent to those arrangements and will need to participate to some extent in their organisation. The relevant arbitral institution may offer help, but this is usually limited.

It is vital that arrangements for the hearing are made well in advance, particularly in circumstances where the tribunal and the parties are based in different jurisdictions. Careful planning is required to ensure that proceedings run smoothly and efficiently. Given that the hearing will have been scheduled for a finite period of time, it is essential that no time is wasted resolving issues that could have been avoided with proper planning or by prior discussion between counsel and the tribunal.

1.1 Place

The geographical location of the hearing may be expressly provided for in the arbitration agreement. If not, it will be determined either by the tribunal or by agreement between the parties, most commonly at the outset of the arbitration. The hearing should be located somewhere that all participants can reach easily, both to minimise the risk of any disruption caused by travel delays and to reduce costs.

The hearing may take place somewhere other than the seat of the arbitration. The applicable arbitration legislation in most jurisdictions and/or the arbitration rules of most arbitral institutions will allow hearings to take place outside of the country of the seat (eg, Article 18 of the International Chamber of Commerce (ICC) Rules of Arbitration 2017 and Article 16 of the Dubai International Financial Centre–London Court of International Arbitration (DIFC-LCIA) Rules of Arbitration 2016). However, the arbitration (and any subsequent award) will still be governed by the law of the seat, regardless of where the hearing physically takes place.

1.2 Video link

Time and cost restrictions may mean that it is more appropriate for some participants to attend the hearing by telephone or video link. The use of Voice over Internet Protocol (VoIP) technology, such as Skype, is also becoming increasingly common. This will require significant forward planning and organisation, but most modern facilities will be able to accommodate this.

When making such arrangements, permission will need to be obtained in good time from the tribunal, even if counsel on the other side is amenable to the proposal. While the international nature of disputes may mean that a video link is the only feasible option, tribunals and counsel will often prefer a witness to be physically present so as to uphold the formality of the occasion or so that their witness statement can be truly tested by live cross-examination (and to ensure that their evidence is not being prompted or otherwise tampered with).

The line and equipment should be tested thoroughly before the start of proceedings. IT technicians should be enlisted wherever possible. It is also worth having a technician on hand during the hearing in case any issues arise once proceedings have started. Consider local time zones in each location that is using the video link to ensure that appropriate support is always available.

A video link feed may have a delay at one or more locations. While this is not a major obstacle, all participants should be aware of the issue and should make allowances for it. If two people are speaking over each other at the same time, for example, others may miss what has been said, including the transcriber. If video links are to be used, it is a good idea for the parties and the tribunal to agree at the start of the hearing how any dialogue with video link participants will work. For example, counsel may wish to leave an accented pause and/or use hand signals at the end of each question in order to let the witness know to start speaking. It may also be useful in certain circumstances to have a party representative alongside witnesses who are giving evidence via video link to minimise complications or confusion associated with time delays or interruptions in the video feed. Representatives of the other party (or parties) should be given the opportunity to also attend the video link with the witness so as to ensure the witness is giving evidence in an independent setting free from coaching or influence.

1.3 **Venue**

The physical venue should be chosen carefully to ensure that it is large enough to accommodate all participants comfortably within the proposed room configuration. You will also need to ensure that all of the necessary facilities and equipment are available.

Many arbitral institutions offer their own or related venues, such as the ICC Hearing Centre in Paris, Maxwell Chambers in Singapore (where the Singapore International Arbitration Centre (SIAC) is based) and the International Dispute Resolution Centre in London (in which the London Court of International Arbitration (LCIA) is based). Other typical venues include specialist dispute resolution centres, hotel conference suites and offices (including those of one of the legal counsels involved).

You should check in advance what room layout the tribunal prefers so as to ensure the space is large enough. The most typical configuration is as illustrated below.

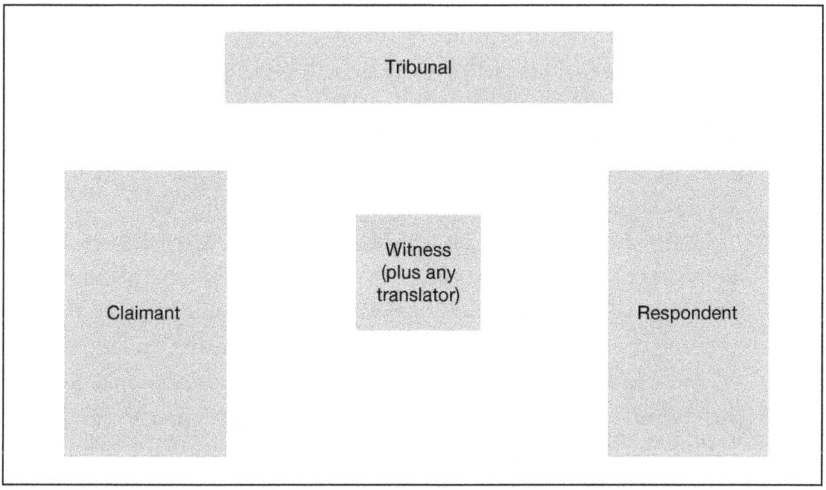

Remember that for most hearings space will also be needed for transcribers. It is worth checking with the transcribers where they would prefer to sit – often they will want to be able to see everybody who is speaking. Equally, if video conference facilities are to be used, thought will need to be given as to where the video will be set up and to ensure that the witness can see all the relevant speakers.

Remember also to plan and check every detail, including internet or wi-fi access, telephone and video-conferencing facilities, power sockets, projectors, microphones, printing facilities, stationery and catering. Make sure you ask well in advance whether any participants have specific access or dietary requirements that you need to accommodate, as this may affect your choice of venue.

The cost of hiring the venue is also relevant and should be discussed with the other side in order to obtain agreement on sharing the costs.

Cross-reference More on the costs of arbitration can be found in Chapter 13.

1.4 Translators and interpreters

The language of the arbitration is usually specified in the arbitration agreement. If not, the general rule is to follow the language in which the arbitration agreement or relevant contracts were made.

Where the dispute relates to a cross-border transaction, there may be documents that need to be translated into the language of the arbitration. Professional translations should be obtained wherever possible to ensure that they are as true to the original language as possible. Each party must procure a translation into the relevant language of any documents or parts of documents on which it is relying. This is an additional, and often significant, cost that will need to be factored in when estimating the total cost of the arbitration. In addition, do not underestimate the length of time required for the translation service to complete the translations, particularly in circumstances where less common language combinations are involved. Always allow plenty of time to avoid paying a premium for an expedited service and to ensure the best quality of translation.

If the first language of a factual or expert witness is not that of the arbitration, it may be necessary to arrange for an interpreter to attend the hearing. The cost of the interpreter will often be shared between the parties. The need for an interpreter should be agreed with the other side as soon as possible to ensure sufficient time to instruct an appropriate professional. Remember that the interpreter will usually require some reading-in time ahead of the hearing so that he or she is familiar with the case and the terminology used. It is also common for the other side to want to approve any interpreter, to ensure that they are with his or her independence and ability.

There are a number of specialist legal services companies today that provide translation and interpretation services.

TIP Consult with witnesses requiring an interpreter to ensure that you engage an interpreter who is a native speaker of the witness' specific dialect to make certain that an accurate interpretation of the witness' evidence is provided during the hearing and for the purposes of the transcript. It is also important to ensure that the interpreter is familiar with the technical and legal terms which will likely arise to ensure they provide an accurate interpretation.

1.5 Transcription

For most final hearings, as well as some interim hearings (eg, if they are particularly long or if there is likely to be an important issue to be discussed and determined), it will be useful to take a verbatim transcript of the proceedings as they occur. This may be either real-time 'simultaneous transcription' – whereby the transcript appears on screen for the parties and tribunal as the stenographer types the spoken words – or a written transcript that is provided at the end of each day of the hearing (or the following morning). Transcripts are particularly helpful where factual and expert witness evidence is heard orally, as they allow counsel and the tribunal to refer to an accurate record of the evidence either during the hearing itself or at a later stage.

As with translation, there are many companies that provide this sort of service for the legal market.

2. Procedure at the hearing

2.1 Opening submissions

Opening submissions, or opening statements, are each party's opportunity to set out in a cohesive and easy-to-follow format the framework of their case and what they intend to prove. It is also common at this point to set out the terms of the remedy being sought. The aim should be to provide the tribunal with a road map of the party's case and a list of the key points which it can easily remember and then mentally check off during the hearing. Note, however, that the opening submission is not an extensive point-by-point analysis of the case. That should be left until the closing submissions, after the oral evidence (if any) has been heard (see further below).

A claimant's opening statement should also include a brief explanation of the facts of the dispute in chronological order. A short introduction to the evidence may also be provided in order to show the arbitrator or tribunal the relevance of the documents and witnesses.

Opening submissions are also an advocate's opportunity to develop a rapport with the tribunal and to get a sense of their style (eg, whether they are likely to be interventionist or passive). It is important not to alienate the tribunal during the hearing by behaving in a manner with which it takes issue.

The format of the opening submission will differ greatly depending on the direction of the tribunal. Some arbitrators will prefer a written opening submission (or skeleton argument), possibly followed by a brief oral opening (eg, one hour maximum). Others will favour a longer oral submission that introduces them to the case and gives them the opportunity to clarify issues at the outset of the hearing. Common practice in international arbitration is to focus on written rather than oral submissions, and to prioritise the time at the hearing for examining factual and expert witnesses. Thus, the tribunal will often ask the parties to produce written submissions in advance of the hearing that briefly summarise the pleadings, evidence and issues to be determined. If the tribunal requires a written opening submission, it may also give some direction as to its format. It may be useful, for example, to leave spaces for the tribunal to be able to write comments.

TIP Consider using technology when presenting opening submissions, for example using slides to structure the presentation, or to display charts, tables or diagrams, or even present photographic or video evidence where relevant.

2.2 Examination of witnesses and experts

Examination is the formal questioning of the factual and expert witnesses. This tends to be divided into four stages:

- direct examination by the party presenting the witness;
- cross-examination by the advocate of the opposing party;
- re-examination by the appointing party; and
- questions from the tribunal.

It is also becoming increasingly popular for expert witnesses to be examined simultaneously, using a procedure called witness conferencing or 'hot-tubbing'. This alternative form of expert witness examination is considered in further detail below.

It is important to establish in advance how exactly the tribunal intends the witnesses and experts to be examined. You will also need to ensure that your witnesses are fully aware of what to expect at the hearing.

(a) Preparing witnesses

Although some witnesses may be familiar with the arbitration process, not all will be. It is therefore extremely important that you explain to your client's witnesses in detail what they should expect from the hearing and how it will work. While in many jurisdictions you should not coach a witness on how he or she should answer questions, it is important to familiarise the witness with the process (eg, the procedure of the hearing, who will ask questions, that they should direct all answers to the tribunal). This will help to calm any nerves and make the witness as comfortable as possible. If you are able to do so, it can be a good idea to show witnesses the hearing room in advance so that they are familiar with their surroundings prior to giving their evidence.

TIP A sample guidance note for witnesses about the hearing process is included in the appendix to this chapter.

Before any examination, a witness should re-familiarise himself or herself with his or her witness statement(s) or expert opinion(s), as applicable. You should also check in advance whether any specific arrangements or facilities (eg, an interpreter) are required. It is also worth appointing one of your legal team to look after the witnesses and ensure that they have everything they need while they are at the hearing.

(b) *Direct examination*

Ordinarily, a witness statement will stand as a witness's 'evidence in chief', and counsel to the party calling that witness will not examine him or her in any detail before opposing counsel's cross-examination. Instead, the witness will be simply asked to confirm who he or she is, that he or she has read and signed their witness statement and that the facts stated in it are true. If any additional facts have since occurred or come to light, or if the witness statement needs to be corrected, counsel may be permitted to raise those additional points and ask the witness some simple questions to cover any new issues ahead of cross-examination. This will usually be at the tribunal's discretion.

(c) *Cross-examination*

The aim of cross-examination is to advance your party's case by challenging or discrediting evidence which conflicts with or hinders your party's case, or by drawing attention to evidence which supports your party's position. On the one hand, it is a valuable tool with which to pick holes in your opponent's case; but on the other hand, it can be an opportunity for the evidence of your own witnesses to be undermined. Much thus rests on the skill of advocates to use cross-examination to their client's best advantage.

Common law versus civil law approach: The style of cross-examination differs between common law and civil law jurisdictions. Proceedings in common law jurisdictions tend to be more adversarial, whereas in civil law jurisdictions they are more inquisitorial. This means that in common law proceedings, as noted above, a witness's statement (or expert report) will stand as his or her 'evidence in chief', which opposing counsel will seek to challenge in cross-examination. It is for each party to present its own evidence to support and prove its case, and to challenge the evidence put forward to the tribunal by the opposition. Counsel from civil law jurisdictions – where it is for the court (and not the parties) to investigate the facts – may be less accustomed to this style. When the two styles are brought together in international arbitration proceedings, the tribunal must reconcile the differences in culture and approach and decide whether to allow any cross-examination, or how it should be conducted. A tribunal of common law lawyers is likely to allow for cross-examination, whereas a civil law tribunal may be less minded to allow it. Nevertheless, cross-examination is normally a part of the arbitral process, with the tribunal retaining the ability to question the witnesses at any time during their testimony (eg, Article 20 of the LCIA Rules and Article 8 of the International Bar Association (IBA) Rules on the Taking of Evidence in International Arbitration).

Style and approach: Cross-examination can be either constructive or destructive. Constructive cross-examination is where the advocate seeks to build or strengthen its case by emphasising favourable evidence from the witness. Destructive cross-examination seeks to weaken evidence which is harmful to the case or to undermine the credibility of the witness in general.

It is important to ensure that all questions posed in cross-examination have been given extensive thought, and have a clear and definite purpose with regard to a specific point at issue. As a general rule, no question regarding a material issue should be put to a witness in cross-examination, unless the answer is reasonably foreseeable, in case it draws out evidence which harms your party's case. Clearly, where there are important issues to address, it may sometimes be necessary to disregard this principle. In this case such questions should be approached with care.

Another way to avoid unexpected or unwanted evidence is to ask closed rather than open-ended questions. Open-ended questions – such as 'How?', 'Why?' and 'Tell me what happened' – seek explanations without a limit on the answer, and give the witness time to reflect and/or potentially provide an unhelpful answer. On the other hand, closed questions require a quick and easy answer – usually a single word (eg, 'yes' or 'no') or a short phrase – and enable the advocate to keep control of the witness and have them support or decline a narrative the advocate puts to them.

A specific form of closed question is the leading question, in which the advocate makes a statement, usually asserting the facts, and invites the witness to agree (or disagree) with that statement. Advocates will often put a string of such questions to the witness, advancing slowly and adding a slightly new element each time (perhaps incorporating a new fact gleaned in a previous answer). In this way they can keep a high degree of control over the answers provided. Another method is to finish a set of questions with a leading question when the advocate has reached the point where he or she knows that he or she will get the key answer he or she is looking for. This creates the maximum impact. However, it is essential to strike the right balance so as to ensure that such questions are not too forceful and avoid giving the tribunal the impression that the advocate is the one giving the evidence rather than the witness.

It is important to be sure of the rules that the tribunal intends to follow. In common law jurisdictions, cross-examination of a factual witness in court proceedings tends to be limited to those issues that a witness has discussed in his or her actual witness statement. (The statement may be deliberately limited in order to take advantage of this.) However, arbitrators tend to be more flexible on what line of questioning they will permit, particularly if they consider it to be important to the issues they are required to determine.

In contrast, in common law jurisdictions, expert witnesses can be asked anything within that expert's expertise, whether it is addressed in his or her written opinion or not. However, in civil law jurisdictions, an expert's cross-examination is limited to those matters addressed in his or her written opinion.

Other tips for advocates to remember when cross-examining include the following:

- Brevity – keep questions as brief as possible and stop as soon you have obtained the desired answer or piece of evidence.
- Clarity – questions should be clear and be put in ordinary, simple language that avoids technical terms. Where this is not possible, the advocate should ensure that the witness understands exactly what is being put to him or her.
- Precision – questions should be precise and should cover only one point at a time.
- Vary the rate of questioning – while advocates should not set out to unbalance a witness, vary the rate of questioning between an ordinary conversational speed of dialogue and more rapid questioning.
- Avoid triviality – concentrate on material issues to avoid diluting the key points. This will also help to keep the tribunal interested.
- Address inconsistent evidence – if a witness gives an answer which is inconsistent with either his or her witness statement or the evidence of another witness (and is harmful to your case), address that inconsistency and seek to challenge it.

(d) Re-examination

Once cross-examination is finished, counsel for the party that called the witness has the opportunity to re-examine that witness. Ordinarily, re-examination is limited to those issues raised in cross-examination and thus counsel will not have an opportunity to raise any issues that opposing counsel did not cover. In addition, questions in re-examination are usually required to be open and not leading, although how strictly this is enforced will depend on the tribunal. Re-examination gives counsel an opportunity to clarify any answers given during cross-examination (ie, if the witness was not given the opportunity fully to explain), and to limit the extent of any damaging evidence that has emerged. However, it can be a double-edged sword, focusing the tribunal's attention on issues where the witness did not answer well (or at least not in favour of the party calling the witness). As such, many advocates will try to avoid a lengthy re-examination, if any.

(e) Questions from the tribunal

The tribunal may ask questions to a witness or expert at any time during direct, cross or re-examination. They may also wait until the end of any re-examination. It is quite usual for members of the tribunal to have come up with questions both when reading the witness's statement in advance and during the hearing itself. It is important that your client's witnesses are warned of this possibility so that they are not surprised by the tribunal's direct approach.

(f) Witness conferencing ('hot-tubbing')

Some tribunals prefer for questions to be put to witnesses by way of witness conferencing, or 'hot-tubbing'. This is an alternative form of questioning, most commonly used with expert witnesses. The tribunal or counsel then put questions to two or more experts at the same time. In this panel-type situation the experts can ask each other direct questions, and the tribunal can interject. Hot-tubbing can highlight the key points of disagreement between two experts, allows them to respond directly to each other's opinion and can act as a form of peer review. It can also save time at the hearing and, accordingly, costs. The obvious disadvantages, however, are that the experts may not have the proper opportunity to explain their written reports, and more confident experts are likely to dominate, which may not support fairness and due process.

In order for a hot-tub situation to work effectively it is important that the tribunal (as well as counsel) is well prepared and familiar with the experts' written opinions. They must have a clear understanding of all of the issues in dispute as it is they, rather than counsel, who will dictate the direction of questioning and discussion. Accordingly, the tribunal will need to prepare in advance the questions it wants the experts to answer. That said, a key advantage of hot-tubbing is that it can help the tribunal to understand complex technical evidence, since this is given in a much more discursive manner and is not restricted by counsel's questions, as is the case in cross-examination.

It is also important that the experts are suitably prepared to ensure that they participate in the debate confidently and are not overshadowed by their counterpart. Critics tend to disagree on whether the hot-tub experience is a more or a less stressful environment for experts than cross-examination – some suggest that an expert is more likely to lose concentration in a hot tub environment and/or will rely on a more dominant expert to speak. They also disagree on whether that is a positive or a negative feature. The most important thing to consider is the suitability of your expert's personality and demeanour. For instance, if your expert speaks confidently, is persuasive and articulate and has had prior experience of witness conferencing, then hot-tubbing may be appropriate. However, if your expert is quite reserved and/or if your client's case is not strong, you may prefer to adopt the standard approach of cross-examination. In any event, the tribunal is also likely to have a view as to whether it wants expert evidence to be heard concurrently.

3. Closing oral submissions versus written post-hearing submissions

Once all witnesses and experts have been examined the hearing will usually move into its closing phase. The tribunal may direct or the parties may have agreed in advance how closing statements are to be submitted. These will be given either orally at the end of the hearing (which then closes the proceedings, save for costs) or in writing in a post-hearing submission. For longer hearings, this decision may not be taken until during the hearing itself, once the parties and tribunal have been able to assess how the hearing is keeping to time and the amount of evidence there is to be discussed in the closing submissions. In contrast to opening submissions, closing submissions are each party's opportunity to present all aspects of its case, and to set out the documentary and oral evidence presented that supports its case and counters that of its opponent. They are also an opportunity to comment on the oral evidence of the witnesses and the experts – for example:

- questioning or affirming their credibility and reliability (as the case may be);
- bringing out the helpful points of the testimony; and
- trying to repair any damage that may have been done.

The advantage of giving closing submissions orally is that advocates can react both to submissions made by their opponent and to any questions posed by the tribunal. Counsel can ensure that the tribunal has understood exactly the case that is being put, and has a proper opportunity to address any harmful points raised by the other side. The disadvantage, particularly if the oral evidence has been substantial, is that closing submissions usually follow immediately after all of the evidence has been heard, thus giving counsel minimal time to prepare.

Written post-hearing submissions, on the other hand, tend to be submitted several days (and sometimes weeks) after the hearing. This gives advocates more opportunity to organise their closing arguments and carry out any additional research or work that is required. Such submissions are inevitably much more substantive, combining all facets of the case into a cohesive argument that attempts to sway the tribunal. They also give a party who may not have performed well in oral submissions at the hearing a chance to correct this in writing. Ideally, a written closing submission should be so persuasive and well written that sections of it can be used by the tribunal to form the basis of its written award.

A tribunal may also require the parties to prepare post-hearing briefs which cross-refer each submission they have made to the applicable evidence. This can be a very time-consuming exercise, and relevant notes should be kept throughout the hearing to make the task easier when the time comes.

Appendix: Sample guidance note for witnesses

[CLAIMANT]

V

[RESPONDENT]

GUIDANCE NOTE FOR [CLAIMANT OR RESPONDENT] WITNESSES
APPEARING AT THE HEARING COMMENCING
ON [DATE] IN [CITY OF VENUE]

Note: this is a template based on standard procedural directions, please ensure to amend it fully to account for any procedural directions issued by a specific tribunal.

1. INTRODUCTION

1.1 The purpose of this note is to provide guidance and a reference for those who will be appearing as a [CLAIMANT OR RESPONDENT] witness in the forthcoming hearing for the arbitration claim brought by [THE OTHER SIDE] against [CLAIMANT OR RESPONDENT] in [CITY OF VENUE].

2. PRACTICAL MATTERS FOR THE HEARING

The Tribunal and the Parties' Counsel

2.1 The case is being heard before a Tribunal of [3] arbitrators: [the Chairman [NAME]; co-arbitrator [NAME]; and co-arbitrator [NAME].]

2.2 [CLAIMANT'S OR RESPONDENT'S] Counsel are [NAME(S)], assisted by [NAME(S)].

2.3 [THE OTHER SIDE'S] Counsel are [NAME(S)], assisted by [NAME(S)].
Hearing Timetable

2.4 The hearing is scheduled to take place between [DATE] and [DATE] at the [COURT/VENUE].

2.5 The hearing will commence on [DATE] and is estimated to run for [NUMBER] working days (Monday to Friday) ending on [DATE].

2.6 The estimated timetable for the hearing is likely to be as follows:
[DATE]:
[Opening submissions]
[DATE]:
[Cross-examination of witnesses]
[DATE]:
[Cross examination of expert witnesses for legal and technical issues]

[DATE]:

[Closing oral submissions]

2.7 All [CLAIMANT OR RESPONDENT] witnesses should be fully available in [CITY OF VENUE] for every weekday between [DATES/MONTH], and possibly more if necessary. We will, however, do whatever we can to ensure that more detailed information is provided once available.

2.8 It is important to note that all witnesses will need to be flexible with their times and dates in [CITY OF VENUE], as it is not possible to predict the speed/progress of the hearing and whether the Tribunal will wish to change the timetable on any days.

2.9 The Tribunal will usually hold a morning session and an afternoon session, with a one-hour lunch break. Witnesses may be interviewed over the course of one or more days.

2.10 We have arranged for suitable [ANY SPECIAL REQUIREMENTS] lunch to be provided for the witnesses in a private room reserved for [CLAIMANT OR RESPONDENT] at the [VENUE].

Language of Proceedings/Interpreters

2.11 The proceedings will be conducted in [English].

NOTE: Please delete as appropriate if an interpreter is not required:

2.12 Interpreters will be available throughout the hearing so, if any witness prefers, [s/he] may give testimony in [LANGUAGE OF CHOICE]. In view of the nature of cross-examination, which is described below, even if the witness is able to answer questions in [English], [s/he] may prefer to communicate in [LANGUAGE OF CHOICE] through the interpreter. This is particularly important if the witness is not confident that [s/he] will be able to understand every question and/or that [his/her] answers in [English] will be clearly understood.

2.13 [The interpreter will interpret simultaneously between [English and LANGUAGE OF CHOICE] for witnesses. This means that they will speak at the same time as the witness, through a microphone and headset.] OR [The interpreter will interpret consecutively between [English and LANGUAGE OF CHOICE] for witnesses. This means that they will wait and listen while the witness speaks, and will then interpret what the witness has said for the Tribunal.] If it is not clear what the interpreter has said, or a witness is unsure that the interpreter has interpreted correctly, then the witness should clarify the position with the interpreter.

2.14 A transcriber will prepare a transcript of everything that is said at hearing which will be available at the end of each day. If necessary, we will be able to review this with each witness to check that any testimony given has been correctly interpreted.

2.15 [There will also be a sound recording made of all [LANGUAGE OF

CHOICE] language testimony, so we can review original testimony to check that the translation is correct.]

2.16 We have requested that the interpreters provide [ENGLISH AND LANGUAGE OF CHOICE] interpretation for any attendees observing the hearing who are not comfortable to listen in [English].

3. PREPARATION BEFORE THE HEARING

3.1 Before attending the hearing to give evidence each witness should review in detail:

3.1.1 their own witness statement, plus all documents exhibited or referred to therein.

3.1.2 the [OTHER SIDE'S] witness statements, and documents exhibited. In particular, witnesses should pay close attention to those issues in the [OTHER SIDE'S] witness statements that are also mentioned in their own witness statements.

3.1.3 Where the [OTHER SIDE'S] witness statement mentions names of [CLAIMANT OR RESPONDENT] witnesses, that [CLAIMANT OR RESPONDENT] witness must be familiar with [THE OTHER SIDE'S] statements and should have enough information to be able to discuss the issue and explain if/why [s/he] disagrees with [THE OTHER SIDE'S] statement.

3.1.4 Where exhibits provided by [THE OTHER SIDE] include letters signed by [CLAIMANT OR RESPONDENT] witnesses, the [CLAIMANT OR RESPONDENT] witness should read the letter, be familiar with its content and the history of the letter/situation. The witnesses should also be familiar with their own testimony as well as [THE OTHER SIDE'S] statements regarding the issue in question.

3.2 Witnesses should remind themselves of what they have said, to place the events into the forefront of their memory. Witnesses will be asked questions about what they said in their statement(s) and it is likely that they will be asked questions about documents attached to their statements and to [THE OTHER SIDE'S] statements.

3.3 There is no substitute for thorough preparation. Further guidance is given below.

4. ADVICE TO WITNESSES FOR GIVING EVIDENCE

4.1 You will be called to the witness seat by [CLAIMANT OR RESPONDENT'S] Counsel, [COUNSEL'S NAME]. You will be asked to affirm, in a manner determined appropriate by the Tribunal, that you commit to tell the truth.

4.2 Your witness statement and the statements of other witnesses, together with all the relevant documents in the case will be available to you throughout, although you will be expected to be able to speak about your witness statement without prompting or reference to it, if possible.

4.3 All documentary evidence to which the Tribunal will be directed by counsel will be in paginated folders referred to as "hearing bundles". One full set of hearing bundles will be on the witness stand and you will be directed to documentation in those bundles during the course of your evidence.

4.4 Your testimony could take up to [one] day, or more in occasional circumstances. It may be spaced over [two] days, depending on the progress of the proceedings.

Direct examination

Note: this to be amended depending on procedural directions

4.5 The Tribunal will have already reviewed your witness statements, so [CLAIMANT OR RESPONDENT'S] Counsel will not question you on issues that are included in your statements.

4.6 You will usually be asked to confirm that you have signed the witness statement and that its contents are true.

4.7 If relevant issues have arisen after your final statement was submitted, [CLAIMANT OR RESPONDENT'S COUNSEL] may start by asking a few basic questions on these points.

4.8 If there are no new points to address, your testimony will start with cross-examination by [THE OTHER SIDE'S] counsel.

Cross-examination

Note: this to be amended depending on procedural directions

4.9 You will be cross-examined by [THE OTHER SIDE'S] counsel [COUNSEL NAME]. [THE OTHER SIDE'S COUNSEL] will ask you questions on points referred to in your witness statement(s), and may also ask you any other questions which [s/he] considers relevant. [S/he] will also put relevant documents before you.

4.10 There is limited opportunity for [CLAIMANT OR RESPONDENT'S] Counsel to intervene in [THE OTHER SIDE'S COUNSEL] cross-examination of you, and you should therefore be prepared to answer all questions.

4.11 [THE OTHER SIDE'S COUNSEL'S] questions will require precise answers. Typically, one issue will be broken down into a large number of questions to take you step by step through a particular time period or subject.

4.12 [THE OTHER SIDE'S COUNSEL] will have a list of questions that [s/he] wishes to ask you, and [s/he] will be hoping to direct you in a certain manner through the questions [s/he] asks. Cross-examination questions are designed to obtain very precise answers.

4.13 It is a common trick for counsel in cross-examination to suggest the answer he wants to hear. He may ask "leading questions", for example, "You agreed to [X] [Y] [Z], that's right isn't it?" or "was it not the case that you did [X]?".

4.14 This may be correct, or not, or there may have been a discussion or some other relevant thing that happened first. Whatever is the case, you should say so.

4.15 It is important not to simply agree with what the questioner has said if you have a fuller response. Also, be careful of being pushed into a "yes" or "no" answer if you do not think that a simple "yes" or "no" answer can be given; ask [THE OTHER SIDE'S COUNSEL] to give you the time to answer the question fully.

4.16 It is not uncommon for some cross-examination questions to feel hostile or difficult. This is designed to make you react negatively. If you feel that the questions are becoming hostile and counsel is trying to push you to say things that you disagree with, you should make it clear that you do not agree with what is being said.

4.17 As noted above, you should be very familiar with your witness statement and with the documents referred to in it. It is essential that you refresh your memory of the underlying documents, and do not confine your preparation simply to reading your own or other witness statements.

4.18 The reason for this is that [THE OTHER SIDE'S] Counsel may show you a document which appears to contradict what you have said in your testimony. If you are familiar with all the documents, there may be another document that you can refer to which helps to clarify the situation, if it is appropriate.

4.19 As a general principle, tribunals tend to put more weight on contemporaneous letters and records of meetings or discussions than on free-standing unprompted recollection of events which happened some years ago. Again, it is extremely important, therefore, that you refresh your memory clearly of how matters were recorded at the time – this may also help you to recall other incidents, matters or discussions that were not specifically recorded.

4.20 It may be the case that letters or records of meetings could be incomplete in some respects, and so you should be prepared to answer questions beyond a particular note of a particular meeting. Also, it is helpful to point out where a document is missing information.

4.21 Please note that in some cases, you may not be the appropriate person to explain a particular document and if so, you should say so and explain why. (This will not necessarily stop [THE OTHER SIDE'S] Counsel from showing it to you and asking for your comments.)

Re-examination

Note: this to be amended depending on procedural directions

4.22 Following cross-examination by [THE OTHER SIDE'S COUNSEL], you may be asked a few supplemental questions by [CLAIMANT OR RESPONDENT'S] Counsel [COUNSEL NAME] on matters arising out of your cross-examination.

4.23 This questioning will not be hostile, and [CLAIMANT OR RESPONDENT'S COUNSEL] will seek to elicit the appropriate answers from you. However, in conducting re-examination, our Counsel will not be allowed to ask "leading questions" which suggest a described answer, as described at paragraph 4.13 above. Instead, you will be asked an open question such as "What did you do then?", "When did you do that?", "Why was this the case?".

4.24 The purpose of re-examination is to give you an opportunity to clarify issues or evidence that may have come across as confused in cross-examination, or to seek to neutralise/set straight misapprehensions or unhelpful inferences that may have been created in cross-examination.

4.25 For example, [THE OTHER SIDE'S] Counsel may have shown you a document which appeared on the face of it to be unhelpful or appeared to contradict what you said in your statement or in cross-examination. In re-examination, [CLAIMANT OR RESPONDENT'S COUNSEL] may then show you other documents addressing the same issue, which will serve to put the original document in its proper context or to show that appropriate action was taken in respect of that original document.

Questions from the Tribunal

4.26 At any time during your evidence, the Tribunal may ask you questions themselves on any matter which they see fit. It is important to listen very carefully to the Tribunal's questions.

4.27 This is especially important for questions asked at the end of your evidence, when there is a tendency for the witness to relax. The Tribunal will be assessing your evidence, and will probably be asking you to explain your position, or explain your recollection, in respect of issues that they regard as important.

4.28 Also think carefully before you answer the Tribunal's questions. Do not be tempted to agree with anything the Tribunal suggests just to "get it over with" or because you feel that you should agree with the Tribunal; it is your evidence and is important that the Tribunal understands your perspective.

General tips on giving evidence

4.29 In addition to the comments on giving evidence above, we hope that you will find the following comments about giving evidence to be of assistance.

- Tell the truth at all times.
- Your evidence is given to the Tribunal, not to Counsel. When answering questions, do so to the Tribunal, not to Counsel. Speak to the Tribunal, and it is important to look at them and focus on them.
- Listen carefully to each question from counsel, pause, and think before answering.
- As a general rule, questions should be answered as concisely as possible. However, do not be pressurised by cross-examination into giving only yes/no answers if to do so would give a false or misleading impression. If appropriate, you can always answer "That is partly right" or "Yes but it does not give the complete picture". You can then request permission to explain.
- If Counsel interrupts you before you have finished answering a question, request if you can complete your previous answer before moving on.
- The key is to remain calm, competent and credible. Avoid a confrontational style. Instead of saying "That is a lie", it is better to say "That is not right, and I would like to tell you why".
- You should not answer a question with another question. An exception would be if you do not understand the question, when it is, of course, perfectly acceptable to ask for Counsel (or the interpreter) to repeat or re-phrase the question, or for clarification.
- If you think that the question is in two parts, it may be desirable to respond separately to each part in turn. If so, explain that you will be doing so.
- If you do not know the answer, say so. Do not speculate unless you are specifically asked to do so.
- If you do not remember something, say so, or qualify your answer to make it clear that it is to the best of your recollection.
- If you are relying on a document rather than your memory, make that clear.
- If you are asked about a meeting or document, you can say that it would be helpful to have the notes of that meeting, or that document, open so that you can see the context, and ask for the page reference.
- If you think a question is unfair you can say so, but you must answer it unless you are told by [OUR] Counsel or the Tribunal not to do so. [OUR] Counsel will object on your behalf if [s/he] feels that a

question is unfair. If you have paused before answering the question, this will give our Counsel an opportunity to object on your behalf.

- If a question refers to a document, make sure that you look at the document before answering. Ask for the page reference and for a moment to read the document. If the question may be directed at a single sentence, you should read the rest of the paragraph or even the whole document (and possibly other documents if, for example, the document is a letter or email in response to another letter or email) before replying. This will give you more time to answer and will enable you to put that part of the document referred to in its proper context.
- Speak loudly enough for the interpreter, the Tribunal and for Counsel to hear.
- It is sometimes tempting to look around for inspiration, given a challenging question. You should resist this temptation and always direct your answers towards the Tribunal.
- The Tribunal will often want to write down notes about your answers, so speak slowly enough for them to do so.
- Take notice of the Tribunal at all times. If it is particularly interested in one of your answers and is writing your responses, allow them time to do so. As mentioned above, when the Tribunal shows such interest you should think very carefully about your answers because the Tribunal obviously considers the point to be important.
- [THE OTHER SIDE'S] Counsel should at all times be polite and respectful towards you, but [s/he] will likely be persistent and will put difficult questions to you. At all times remain calm and collected. You should be courteous even if you feel irritated by the questions. If opposing Counsel is going too far, [CLAIMANT OR RESPONDENT'S] Counsel will interject on your behalf if [s/he] feels it is appropriate to do so.
- Keep calm throughout. If you become heated you may lose control over your answers.
- It is a question of balance, but you should not be too compliant either: if you are too compliant you might find yourself agreeing too much. In particular, try to avoid taking an adversarial approach to [THE OTHER SIDE'S] Counsel. [S/he] may seek to exploit this to trip you up, or to encourage flippant or rash answers.
- [THE OTHER SIDE'S] Counsel may ask how your statement was prepared. The details of this process are, for the most part, legally privileged and need not be disclosed to the Tribunal. It is usual for your written statement to be prepared by [LAW FIRM] following meetings between you and [LAW FIRM], and according to documents

and evidence provided to [LAW FIRM] by you. Although the statement was not written directly by you, you reviewed its drafts agreed to the final version. If asked, there is no harm in making the position clear to the Tribunal.

Attendance at the hearing after your testimony

Note: this to be amended depending on procedural directions

4.30 You may observe the testimony of [THE OTHER SIDE'S] witnesses if you wish.

4.31 You may only observe the testimony of [CLAIMANT OR RESPONDENT'S] witnesses once you have completed your own testimony, but you will not be allowed to hear [CLAIMANT OR RESPONDENT'S] other witnesses before you have given evidence.

4.32 Witnesses who have already given their evidence should not speak to witnesses who have not yet given their testimony.

If you have any questions about the contents of this note or on the proceedings generally then please do not hesitate to discuss these with [LAW FIRM CONTACT DETAILS].

[DATE]
[LAW FIRM]

13. Costs

1. Overview

Costs in international arbitration proceedings may be substantial. Unlike in court proceedings, where the costs of the judge and the administration of the proceedings by the court office may be partly or wholly met by the state, in international arbitration proceedings all of the costs are borne by the parties. It is therefore important to keep track of costs in international arbitration proceedings as, if left untended, they can become greater than the amount that is in dispute.

The costs of an arbitral proceeding usually fall into two broad categories: the costs of the arbitration and the costs of the parties' legal representatives.

The costs of the arbitration can be divided further into the administrative costs of the arbitration institution (if there is one), and the tribunal's fees, including the fees of any administrative assistant or experts appointed by the tribunal. Arbitrators will normally expect to be paid for their work and for reasonable expenses, regardless of the outcome of the dispute. Other expenses, such as venue hire, transcription services and translations, may also fall under costs of the arbitration, particularly where they are organised through the institution and/or paid for by the advances on costs held on behalf of the parties. More commonly, however, the parties will each agree to pay half of such costs as they arise, while reserving the right to claim these costs back from the other side should they ultimately succeed in the arbitration.

Parties' legal costs form the greatest proportion of the costs of an international arbitration proceeding. In addition to the fees of legal counsel, they include reasonable expenses incurred by the parties' representatives (eg, photocopying, travel), as well as the fees of party-appointed experts and so on, and can amount to a significant percentage of the total amount in dispute. It is common practice for the winning party to claim the costs that it has incurred (both costs of the arbitration and legal costs) from the losing opponent. This can mean the losing party paying not only its own legal costs and share of the costs of the arbitration, but also a significant portion of those of the other side. As such, applications for costs (whether seeking to maximise the percentage of your costs that your opponent will pay, or to minimise the percentage of the other side's costs that you may be required to pay) may be as important as the primary dispute.

A survey conducted by the Chartered Institute of Arbitrators in 2011 covering 254 arbitrations conducted between 1991 and 2010 revealed the following:

- party costs in common law countries averaged £1.348 million, compared to £1.521 million in civil law countries;
- 74% of party costs were spent on external legal costs; and
- 60% of the costs of the arbitration were spent on the arbitrators' fees, with the remainder on the costs of transcripts, hiring the hearing venue and other arbitral and miscellaneous expenses.

2. Costs of arbitration

Where the parties have chosen institutional arbitration, the institution's rules normally set out the method for determining the tribunal's fees.

Under Article 36 of the International Chamber of Commerce (ICC) Rules on Arbitration, for example, soon after filing the Request for Arbitration the claimant must pay a provisional advance intended to cover the costs of the arbitration up to the drawing up of the Terms of Reference. Once the tribunal is constituted, the ICC Court will normally determine the full amount of the advance on costs to cover the fees and expenses of the arbitrators and the administrative expenses of the ICC for the entire arbitration. This is payable in equal shares by the parties (the claimant's provisional advance will be considered as a partial payment towards this amount). The amount of the advance on costs is determined, as set out in Appendix III to the ICC Rules, with reference to the amount in dispute between the parties. This means that a small claim can be run relatively cheaply, while larger claims will be substantially more expensive, regardless of the complexity of the dispute or the time spent by the tribunal. Most of the major arbitration institutions (eg, the Arbitration Institute of the Stockholm Chamber of Commerce (SCC), the Singapore International Arbitration Centre (SIAC), the Hong Kong International Arbitration Centre (HKIAC) and the Swiss Chambers of Commerce) adopt this method.

The London Court of International Arbitration (LCIA) employs a different method. Under Article 24 of the LCIA Rules, the LCIA Court may direct the parties to make one or several interim or final payments on account towards the costs of the arbitration. These deposits are made to and held by the LCIA and from time to time may be released to the arbitrator(s), any expert appointed by the arbitral tribunal and the LCIA itself as the arbitration progresses. The LCIA's charges, and the fees charged by the tribunals it appoints, are not based on the sums in dispute, but are calculated by reference to work done by the tribunal or the LCIA administrative staff. These will be charged at hourly rates appropriate to the particular circumstances of the case, including its complexity and the special qualifications of the arbitrators. Unlike the ICC method, the cost of the arbitration will therefore depend on the complexity of the dispute and the amount of work that the tribunal is required to undertake, rather than the amount in dispute: a very substantial monetary claim (and/or counterclaim) does not necessarily mean a technically or legally complex case. The LCIA Court checks the fees incurred to ensure that they are fair and reasonable for the circumstances of the case. *Ad hoc* arbitrations will normally follow the LCIA method of 'time spent' (although without an institution to keep a check on the reasonableness of the fees).

It is common in *ad hoc* arbitrations to use an arbitral institution to hold payments on account of costs. Although institutions such as the ICC, SIAC and LCIA do not administer the arbitration in these instances, they have the administrative infrastructure in place to hold any deposits. An arbitral institution provides a neutral organisation that is trusted by both the tribunal and the parties to hold the moneys until the arbitration is over. However, there is no requirement for arbitration costs to be held in this way and an alternative may be agreed. For example, the funds could be held in an escrow account or in a solicitor's trust account pending resolution of the dispute.

Besides the different methodologies used to calculate the fees payable, the cost and expense of arbitrating in different arbitral institutions using the same methodology can vary greatly, as the following table based on the ICC model demonstrates.[1]

Amount in dispute	ICC	Swiss Chambers	SCC	SIAC
€50,000	€23,015	€13,766	€29,900	€16,704
€500,000	€96,007	€85,094	€77,165	€81,536
€1,000,000	€141,472	€125,304	€107,065	€121,235
€5,000,000	€307,017	€250,096	€230,690	€225,400
€50,000,000	€612,967	€572,161	€427,915	€506,416

The ICC will reduce arbitrators' fees by between 5% and 20% or higher where there is an unjustified delay in rendering an award after the final hearing,

1 Examples calculated using the respective institution's online calculator, May 2018.

though there may be differences of view between the parties and the arbitrators as to what can justify a delay.

> **TIP** Calculate the estimated arbitrators' fees and administrative costs of institutional arbitrations by using the online calculators available on each of the arbitral institutions' websites.

3. Applications for costs

It is standard practice for parties involved in litigation or arbitration to ask the court or arbitral tribunal for an award of costs (ie, that the other party pay the legal and other costs incurred) as part of the prayer for relief set out in the statement of claim or defence.

Such applications are usually dealt with at the end of an arbitration proceeding, either following the award on the merits (when it is clear which party has succeeded), or as part of the final post-hearing submissions.

However, parties may apply for costs at other times, particularly where there have been interim applications or a challenge to jurisdiction. It is appropriate when making such interim applications also to include a request for costs in the prayer for relief sought on that application.

> **TIP** Remember to include requests for costs in all applications and pleadings. If a party does not ask for its costs, then the tribunal may well make no orders as to them. This may mean that the successful party will then have to make an application to the courts of the seat for an order as to costs (assuming that this is permitted under the relevant legislation or procedural rules). This is likely to result in significant additional costs being incurred.

3.1 Methodologies for allocating and assessing costs

As with many aspects of international arbitration, the parties are always entitled to agree between themselves on the allocation of costs incurred. However, in reality, parties are rarely able to agree on these matters at the end of a hard-fought arbitration. Responsibility for allocating and assessing costs therefore usually falls to the tribunal. It should also be noted that in some jurisdictions (eg, England and Wales), attempts to agree on the allocation of costs prior to a dispute arising may be invalid.

Approaches to the allocation of costs vary in different legal systems around the world. In England and Wales, and other common law countries, it is generally accepted that the winning party's reasonable costs are paid by the losing party; that is, costs follow the event. This is also the predominant practice in international commercial arbitration. In some countries, however, such as the United States, the usual practice is for parties to bear their own costs. In yet other legal systems, cost allocation may reflect the degree of success of the claims brought in the case.

The approach to assessing the amount of costs payable also varies. In Germany, for example, how much of an attorney's legal fees is recoverable in court proceedings is fixed according to a scale determined by the government. In England and Wales, however, the court will determine whether the legal costs incurred by the successful party are reasonable and proportionate taking into account the amount of the claim, the importance of the case to the parties, the complexity of the matter, and the financial position of each party. There is also discretion to order 'indemnity costs' in appropriate cases, such as where the conduct of a party to a dispute, or the management of the legal proceeding by that party's legal representatives, caused unnecessary costs or delays to be incurred in that proceeding. An order for indemnity costs will result in a higher portion of a party's costs being recoverable, as there is no requirement that the costs are proportionate so long as they are reasonable.

In international arbitration, the tribunal's power to award and allocate costs depends on the agreement of the parties, including its choice of procedural rules and the relevant applicable law governing the arbitration agreement. Nevertheless, the tribunal is generally granted broad discretion to allocate costs between the parties. However, it has no power to award costs against a non-party.

TIP When making (or defending) a claim for costs, it is worth bearing in mind the relevant costs rules of the courts of the seat. They may be useful in persuading the tribunal of your position, particularly if you are asking for something different from the 'normal' position (eg, indemnity costs).

The tendency under most institutional arbitral rules and the United Nations Commission on International Trade Law (UNCITRAL) Rules is for the losing party to pay the winning party's costs. However, the tribunal may take into account various aggravating or mitigating factors when deciding to award costs. These may include the level of success of a claim, the behaviour of the parties towards the efficient conduct of the arbitration or the pursuit of unnecessary or unmeritorious arguments by one of the parties. An example of where a successful party may not obtain an award of costs is where that party has claimed a significant amount and is successful in establishing a breach of contract, but the tribunal determines that the party is entitled only to nominal damages because it has suffered no loss.

3.2 Costs of third-party funding

An increasing number of parties are using third-party funding to finance the costs of arbitration. Third-party funding can take a number of forms, but typically involves an external investor providing money to cover a claimant's counsel's fees, arbitrators' fees and disbursements such as arbitral administration fees. If the party loses the case, it does not have to repay these amounts to the funder. But if the party wins its case, the funder is entitled not only to be repaid its outlay, but to a sizeable return. This can be calculated as a proportion of the damages awarded or as a multiple of the funds provided, or under a formula where the greater of two options becomes payable. Funders typically look for a return of three or four times the amount of the funding, meaning that it is a very expensive way to fund an arbitration. Funding of defendants is possible but far less common: if a defendant does not have the funds to pay its own legal costs, it is unlikely to be able to pay the funder in the event it succeeds in the arbitration.

Cross-reference For more on obtaining funding, see Chapter 5.

In jurisdictions where the winning party usually recovers its costs from the losing party, funders of unsuccessful claimants may well be ordered by the courts to pay the defendant's costs. In England and Wales, for example, it is well established that a person who funds a party's case is liable to pay the other side's costs up to the amount that they have contributed in the litigation. In reality most funders require the party they are funding to obtain 'after the event' insurance to cover any adverse costs order. In arbitrations, the tribunal has no ability to order a non-party to pay any costs and funders are therefore not at risk of having to pay the other side's costs. This has led to a rise in the number of defendant parties applying for 'security for costs' orders to protect their costs position when faced with a seemingly impecunious claimant. Where a tribunal makes a security for costs order, the claimant must pay the amount ordered to the arbitral institution to hold in escrow as security against any final order for costs made in favour of the defendant. Many arbitrators are generally opposed to ordering security for costs, which is a concept founded in English court procedure and only covered in most institutional rules through general provisions for interim measures.

Cross-reference For more on security for costs, see Chapter 10.

Views differ as to the way in which funding should be addressed by tribunals when it comes to issues of costs. It is widely accepted that a party's costs should be recoverable notwithstanding that the party has had third-party funding. It is also generally accepted that where recovery of costs is limited to 'incurred' costs, the obligation on the funded party to reimburse the funder in the event of a successful outcome is sufficient for a tribunal to find that the party's costs have been 'incurred'.

More difficult is the question of whether the 'success fee' payable to the funder should be recoverable from the losing party. In general, it will not, as how a party raises finance to cover the costs of an arbitration will be a matter for each party. However, the English High Court has upheld a decision by a sole arbitrator to award the winning party its costs of funding, finding that compatible with the Arbitration Act 1996. In that case, *Essar Oilfields Services Ltd v Norscot Rig Management Pvt Ltd* [2016] EWHC 2361 (Comm), the arbitrator found Essar to have "set out to cripple Norscot financially", forcing them to enter into the funding agreement in order to assert their rights. With the precedent established, more parties may seek to argue that the substantial costs of funding (including success fees) should be recoverable from their opponents, but it is doubtful that many arbitrators will follow this lead.

3.3 Costs submissions

It is common practice for parties to make submissions in writing as to costs. Ordinarily, the party seeking its costs will make an application, the respondent to the application will be given the opportunity to respond and the applicant may be permitted to reply. However, since submissions may be made before the award on the merits is rendered, both parties may be required to apply for their costs on the assumption that they might win.

Determining costs is effectively a two-stage process: the decision of the tribunal on which party is liable to pay which elements of the other party's costs; and the determination (either by the tribunal, or by the local court if the tribunal refuses to do so) of the amount of those costs to be paid. These two stages may be particularly noticeable where costs submissions are to be given before the award is rendered, as the tribunal may only decide on liability for costs at that stage and then seek submissions on the amounts thereafter. Where costs submissions are provided after the award is rendered, the tribunal will ordinarily decide on both liability and the amount to be paid in a separate costs award.

Complex costs situations may call for a more tailored approach. This is particularly true of multi-party arbitrations. For example, several parties may be partially successful against one or more of the other parties. Or a claimant in a multi-party arbitration may settle its claims against one respondent with no order as to costs, but proceed against the second respondent before seeking the costs of the whole arbitration against the second respondent. Where these types of complex costs issues arise, the parties' submissions will be even more important.

(a) Pre-award costs submissions

As noted above, costs submissions may be requested from the tribunal before the award on the merits is issued, in order that the decision on costs (or at least liability for costs) can be included in that same award. As the parties will not know at that stage who has succeeded or the extent to which the claims or counterclaims have succeeded or failed, the costs submissions will be somewhat speculative.

In this situation, it is normal for each party to make an application in its post-hearing submissions for its costs to be paid by the other side, on the assumption that it wins. The tribunal may also ask the parties to set out the costs that each has incurred to the date of their submissions (eg, if the tribunal intends to deal with both liability and the amount of costs in its final award). The parties may also want to include the reasons why they believe the other side should not recover all of its costs should it succeed. However, these can only be based on the counterparty's conduct during the arbitration, since the actual detail of that party's costs (eg, hourly rates, activities undertaken, time spent on each activity) will not be known until detailed costs submissions are exchanged.

TIP If putting in costs submissions pre-award, you may want to consider having two rounds of submissions, with the first round setting out each party's claims for its costs should it win, and the second setting out each party's objections to the other side's costs should it lose.

The advantage of putting in the costs submissions pre-award is that the parties will receive one final award which deals with both the merits and costs. This is simpler for enforcement purposes. Nevertheless, the tribunal may deal only with liability for costs in the final award, and deal with the amount of costs to be paid in a separate costs award thereafter. However, this can still be useful for the parties as a basis from which to negotiate the amount of costs to be paid.

The disadvantage is that greater costs may be incurred on the submissions as both parties are speculating on the result. In addition, unless two rounds of submissions are permitted, the losing party may not have adequate opportunity to object to the costs claimed by the winning party.

(b) Post-award costs submissions

It is more common for costs submissions to be filed after the award on the merits has been issued, when it is clear which of the parties has been successful.

This means that only one party need set out its claims for costs, with the losing party then setting out its objections. The claiming party is usually given a chance to reply to those objections. A separate award on costs is then issued.

The advantage of this method is that the parties know the position on the merits and can tailor their submissions appropriately. This is particularly useful if one party has succeeded overall, but lost on a particular issue which involved considerable cost, or if only nominal damages have been awarded. The costs incurred in making these submissions will also likely be lower as both parties are not required to set out their claims for costs (or their objections) or prepare schedules of their costs (which, in a complex arbitration, can involve significant time and cost). Both the claims and objections can be more targeted.

The disadvantage is that this may prolong the arbitration considerably. In some cases, it may take months (or even years) after the award on the merits has been rendered to obtain an award on costs. Equally, if the matter is particularly complex, the tribunal may decide (or the parties may request) a hearing to deal with the issue of costs. This will increase both the time and costs involved.

(c) ***Applicant's submissions***

The applicant's submissions will ordinarily set out:

- The basis on which it claims that its costs should be awarded – for example, because it is the winning party (defining the issue/event that it won) and the relevant rules or law provides for the losing party to pay the winning party's costs.
- How it claims the payment of costs should be allocated – ordinarily, the applicant will request that the counterparty should pay all of its reasonable costs. In practice, because the applicant is also likely to claim that all of its costs are reasonably incurred, this usually means that the applicant is effectively claiming to recover all of its costs.
- On what basis the applicant claims that the costs it incurred are reasonable, bearing in mind the amount in dispute, the complexity of the dispute, the way in which the legal team has been organised or particular issues have been handled (eg, less time incurred by senior (more expensive) fee earners, document management handled by junior fee earners/trainees).
- Details of any without-prejudice offers made that may be relevant – if, for example, an offer had been made by the successful party to settle which was rejected by the other side and that offer was then beaten, the successful party may want to argue that it should be awarded a greater proportion of its costs as they would not have been incurred had the offer been accepted.

TIP Where costs submissions are made before the award on the merits is rendered, it is usually inappropriate to refer to without-prejudice offers. To avoid this, you can either ask for costs submissions to be made after the award on the merits is rendered or suggest that the costs submissions are served 'sealed' and are not opened by the tribunal until after the award on the merits has been determined.

- Any vexatious conduct or bad behaviour on the part of the other side, which may justify a greater costs order (eg, indemnity costs).
- The level of those costs – this will normally involve attaching a sufficient

breakdown of the activities undertaken during the arbitration and the hours spent/costs incurred in relation to each activity. The level of detail required will usually depend on the tribunal. An example of a simple schedule of costs is set out in the appendix to this chapter. The tribunal may also require evidence in the form of invoices as proof that the costs claimed have been incurred (particularly in relation to disbursements such as travel costs or expert's fees), although this is relatively unusual. However, under the indemnity principle, a party cannot claim more costs than it has actually paid or is liable to pay.

TIP When recording time throughout the life of the arbitration, bear in mind that you may need to create a schedule of costs at the end of the proceeding. Be sure in your time entries to identify clearly the activities undertaken and the time spent on each.

(d) ***Respondent's submissions***

The respondent to the application must be given an opportunity to make submissions in response. These will usually include:

- Specific challenges to individual items claimed – for example, the hourly rates used being too high, the amount of time spent on particular activities being excessive and any apparent duplication of work between the members of the legal team.
- Challenges to any parts of the case which the applicant party lost and thus should not be entitled to receive costs on – for example, if an interim application for a freezing order was made and was not successful, the respondent party will normally want to argue that the costs of that application should be borne by the applicant as the loser of the application.
- Reference to any without-prejudice offers made by the respondent party which the applicant party did not succeed in beating in the final award – in these circumstances, the respondent party would normally argue that the costs incurred because that offer was not accepted could have been entirely avoided. Therefore, the applicant should not only not be entitled to its costs for that period, but should also pay the respondent's corresponding costs.
- Any bad behaviour or vexatious conduct throughout the arbitration on the part of the applicant which would justify reducing the level of costs to which they ought to be entitled.

3.4 Tribunal's consideration of parties' submissions

The tribunal will normally consider a number of factors when assessing submissions on costs. Usually, it will seek to determine whether the costs sought by the party are reasonable taking into account the circumstances of the case.

In making such an assessment, it will often consider:

- the extent to which the party seeking costs has been successful or unsuccessful in its claims;
- the complexity of the issues involved in the case;
- the amount and nature of the dispute;
- the duration of the proceedings; and
- whether the costs claimed are proportionate. (For the purposes of comparison, the tribunal may ask for the other side to provide their costs, if they have not already been volunteered.)

The tribunal may also alter the amount of costs it is willing to order to take into account the conduct of the parties. For example, if a party has engaged in dilatory tactics by initiating or defending hopeless claims, or bringing unjustified challenges against members of the tribunal, the tribunal is likely to reflect any resulting additional costs incurred in its costs award.

Exaggerated claims may also lead to unnecessary costs and are likely also to affect the total amount of the tribunal's costs award. This is not only because the administrative and legal costs of arbitration proceedings are often directly linked to the amount in dispute (particularly if participating in an institutional arbitration using the ICC model as described above), but also because respondent parties will make decisions on whether to continue to defend the claims brought against them (and how much money to invest in doing so), or to seek settlement, based on the amount in dispute. Exaggerated claims are more likely to prolong the arbitration unnecessarily and increase costs.

Generally speaking, the tribunal's objective will be to ensure that its costs award does justice to both parties and is fair, reasonable and proportionate to the circumstances of the case. Submissions on costs should seek to establish these factors. Where costs can exceed millions of dollars and amount to a significant percentage of the amount in dispute, the award on costs can be as important to achieving justice between the parties as the award on the merits itself.

3.5 Timing of awards of costs on interlocutory applications

As noted above, it is sometimes appropriate to ask the tribunal to make an award on costs at the end of an interlocutory application. However, tribunals are often reluctant to make such an order.

The costs incurred by the parties on interlocutory applications are usually assessed and allocated at the end of the entire proceeding rather than at the end of the interlocutory application. This is often because the tribunal will consider that its duty to ensure relative justice between the parties includes waiting until the end of the proceeding to determine issues on costs in order that it can consider properly who should bear the overall cost of the proceeding.

For example, if a claimant unsuccessfully defends an interlocutory application brought by the respondent during the proceeding, but ultimately succeeds on the merits of its substantive claim at the final hearing, it might not be fair to award the costs of the interlocutory application to the respondent.[2] The rationale for this is that if the respondent had not breached its legal obligations in the first place, the entire proceeding would not have been necessary and no costs would have been incurred. On this view, therefore, it may be more appropriate to look at the overall allocation of the costs of the entire proceeding rather than to take each application on an individual basis.

The disadvantage to this approach, however, is that the claimant or respondent may incur significant costs in applying for or defending interlocutory matters and end up 'out of pocket' for a considerable period of time. As such, if a party has been put to considerable expense in successfully applying for or defending an interlocutory application that was brought (or defended) vexatiously or merely to delay proceedings or otherwise cause inconvenience, it may be appropriate for a tribunal to make an interim costs order.

2 This is particularly true if the result on the merits would mean that the respondent should, in fact, not have won on the interlocutory application.

Appendix: Sample schedule of costs

A. [Institution]/tribunal costs		
Amount paid by claimant:		
– Registration fee	US$3,000.00	
– Preliminary advance on costs	US$14,500.00	
– Balance of claimant's share of final advance	US$10,000.00	
Sub-total	US$27,500.00	£17,546.40[3]
B. Legal costs – [law firm]		
Work done on documents, including Request for Arbitration, Terms of Reference, Procedural Order No. 1, witness statements, documentary evidence, costs submissions, etc:		
– Partner, 5.9 hours at £500 per hour	£2,950.00	
– Associate, 36.1 hours at £350 per hour	£12,635.00	
– Trainee, 11.1 hours at £175 per hour	£1,942.50	
– Paralegal, 1 hour at £100 per hour	£100.00	
Sub-total: 47.8 hours	£17,627.50	
Attendances on other side:		
– Partner, 1.9 hours at £500 per hour	£950.00	
– Associate, 6.5 hours at £350 per hour	£2,275.00	
Sub-total: 8.4 hours	£3,225.00	

continued on next page

3 For comparison purposes, a sterling equivalent has been calculated on exchange rate of [x] as at [date].

B. Legal costs – [law firm] *continued*		
Attendances on client, including witnesses: – Partner, 4 hours at £500 per hour – Associate, 7.4 hours at £350 per hour Sub-total: 11.4 hours	 £2,000.00 £2,590.00 £4,590.00	
Attendances on ICC and tribunal: – Partner, 1.4 hours at £500 per hour – Associate, 7.4 hours at £350 per hour Sub-total: 8.8 hours	 £700.00 £2,590.00 £3,290.00	
Preparation for and attending Terms of Reference Hearing and preparing note of same: – Associate, 2 hours at £350 per hour – Trainee, 3.6 hours at £175 per hour Sub-total: 5.6 hours	 £700.00 £630.00 £1,330.00	
Total fees (82 hours)		£30,062.50
C. Disbursements		
Disbursements: Photocopying Courier charges Company search	 £18.55 £70.01 £140.01	 £228.57
TOTAL		**£47,837.47**

14. After the hearing

1. The award

The award records the tribunal's decision on the substantive issues raised. As such, it differs from a procedural ruling, which will generally deal with case management issues. These can be reopened during the course of the arbitration. Awards, in contrast, cannot be appealed to the tribunal. Any challenge must be dealt with by the national courts, either at the seat of the arbitration or at the place where enforcement is sought. These options are both discussed further below. Subject to the limited grounds of challenge, an award is final and binding between the parties. As a consequence, a claimant cannot bring the same claims in a different arbitration or court proceedings.

TIP When drafting the Request for Arbitration and Statement of Claim it is important to consider all of the losses that the claimant has suffered and any future or continuing ones that might be incurred. The claimant may be unable to recover losses that are not included in these documents as part of the arbitration, and may then be barred from recovering them as part of another claim unless they arise from a new cause of action.

A number of institutional rules – including those of the London Court of International Arbitration (LCIA), the International Centre for Dispute Resolution (ICDR) and the United Nations Commission on International Trade Law (UNCITRAL) – do not give a time period in which the award should be provided. However, in most instances the tribunal is required to proceed in a timely and efficient manner. Other rules, such as those of the International Chamber of Commerce (ICC) and Stockholm Chamber of Commerce Institute (SCC), set a time limit. The ICC requires that the award be provided within six months of the Terms of Reference, while for the SCC the time limit is six months from the date on which the arbitration was referred to the tribunal. Nevertheless, both of these periods can be (and often are) extended by the ICC Court and the SCC Board, respectively.

It should also be remembered that most institutional rules require that the award is confidential. The parties should not, therefore, disclose or otherwise publicise it.

1.1 ICC checklist

Most institutional rules give no guidance, to either the arbitrators or the parties, on the key information that should be provided in the award. However, the ICC has recently issued a checklist to assist arbitrators when drawing up the award. This suggests including details such as the identities of all of the parties, the details of the arbitration agreement, the procedural history, any jurisdictional decisions and the substantive decision disposing of the parties' claims.

Although the checklist does not have the same status as the ICC Rules and is not mandatory or binding upon the tribunal, it is hoped that it will improve the quality and efficiency of awards produced by busy arbitrators. The ICC Court will review draft awards against this checklist, among other things; it is yet to be seen whether this practice will be adopted by other institutional bodies (although it is noted that the International Bar Association (IBA) has produced a Toolkit for Award Writing for practitioners drafting their first awards). A further distinctive feature of ICC arbitration (currently shared only by the China International Economic and Trade Arbitration Commission (CIETAC)), which is designed to improve the quality of awards, is that all awards are scrutinised by the ICC Court for any errors of form or substance at its monthly plenary sessions. However, the tribunal is not required to accept the ICC Court's view on substantive issues.

In addition to the guidance provided in the ICC checklist, most institutional rules require the tribunal to detail in the award the reasons for its decision, unless the parties agree otherwise. While it is rare in most international commercial arbitrations for the parties to agree to dispense with reasons (unless they want to expedite publication of the award), it is a common approach in maritime arbitration. Here the usual practice is for the parties to agree that the tribunal will provide 'confidential reasons' separate from the award.

TIP Any agreement to dispense with reasons in the award should be considered carefully, as it may reduce a losing party's ability to challenge the award (see below). For example, under the Arbitration Act 1996, an agreement to dispense with reasons will remove the right to appeal the award on a point of law (although this option is often removed in any event by the arbitral rules, such as those of the ICC and LCIA). A lack of reasons in the award may also make it more difficult to raise a challenge on the basis of serious irregularity.

The award must also comply with any requirements of the laws of the seat of the arbitration, to the extent that these are not legally excluded by the arbitration agreement or institutional rules. In most cases these laws will require, at minimum, that the award be in writing, be signed by all of the arbitrators (or by a majority, with reasons given for the failure of an arbitrator to sign) and give the date and place of the award. This is the position, for example, under the English Arbitration Act 1996 (Section 52).

2. Enforcing the award

Obtaining a favourable award from an arbitral tribunal may only be half the battle. If the other party refuses to comply with the award voluntarily (normally after being served with a written demand for payment), steps will need to be taken to enforce the award. The critical question when faced by a recalcitrant losing party is whether an award that has been obtained, often at great expense, can be enforced in a country (or countries) where that party holds suitable assets against which the award can be enforced. The good news, however, is that research by Queen Mary University and PricewaterhouseCoopers on corporate attitudes to the recognition and enforcement of arbitral awards ("International Arbitration: Corporate Attitudes and Practices 2008") has concluded that most arbitral awards are voluntarily complied with by the losing party, making enforcement unnecessary.

TIP Before incurring legal fees on formal enforcement procedures, it is worth considering whether the opposing party can be persuaded to voluntarily honour the award by indirect or informal means. These may include exerting commercial pressure by threatening to cease trading, negotiating a reduction in the size of the award in order to avoid the legal costs of enforcement action or applying reputational pressure. The threat of enforcement action in an arbitration-friendly country may also be enough to encourage voluntary payment. If negotiating a reduced payment, it is important to ensure that any agreement does not amount to a waiver of the right to enforce the award for the entire sum or register it as a judgment at the courts of the seat until payment is received.

As well as the standard final award, other types of award may be recognised for enforcement:

- Partial awards – these dispose of some, but not all, of the issues in dispute, such as a decision on the main issue between the parties, with any smaller claims or counter-claims being reserved; or a decision on jurisdiction with the decision on the merits to follow later.
- Provisional awards – for example, interim awards for security for costs. These can be recognised only if the parties have specifically agreed that the tribunal can make them. As noted in Chapter 2, more and more institutional rules are now recognising the importance of interim awards, including the ICC, SCC and UNCITRAL. This type of award also includes emergency arbitration awards, whereby because of the need for a speedy decision, an emergency arbitrator is appointed and makes an

award in a very short period of time. Both the ICC and the SCC Rules provide for emergency arbitrators.

- Agreed awards – these are effectively settlement agreements between the parties in the form of an award from the tribunal. They are available under most institutional rules. The advantage of asking a tribunal to record the settlement in an award is that it will benefit from the enforcement provisions of the Convention on the Recognition and Enforcement of Foreign Arbitral Awards 1958 (the 'New York Convention') (discussed below). As such, it is considerably easier to enforce than a standard settlement agreement, which may require further arbitration and/or litigation.

TIP Not all jurisdictions recognise partial or other non-final awards. Before seeking such an interim award, it is worth checking the position in the country where any enforcement may be required.

2.1 New York Convention

As discussed in Chapters 2 and 3, one of the major advantages of arbitration is the relative ease of international enforcement provided by the New York Convention. While national court decisions are enforced internationally by an often inadequate and complex patchwork of treaties, the New York Convention allows arbitration awards to be enforced in almost 160 countries.[1] For this reason, arbitration provides far greater certainty and uniformity of enforcement than a court judgment.

The New York Convention requires the national courts of signatory states to recognise and enforce arbitral awards made in other states. This general provision can be limited, however, such that only awards made in states that are also a party to the Convention are enforceable. A number of states, including China, France, Germany, India, the United Kingdom and the United States, have adopted this reservation – it is therefore important to check that both the seat of the arbitration and the country in which enforcement is sought are parties to the Convention.

It should be remembered that enforcement of an arbitral award is governed by the national laws and procedures of the country in which enforcement is sought. These vary greatly, even between countries that are members of the New York Convention. So too does the overall approach to enforceability of foreign awards. Some notable jurisdictions in Africa, the Middle East, Central Europe and the Far East present significant challenges to enforcement. As such, the New York Convention is not a panacea to any potential enforcement issues. An

1 As at the time of writing, 159 states have ratified the New York Convention. A full list can be found at www.uncitral.org/uncitral/en/uncitral_texts/arbitration/NYConvention_status.html.

arbitral award may be easier to enforce than a foreign court judgment, but this does not necessarily mean that it will be simple.

TIP When enforcement is to be made against assets in a number of different countries, it is important to coordinate these actions in order to ensure that the award debtor is not tipped off and able to move or protect its assets. It is particularly important to ensure that all necessary documents (and translations if required) and all administrative or court fees are in place before giving instructions to enforce in each jurisdiction simultaneously. It may also be likely that some jurisdictions will require original, engrossed copies of the award to be filed with an enforcement application. If this is the case, liaise early with the relevant institution (or the tribunal in *ad hoc* instances) with respect to requesting further copies and/or letters confirming the authenticity of the award.

2.2 Formal requirements

In England, Wales and Northern Ireland, Sections 100 to 103 of the Arbitration Act 1996 deal with the recognition and enforcement of foreign arbitral awards made under the New York Convention.[2] An award made in another Convention state can be enforced using the tools available for enforcing court judgments, but only once a court has recognised the award. As such, recognition and enforcement of the award are two separate steps.

In order to have the award recognised, the claimant must apply to the court by way of an arbitration claim form. Unlike a normal claim, this is an expedited process and can be made without giving notice to the other party. The court may order that it should be served on the other party, although this is rare.

TIP Before deciding to have an award recognised and enforced, it is important to ensure that the time limit for enforcement action in the relevant country has not passed. As with other issues of national law and procedure, these vary from country to country. The United States, for example, has a limit of three years from the date of the award, while the United Kingdom has a limit of six years from the date of the award. France, in contrast, has no limit at all. Of course, these periods relate to the limits in these jurisdictions to enforce an award. This is different from if the winning party wishes to rely on the award to preclude claims or issues from being raised in other proceedings (eg, by way of *res judicata* or *issue estoppel*).

A number of formal requirements must be met under the English

2 Note that the Arbitration Act does not apply in Scotland, where enforcement is governed by the Arbitration (Scotland) Act 2010.

Arbitration Act, in accordance with the New York Convention, before an award can be recognised. The arbitration claim form must be accompanied by written evidence (in the form of a witness statement from the acting solicitors or in-house counsel), which exhibits certified copies of the award and the arbitration agreement (or certified translations if they are in a foreign language). The witness statement itself must state the name and usual or last known place of business of the party against which enforcement is sought and the extent, if any, to which the award has been complied with. The claim form and written evidence should also be accompanied by a draft order for permission to enforce the award for the court to approve. A court fee is also payable.

TIP If the award includes a provision of interest any part of which applies to a period after the date of the award, this can be recovered only if the arbitration claim form is accompanied by a certificate of interest providing the following details:

- whether simple or compound interest has been awarded;
- the rate of interest;
- the date from which the interest was awarded and details of any rests that were provided; and
- a calculation showing the total amount claimed on the date on which the claim for permission to enforce the award was made (ie, capital plus interest to that date) and any future interest at a daily rate.

Once the court has given permission for the award to be recognised, the order recording this must be served on the award debtor by sending it to its last place of business. Unlike most court documents, this order can be served outside the United Kingdom without first obtaining the court's permission. Once the order has been served, the award debtor has 14 days (or however long the court sets, if the order is served outside the United Kingdom) to apply for it to be set aside on the basis that the award is not properly enforceable. (The grounds for challenging enforcement are dealt with in more detail below.) Enforcement action cannot be taken until either this period has passed or the award debtor's application to set aside has been rejected.

The above procedure is based on the requirements of the New York Convention, so a similar procedure is found in most jurisdictions – although precise requirements and time limits will, of course, vary.

2.3 Execution, or getting the money

As noted above, having a court recognise the award is only the first part of the enforcement process. In order to get the money which has been awarded, a party must use the enforcement machinery provided by the laws of the relevant country to enforce its own national court orders. As with the procedure for having the award recognised, the tools available for enforcement will vary greatly from country to country. Some will have more effective mechanisms and a greater range of assets that can be enforced against than others. The practical first step is to locate any assets; and it is often advisable to engage a specialist investigations company to help with this process.

TIP In most jurisdictions a variety of enforcement routes will be available to an award creditor, with different costs and chances of recovery for each. When considering enforcement options (including the jurisdiction(s) in which to begin enforcement action), it is worth performing a cost/benefit analysis against each available option in order to ensure that the most effective steps are taken.

TIP If not already obtained during the course of the arbitration, it may be necessary to consider whether a freezing order is required to stop any potential dissipation of assets. This should be sought at the same time as the application to recognise the award is made, in order to avoid tipping off the counterparty about the proposed enforcement action.

3. Challenging enforcement at the place where it is sought

As noted, one of the major advantages to international arbitration under the New York Convention is that enforcement of an award can be challenged in a Convention state only under the seven exhaustive grounds contained within Article V of the Convention. Furthermore, if national laws are more favourable to enforcement than the Convention, it is generally possible to rely upon these to limit the grounds of challenge even further. The consequences of this are discussed further below.

The seven grounds provided by the Convention are as follows.

3.1 Incapacity or invalidity

This ground applies where the party to the arbitration agreement was, under the law applicable to it, under some incapacity; or where the arbitration agreement was not valid under the law to which the parties subjected it (or, if this is not clear, under the law of the country where the award was made).

Incapacity is a very rare ground for challenging enforcement and is likely to apply only in commercial contexts where a party is prohibited under its national laws from entering into an arbitration agreement.

Invalid arbitration agreements are also relatively rare. This ground should be judged on the law that applies to the arbitration agreement. This will usually be the seat of the arbitration or the governing law of the underlying contract in which the arbitration agreement is located.

> **TIP** A growing body of case law in England suggests that the governing law of the contract will not automatically be the governing law of the arbitration agreement. English courts have held that English law should determine the validity of an arbitration agreement which provided for arbitration in London, even though the governing law of the rest of the contract was Brazilian law (and both parties to the contract were Brazilian entities). This is another reason why the parties should consider carefully the drafting of the arbitration agreement and the seat of the arbitration.

3.2 Improper notice or inability to present case

A party may challenge recognition or enforcement of an award if it was not given proper notice of the appointment of the arbitrator or of the arbitration proceedings, or was otherwise unable to present its case.

This ground is designed to ensure that the arbitration has been carried out with due process and that all of the parties listed in the award have had a fair opportunity to be heard. 'Proper notice' requires the party bringing the arbitration to comply with any notice provisions in the arbitration agreement. However, this is not enough: actual notice is also often required and is a safer way to ensure the actual notice of procedure.

The authors have previously successfully challenged an attempt to enforce an arbitration award in England where the arbitrator had made the award payable both by the company that was a party to the arbitration agreement and by its parent company. The parent company had not been notified of the arbitration and had not been given the opportunity to make submissions during the hearing.

3.3 Award goes beyond the scope of the submission to arbitration

This ground applies where the award deals with a difference that is not within the terms of the submission to arbitration or contains decisions on matters beyond its scope.

This ground ensures that the tribunal deals only with issues that are referred to it by the parties. If the court can identify particular areas of the award that go beyond the tribunal's jurisdiction, it can refuse to enforce these elements while maintaining those parts of the award that are within its scope. Partial enforcement of an award is therefore possible.

3.4 Improper procedure or tribunal composition

A challenge to the recognition or enforcement of an award may be made if the composition of the tribunal or the arbitral procedure was not in accordance with the agreement of the parties or, where applicable, the law of the country in which the arbitration took place.

The basis of this ground is that an award should be valid only where the procedure adopted by the tribunal has followed that agreed by the parties. This is normally the procedure set out in the arbitration agreement or in the rules chosen to apply. However, a challenge under this ground should succeed only where the procedural irregularity was significant enough to have had a potential impact upon the decision reached by the tribunal.

TIP A party may lose its right to challenge an award due to a procedural breach of the parties' arbitration agreement if it does not object to such a breach within a reasonable period of time.[3] As such, it is important that any disagreement as to procedure is communicated to the tribunal in writing and in a timely manner.

3.5 Award is not yet binding or has been set aside or suspended

Recognition or enforcement of an award may be challenged if the award has not yet become binding on the parties, or has been set aside or suspended by a competent authority of the country in which, or under the law of which, it was made.

An award is generally binding as soon as it is made. (In the case of ICC and CIETAC arbitrations it must be approved by the institutional body first.) The laws of the seat of the arbitration may also require certain steps to be taken in order to make the award binding.

As noted below, where an award is successfully challenged under the laws of the seat of the arbitration, the general approach is that enforcement will not be permitted in another country. However, there is some debate in relation to this point in the international arbitration community, particularly where national laws are more pro-enforcement than the New York Convention. In this regard, it should be noted that French national law does not allow for arbitral awards to be set aside. As such, French courts can (and do) enforce international arbitration awards that have been set aside by the courts of the seat of the arbitration.

In England, where there is a claim to set aside an award in a foreign court, the Arbitration Act allows for any application to have the award recognised or enforced to be adjourned until a decision is made by the foreign court. However, this fails to recognise that in most cases the application to have the award recognised will be made without notice to the other party. As such, the challenge to the award may not come to the court's attention until after recognition has been granted. If this is the case, the award debtor can apply to the English court to request a stay of execution until the foreign court has made its decision. The court will not, however, order a stay as a matter of course, so

3 This is the position, for example, under Section 73 of the English Arbitration Act 1996.

as to ensure that the process is not abused by parties that are seeking to delay enforcement. A stay will be awarded only if:

- the challenge in the foreign court is *bona fide* and not simply a delaying tactic;
- the challenge has a real prospect of success; and
- the delay and prejudice resulting from the adjournment will be minimal.

The authors have experience of successfully resisting such a stay on the basis that the challenge being made to the award in the foreign jurisdiction not only was a delaying tactic, but was also susceptible to bias in the courts of that jurisdiction in favour of the award debtor. The English court was, in those circumstances, willing to grant a stay only if the award debtor put up security for most of the amount of the award (which it did not).

In 2017, the UK Supreme Court (in IPCO (*Nigeria Limited v Nigerian National Petroleum Company* [2017] UKSC 16) considered Section 103 of the Arbitration Act, which follows Articles V and VI of the New York Convention, and clarified that these provisions do not permit a court to order security in the amount of the award as a condition for challenging enforcement. The court may only order security in the amount of the award in the circumstances of Article VI of the New York Convention, as found in the Arbitration Act at Section 103(5), ie, in the case of an adjournment pending a challenge to the award in the jurisdiction in which the award was made.

3.6 Matters that cannot be settled by arbitration

Whether or not a matter is capable of being dealt with by arbitration is determined by the law in the country in which enforcement is sought. In England, matters that cannot be arbitrated include:

- issues affecting the legal status of the parties;
- issues affecting the legal status or rights of third parties; and
- awards which are not quasi-judicial in nature, such as mediations or valuations.

3.7 Award is contrary to public policy

Recognition or enforcement of an award may be refused where it would be contrary to public policy to permit it. This is the ground most frequently used by parties seeking to oppose enforcement of an arbitral award. However, it is difficult to prove, and controversial. There has been much debate about the definition and extent of public policy interests and how this ground has been interpreted by various national courts. In general, the ground is construed narrowly in pro-arbitration countries. Such jurisdictions now often distinguish between potentially variable domestic policy issues and the more generally applicable standard of 'international public policy', which focuses upon basic notions of morality and justice.

In England, the courts have stated that in general the only matters contrary to the idea of international public policy are those that meet with universal condemnation such as corruption or fraud. However, the exception is issues that may cause the United Kingdom to breach its treaty obligations and, in particular, the enforcement of EU competition laws. An award that is contrary to these laws can therefore be annulled by the English courts even though breach of the national competition law regime is not a ground for annulment.

Issues can arise, however, in relation to local application of the public policy ground in countries that are not pro-arbitration. In these jurisdictions, the lack of a definition of public policy can lead to this ground being construed very widely. Any conflict between the award and the country's national laws may therefore become a reason to annul the award. Consequently, the public policy ground can become a way to review the merits of the award via the back door.

TIP Given that public policy can be a vague concept, particularly in less pro-arbitration countries, it can bring serious uncertainty and unpredictability to the arbitral process. This can encourage recalcitrant parties to challenge enforcement. In order to minimise and mitigate this risk it is important to consider any potential public policy issues before commencing arbitration. If necessary, advice should be sought from legal counsel in the jurisdictions in which the other party has assets.

The different local practices of the various New York Convention states can raise other uncertainties in relation to enforcing arbitral awards. Some states, for example, may not have fully incorporated the text of the Convention into their national laws, creating conflicts between the two. Some national courts may have little or no experience of dealing with the Convention's grounds for challenge and their usual interpretation in international arbitration, and may lack the proper judicial machinery to ensure effective enforcement. National courts may also be biased towards the award debtor (since they are often local to the jurisdiction in which enforcement is sought, whereas the award creditor seeking enforcement may have no presence in that jurisdiction). The court process may also be inefficient or may allow for numerous appeals, thus adding significant delay to any enforcement action. All these issues should be considered when entering into the arbitration agreement.

The New York Convention places the burden of proof for any challenge firmly upon the award debtor. In general, the award creditor need only provide to the court the documents necessary for recognition of the award (as discussed above). The exceptions to this position are grounds six and seven – matters that cannot be settled by arbitration and awards that are contrary to public policy – which a court can raise of its own initiative.

If a court decides to refuse to recognise or enforce an award, the award itself is not invalidated or annulled. The award creditor can still seek its enforcement in any other jurisdiction where the award debtor holds assets. The effect of a refusal to recognise or enforce is therefore limited to the country in which the order is made.

4. Challenging the award at the seat of the arbitration

Unlike a challenge to the enforcement of an award, a challenge to the award itself is normally commenced before any enforcement action is taken. However, given that most arbitral rules do not allow for any internal appeals process, either to the original tribunal or to another appellate arbitral body, challenging an award is generally the preserve of the national courts of the seat of the arbitration. The exception to this is arbitrations before the International Centre for Settlement of Investment Disputes (ICSID), which allows awards to be appealed to an *ad hoc* annulment panel convened by the ICSID itself. It is also possible for parties to agree to an internal appeals process in the arbitration agreement. This is very rare, however, as a right to appeal is not common practice in international arbitration, since it is felt that an appeals process diminishes the certainty that arbitration brings.

TIP Parties may manage the risk of a challenge to the award by asking the tribunal to seek the parties' agreement on issues that may give rise to a potential challenge, such as the appointment of the arbitrators, the tribunal's jurisdiction to hear the dispute and any procedural rulings that are made. Any such agreement can be recorded by the tribunal either in the Terms of Reference or in some other procedural order. If this is signed by both parties, it may amount to a waiver of a right to challenge on the grounds of procedural irregularity or lack of jurisdiction, or at least make any challenge more difficult to sustain.

Because the regime applicable to challenging an award is that of the seat of arbitration, the scope of challenge varies from country to country. In general (and particularly in countries which are pro-arbitration), the grounds for challenging an award are very limited. Nevertheless, as with a challenge to enforcement, it is worth considering the various national practices which can affect a challenge. For example, in Switzerland there is no ability to appeal the decision of the court of first instance, whereas in England the challenge can be appealed all the way to the Supreme Court.

Although in general there are limited grounds upon which a challenge can be made (limited usually to grounds based on a lack of jurisdiction or a serious procedural irregularity, such as bias), some countries give greater powers to the courts, such as a right to appeal the tribunal's award on a point of law. This ground is available in England, even though England is generally considered to be pro-arbitration. While the parties are free to opt out of this provision – and most institutional rules, including the ICC and LCIA Rules, contain an automatic opt out – the availability of an appeal on a matter of law is controversial within the international arbitration community, since the ability to review a tribunal's substantive decision undermines the principle that an arbitral award should be final and binding.

TIP The variety of options available for challenge in different jurisdictions again demonstrates the importance of considering these issues when determining the seat of the arbitration in the arbitration agreement. If a party's primary concern is finality and certainty, choosing a seat with fewer grounds for challenge may be appropriate. This also shows the importance of considering the interrelationship between the arbitration agreement and/or institutional rules and the laws of the seat of arbitration. For example, while the ability to appeal on a point of law in England is effectively removed by the ICC and LCIA Rules, this is not the case under the UNCITRAL Rules. Furthermore, in certain jurisdictions, such as Switzerland, it is possible to agree to dispense with all of the available grounds for challenging an award (although any such agreement should clearly be considered with care).

There are three ways in which an arbitral award can be challenged in England under the Arbitration Act 1996:

- a challenge to the tribunal's jurisdiction (Section 67);
- a challenge due to serious irregularity either in relation to the tribunal, the proceedings or the award (Section 68); and
- an appeal on a point of law (Section 69).

As mentioned above, an appeal on a point of law can be contracted out of by agreement of the parties; however, the grounds under Sections 67 and 68 of the Arbitration Act (which are often also available in other jurisdictions) are mandatory and cannot be removed by agreement of the parties.

4.1 Challenging an award in England for lack of jurisdiction

Section 67 of the Arbitration Act allows an award to be challenged on the basis that the tribunal does not have jurisdiction to deal with the dispute, either because the arbitration agreement is invalid, the tribunal has been incorrectly constituted or the dispute is outside the scope of the arbitration agreement. It is important to note that English courts have held that an error of law by the tribunal will not amount to a lack of jurisdiction. This is a key decision as it stops an appeal on a point of law being brought under Section 67 when the parties have contracted out of Section 69.

The award may be either the final award or a preliminary one dealing with the tribunal's jurisdiction. In the latter case, the challenge does not preclude the tribunal continuing to hear the dispute and issuing a final award pending the court's decision.

As with an application to have an award recognised, an application to challenge an award must be made using an arbitration claim form, using the expedited claims procedure for arbitration disputes. However, unlike an application to have an award recognised, the challenge must be served before the court makes any decision and within one month of the arbitration claim being issued. An application under Section 67, 68 or 69 must be made within 28 days of the date of the award.

TIP It is important to note the date of the award, as this is the date from when the time limits for a challenge or for correction (as discussed below) run. Special care needs to be taken if seeking to challenge a preliminary award (either in respect of the tribunal's jurisdiction or in relation to part of the dispute), as the relevant time limits run from the date of the preliminary award and not that of the final award.

The arbitration claim form should set out the details of the award and the grounds on which it is challenged, and state the remedy sought. The claim form should be accompanied by a supporting witness statement setting out the facts that show that the tribunal lacks jurisdiction. The other party then has 21 days to enter any evidence in response.

If a final award is being challenged, the award creditor (ie, the defendant to the challenge to the award) can apply to the court for any money payable by the award debtor to be secured pending determination of the challenge. The English courts have not been consistent in their approach on this matter. However, the preferred view appears to be that security will be required only if the challenge to the award is weak or lacks substance, such as might be demonstrated if it was clear that an award had been made in circumstances where there was a valid arbitration agreement.

The nature of a hearing under Section 67 is that the entire case regarding the tribunal's jurisdiction is reheard – including any relevant factual background and submissions as to points of law – rather than simply reviewing the tribunal's decision. However, depending on how closely linked they are with the issue of jurisdiction, this need not involve a re-hearing of the merits. In addition, the English courts have held that material that was not put before the tribunal can be relied upon in a challenge under Section 67. The consequences of this are that a challenge under Section 67 is often costly and time consuming.

The court can either confirm, vary or set aside the award. When an award is set aside, it ceases to exist and cannot be enforced in any jurisdiction which recognises this (although note the exception to this rule under French law discussed above). Consequently, it would be necessary to begin the arbitral process afresh in order to obtain an enforceable award. However, if the court holds that the arbitration agreement is invalid or that the dispute is outside of its scope, it will not be possible to start another arbitration. The claim would need to be pursued through normal court litigation.

TIP If an award is varied by the courts, this may create enforcement issues. Although the court's decision takes effect as part of the tribunal's award, there is no mechanism by which the court can amend it. As such, the court must issue an order alongside the award. Because the court order is not covered by the New York Convention, this raises concerns about the enforcement of such hybrids. In addition, the power to vary a tribunal award is not present in the arbitral laws of many other countries, meaning that the court order is less likely to be enforced.

4.2 Challenging an award in England for procedural irregularity

Section 68 of the Arbitration Act allows a party to challenge an award if there has been a serious irregularity – in relation to either the proceedings, the tribunal or the award – that has caused serious injustice to the applicant. This is designed to remedy procedural failings. As with Section 67, the English courts have held that this section cannot be used to correct errors of law where the parties have agreed to opt out of the provisions of Section 69.

Section 68 contains an exhaustive list of the types of irregularity that can be challenged. These are:

- The tribunal failing to comply with its Section 33 duty to treat the parties fairly and impartially. This includes giving each party the opportunity to put its case and respond to the other party's case, and adopting a suitable procedure for the arbitration. However, the court will intervene only where it is clear that such irregularity has led the tribunal to reach a decision which no reasonable tribunal would have done.
- The tribunal exceeding its powers. As noted above, the courts have held that if the tribunal makes an error in exercising its powers (ie, by making an error of law), this does not mean that it has exceeded its powers under Section 68. Instead, this ground is limited to occasions when the tribunal acts outside the powers granted to it, such as if it appointed an expert of its own volition when the parties had agreed that it should not be able to do so.
- The tribunal failing to adhere to the procedures agreed to by the parties.
- The tribunal failing to deal with all of the issues put before it. This is not a prohibition on partial awards, but instead relates to a failure by the tribunal to deal with all arguments raised by the parties on the relevant

issues. However, a tribunal is not forced to deal expressly with every point raised by the parties, as the courts will focus only upon the essential issues.

- Uncertainty or ambiguity in the award or a failure to comply with the requirements of an award that create difficulties in its enforcement. In order to rely upon this ground, the party must have first unsuccessfully requested that the tribunal correct the award (as discussed further below).
- Procurement of an award by fraud or in a way that is contrary to public policy. There must be a causal link between the fraud and the award; if the award would have been the same without the fraud, the court will reject the challenge.
- Any irregularity in the award which is admitted by the tribunal. This is designed to deal with issues that cannot be addressed or corrected under the rules of the arbitration.

As can be seen from the above list, anyone seeking to challenge an award under Section 68 faces a high hurdle in establishing that there has been a serious irregularity. This is in keeping with England's pro-arbitration stance. Furthermore, even if it can be shown that a serious irregularity has occurred, the applicant must also show that this has caused a substantial injustice. (It is also not possible to aggregate a number of minor issues that are not, of themselves, a substantial injustice.) This ground is designed to stop claims that are weak or merely technical in nature. By way of example, in a case in which the authors were involved, the court found that evidence had been withheld from the tribunal by fraud, but did not set aside the award because the applicant could not show that there was a probability that the evidence would have caused the tribunal to change its decision had it been produced.

The procedure for making a challenge under Section 68 is much the same as that for Section 67, except that the claim form and supporting evidence must also be served upon the tribunal by sending it to each of the arbitrators. Any of the arbitrators may apply to be made a defendant to the proceedings or submit written evidence to the court. The court also has the power summarily to dismiss the application of its own volition if it believes it has no real prospects of success, although this decision can be appealed. The security provisions described in relation to Section 67 are also available.

If the application is successful, the court can either remit the award to the tribunal or set it aside. Remission is the primary remedy and will be applied unless the court is satisfied that a full rehearing is required or that there are issues of bias or incompetence by the tribunal. Once remitted, the tribunal must produce a new award within three months, or such other period as the court orders.

4.3 Challenging an award in England on a point of law

As noted above, the parties can agree to contract out of the provisions of Section 69. Many institutional rules, including those of the ICC and LCIA, automatically provide for this (although the UNCITRAL Rules do not). If it is not opted out of, Section 69 allows an award to be challenged on the basis that the tribunal has made an error of interpretation of law (but, crucially, not fact) if the following criteria are satisfied:

- It is a question of English law.
- It arises out of the award. That is, a challenge cannot be brought on a point of law which was not raised before the tribunal.

Even if these grounds are met, a challenge under Section 69 can be brought only if all the parties to the arbitration agree to such challenge being made (this is a separate agreement to the agreement that Section 69 should apply as a ground of challenge to the arbitral award, and as such is rare in practice) or if the court approves. Permissions to bring a challenge will be given only if:

- the question of law will (not may) substantially affect the rights of one of the parties (ie, if the decision is reversed it will make a significant difference to the size of the award);
- on the basis of the tribunal's findings on the facts (which, as noted above, the court cannot challenge):
  - the tribunal's decision on the point of law is obviously wrong; or
  - the decision is open to serious doubt and the point of law is one of general public importance; and
- it is just and proper in the circumstances for the court to decide the point.

The provision relating to general public importance is key. It lowers the threshold for gaining judicial approval from the award being obviously wrong to open to serious doubt. This ground has not been fully defined by the courts, but appears to distinguish between points of law that have general applicability (eg, the construction of a clause in a standard form contract) and those that relate only to the particular circumstances of the dispute in question.

As with those under Sections 67 and 68, a challenge under Section 69 is made by way of an arbitration claim form. However, there are a number of unique procedural steps. This is because it is normally a two-stage process, with the court first considering whether to give permission for the challenge to take place (normally on paper) before hearing the arguments on the point of law. The procedure is also designed to streamline the process. The key procedural differences are as follows:

- The arbitration claim form must be accompanied by a skeleton argument, which should be no longer than 15 pages.

- Written evidence should be provided only if it is necessary to show that the grounds for permission are met and to the extent that this is not clear from the award itself.
- The only documents that can be exhibited in the written evidence are the award and any documents (eg, the contract) which are referred to in the award.
- The application documents must also be served on the tribunal, by sending them to each of the arbitrators. Any of the arbitrators may apply to be made a defendant to the proceedings or submit written evidence to the court.
- If the other party wishes to oppose the application, it must file a respondent's notice setting out the grounds (although not the arguments) upon which the award should be upheld. This must be filed within 21 days of the claim being served and must also be accompanied by a brief skeleton argument and any written evidence that is necessary.
- The applicant can, if it wishes, serve brief evidence in reply to the respondent's notice within seven days.
- The court may summarily dismiss the application if it believes it has no real prospects of success. It may also refuse permission to challenge having reviewed the papers. Either of these decisions can be appealed.

If the court gives permission for the challenge to go ahead, it may then confirm the award, vary it, remit it to the tribunal or set it aside.

TIP Although some time has been spent some here dealing with the various grounds for challenging an award where England is the seat of the arbitration, it should again be stressed that England is a pro-arbitration country. As such, successful challenges are rare. Consequently, it is important to consider carefully the merits of making a challenge before making any application. If the court decides that the application is weak or was made for tactical reasons, it is likely to make a costs order against the applicant. To this end, in addition to the award creditor seeking security for the amount of the award, it can also seek security for the costs of dealing with the challenge.

5. Correcting an award

All major institutional rules allow for the correction of typographical, clerical and computational mistakes in an award, following an application either by the party or by the tribunal itself. A correction to an award is part of the original arbitration and is therefore performed by the original tribunal. The correction process cannot be used, however, to change the tribunal's findings of fact or law.

In general, any application to correct an award should be made as soon as possible and some rules provide a strict timeframe for such applications (eg, under LCIA Article 27.1, parties have 28 days from receipt of any award to request a correction). It should also be noted that any applicable time limit for making a challenge to an award may run from the date of the award, notwithstanding any application for a correction. Parties should therefore review the award carefully for any mistakes as soon as it is received, and deal with any applications for correction promptly.

15. Table comparing key provisions of arbitration rules

Readers should note that this is a simplified guide intended to provide an overview of the similarities and differences between some of the major institutional and *ad hoc* international arbitration rules. It is not intended as, and should not be used as, a substitute for a review of the relevant rules. Information presented correct as at September 2018.

15. Table comparing key provisions of arbitration rules

	ICDR 2014	SCC 2017	ICC 2017	ICSID 2006*	LCIA 2014	
Deemed start date of arbitration	**Article 2.2** Day on which Administrator receives the Notice of Arbitration.	**Article 8** Day on which SCC receives Request for Arbitration.	**Article 4(2)** Day on which Request is received by Secretariat.	**Rule 6(1)** Day on which the Secretary-General notifies parties that all the arbitrators have accepted appointments.	**Article 1.4** Date of receipt by the Registrar of Request.	
Default deadline for response	**Article 3(1)** Within 30 days after commencement of arbitration.	**Article 9(1)** Set by Secretariat.	**Article 5(1)** Within 30 days from receipt of Request by Secretariat.	**Rule 31** Time limits for filing memorial and counter-memorial set by tribunal.	**Article 2.1** Within 28 days from start of arbitration.	
Default number of arbitrators	**Article 11** Sole arbitrator unless parties have agreed otherwise or Administrator determines three are appropriate.	**Article 16** None; where parties have not agreed on number of arbitrators, the Board shall decide on whether sole or three arbitrators.	**Article 12(2)** Sole arbitrator unless it appears to the Court that dispute is such to warrant three arbitrators.	**Article 37** Three arbitrators unless agreement as to number by parties.	**Article 5.8** Sole arbitrator unless the parties have agreed otherwise or if LCIA Court determines that in the circumstances, a three arbitrator tribunal is appropriate (or exceptionally, more than three).	

UNCITRAL 2013	CIETAC (Bejing) 2015	HKIAC 2013	Swiss 2012	WIPO 2014	SIAC Rules 2016
Article 3.2 Day on which Notice of Arbitration received by respondent.	**Article 11** Date on which Request is received by the Arbitration Court.	**Article 4.2** Date on which copy of Notice of Arbitration received by HKIAC.	**Article 3.2** Date on which Notice of Arbitration is received by Secretariat.	**Article 7** Date on which the Request for Arbitration is received by the Centre.	**Rules 3.3** Date of receipt of complete Notice of Arbitration by Registrar.
Article 4.1 Within 30 days of receipt of Notice of Arbitration by respondent.	**Article 15** Within 45 days of receipt of Notice of Arbitration by respondent.	**Article 5.1** Within 30 days from receipt of Notice of Arbitration by respondent.	**Article 3.7** Within 30 days of receipt of Notice of Arbitration by respondent.	**Article 11** Within 30 days from date on which respondent receives the Request for Arbitration.	**Rule 4.1** Within 14 days of receipt of Notice of Arbitration by respondent.
Article 7 If the parties have not previously agreed on the number of arbitrators, and if within 30 days after receipt by the respondent of the Notice they have not agreed there shall only be one, then three arbitrators will be appointed.	**Article 25** Unless otherwise agreed by parties or provided for in rules, the tribunal shall be composed of three arbitrators.	**Article 6** Unless parties agreed, HKIAC decides whether a sole arbitrator or three arbitrators should be appointed.	**Article 6** Unless parties agreed, Court shall decide on whether sole arbitrator or three arbitrators, taking into account all circumstances. General rule is that there shall be a sole arbitrator unless complexity and/or amount in dispute justify three.	**Article 14** Unless parties agreed, a sole arbitrator except where Centre in its discretion determines that in view of all circumstances, three arbitrators is appropriate.	**Rule 9.1** Unless parties agreed otherwise, sole arbitrator or it appears to Registrar that the circumstances warrant three arbitrators.

15. Table comparing key provisions of arbitration rules

	ICDR 2014	SCC 2017	ICC 2017	ICSID 2006*	LCIA 2014	
Default appointment of a sole arbitrator	**Article 12(3)** By Administrator if parties have not agreed on procedure for appointment or agreed on selection within 45 days of commencement of arbitration.	**Article 17(3)** Board shall make appointment if parties fail to jointly appoint within 10 days.	**Article 12(3)** By Court if parties fail to nominate within 30 days from date when Request received by other party or within such additional time as allowed by Secretariat.	**Article 38; Rule 4** If tribunal not constituted within 90 days after notice of registration of request dispatched by Secretary-General or such other period as parties agree, Chairman shall at request of either party and after consultation with parties, appoint arbitrator.	**Article 5.6** By LCIA after receipt of response or, if no response, 35 days from the start of arbitration.	
Default appointment of three-member tribunal	**Article 12(5)** By Administrator if parties have not agreed otherwise no later than 45 days after commencement of arbitration.	**Articles 17(4), (5)** Board shall make appointments where parties fail to appoint arbitrator(s) within stipulated time period.	**Articles 12(4), (5)** Each party nominates one arbitrator; Court shall make appointment where party fails to do so. Unless parties agree on procedure for third arbitrator (president), Court shall appoint. If parties fail to appoint third arbitrator, Court shall do so.	**Article 38; Rule 4** If tribunal not constituted within 90 days after notice of registration of request dispatched by Secretary-General or such other period as parties agree, Chairman shall at request of either party and after consultation with parties, appoint arbitrators.	**Article 5.6, 5.8** By LCIA after receipt of response or, if no response, 35 days from the start of arbitration.	

	UNCITRAL 2013	CIETAC (Bejing) 2015	HKIAC 2013	Swiss 2012	WIPO 2014	SIAC Rules 2016
	Article 8 Joint appointment within 30 days, otherwise by appointing authority using list procedure.	**Articles 28 and 27(2)-(4)** Joint appointment process to begin within 15 days from respondent's receipt of Notice of Arbitration; otherwise appointed by Chairman of CIETAC.	**Articles 7.1(b) and 7.2** Joint appointment within 30 days from HKIAC's decision that sole arbitrator; otherwise HKIAC appoints.	**Article 7.3** If parties fail to designate sole arbitrator within time limit, Court shall proceed with appointment.	**Articles 16 and 19** If parties fail to nominate jointly within agreed time limit or within 30 days of commence-ment, Centre shall make appointment under Article 19.	**Rule 10** If, within 21 days of commencement or within agreed period/period set by Registrar, parties not agreed or party so requests, President appoints.
	Article 9 If within 30 days of first party receipt of a party's nomination of appointment, other party does not notify of its appointment, appointing authority will appoint. If within 30 days of appointment of second arbitrator, two arbitrators not agreed on presiding arbitrator, shall be appointed in accordance with Article 8.	**Article 27** Joint appointment process to begin within 15 days from respondent's receipt of Notice of Arbitration; otherwise appointed by Chairman of CIETAC.	**Article 8** Appointment process begins within 15 days of HKIAC's decision that three arbitrators to be appointed. Where party fails to designate arbitrator and/or two arbitrators fail to designate presiding arbitrator, HKIAC appoints.	**Article 8** If parties fail to designate an arbitrator within the time limit and/or the two arbitrators so appointed fail to designate presiding arbitrator, Court shall appoint.	**Articles 17 and 19** If parties do not make nominations within applicable time periods, Centre shall make appointments under Article 19.	**Rule 11** If party fails to nominate within 14 days of receipt of other party's nomination or within agreed period/period set by Registrar and/or parties fail to nominate third arbitrator, President shall appoint.

	ICDR 2014	SCC 2017	ICC 2017	ICSID 2006*	LCIA 2014
Default restrictions on arbitrators where parties with different nationalities	**None but see Article 12(4).** **Article 12(4)** In making appointments, Administrator may appoint nationals of a country other than that of the parties either at request of any party or on own initiative.	**Article 17(6)** Where parties of different nationalities, sole arbitrator or Chairperson shall be of a different nationality than parties unless parties agreed otherwise or Board deems it appropriate.	**Article 13(5)** Sole arbitrator/ president shall be of nationality other than those of the parties. However, in suitable circumstances and provided no party objects, sole arbitrator/ president may be chosen from country of which any of the parties is a national.	**Article 39; Rule 1(3)** Majority of arbitrators shall be nationals of States other than Contracting State party to dispute and Contracting State whose national is party to dispute. Derogation permitted if appointment of tribunal members agreed by parties. Where tribunal is to consist of five or more members, nationals of either States may not be appointed if to do so would result in a majority of arbitrators of those nationalities. Also see Rule 3(1).	**Article 6.1** Sole arbitrator or presiding arbitrator shall not have same nationality as any party unless parties who are not of same nationality as candidate all agree otherwise.
Time limit for challenging arbitrator	**Article 14(1)** Within 15 days after being notified of the appointment or within 15 days after becoming aware of circumstances giving rise to challenge.	**Article 19(3)** Within 15 days from becoming aware of relevant circumstances.	**Article 14(2)** Within 30 days from appoint-ment/confirm-ation or within 30 days from becoming informed of relevant facts and circumstances.	**Rule 9** Promptly, and in any event before the proceeding is declared closed.	**Article 10.3** 14 days from appointment or, if later, 14 days from becoming aware of grounds.

	UNCITRAL 2013	CIETAC (Bejing) 2015	HKIAC 2013	Swiss 2012	WIPO 2014	SIAC Rules 2016
	None but Article 6.7 provides that the appointing authority shall take into account advisability of appointing an arbitrator of a nationality other than the nationality of the parties.	**Article 30** When appointing arbitrators, the Chairman shall take into consideration, *inter alia*, the nationalities of the parties.	**Articles 11.2 and 11.3** General rule that where parties to arbitration are of different nationalities, sole/presiding arbitrator shall not have same nationality unless specifically agreed by parties. In appropriate circumstances and provided none of parties object within time limit, sole/presiding arbitration may be of same nationality.	None.	**Article 20** Any agreement by parties on nationality of arbitrators to be respected. If parties not agreed on nationality of sole or presiding arbitrator, such arbitrator shall, in absence of special circumstances, be a national of country other than parties.	None.
	Article 13 Within 15 days from notification of appointment or within 15 days of becoming aware of relevant circumstances.	**Articles 32.1 and 32.3** Within: (a) 10 days of receipt of Declaration and/ disclosure of arbitrator; (b) within 15 days from notice of tribunal being formed; or (c) within 15 days from becoming aware of reason or challenge but no later than conclusion of last oral hearing.	**Article 11.7** Within 15 days from appointment or within 15 days from becoming aware of circumstances for challenge.	**Article 11** Within 15 days after the circumstances giving rise to the challenge became known to that party.	**Article 25** Within 15 days after being notified of appointment or within 15 days of becoming aware of the circumstances for challenge.	**Rule 15.1** Within 14 days of notice of appointment or within 14 days of becoming aware of circumstances for challenge.

	ICDR 2014	SCC 2017	ICC 2017	ICSID 2006*	LCIA 2014
Joinder	**Article 7** Permitted but no additional parties may be joined after the appointment of the arbitrator unless all parties, including the additional party, otherwise agree.	**Article (13)** On request by party to Board; Board to decide after considering certain matters including jurisdiction and, where claims made under more than one arbitration agreement, after consultation with parties.	**Article 7(1)** On request by a party to Secretariat. No additional party may be joined after the confirmation or appointment of any arbitrator, unless all parties, including the additional party, otherwise agree.	**Article 46, Rule 40** If requested by the party, the tribunal may determine any incidental or additional claims or counterclaims arising directly out of the subject-party provided they are within the scope of consent by the parties and are otherwise within the jurisdiction of the Centre.	**Article 22.1(viii)** Only on application by a party and consent of applicant and new party required.
Consolidation	**Article 8** On request by party, Administrator may appoint a consolidation arbitrator who has power to consolidate provided certain conditions met. Decision to consolidate made after considering all relevant circumstances.	**Article 15** On request by party, the Board may decide to consolidate a newly commenced arbitration with a pending arbitration if certain conditions are met and after consultation with parties and tribunal.	**Article 10** On request by party, ICC Court may consolidate two or more arbitrations pending under SCC Rules into a single arbitration provided certain conditions are met and after taking into account any circumstances Court considers relevant.	**Article 46, Rule 40** If requested by the party, the tribunal may determine any incidental or additional claims or counterclaims arising directly out of the subject-party provided they are within the scope of consent by the parties and are otherwise within the jurisdiction of the Centre.	**Article 22.1(ix) and (x)** On request by any party but subject to conditions depending on consolidation sought.

	UNCITRAL 2013	**CIETAC (Bejing) 2015**	**HKIAC 2013**	**Swiss 2012**	**WIPO 2014**	**SIAC Rules 2016**
	Article 17.5 On request by party and only if third party is party to arbitration agreement. Is not permitted if would cause prejudice to any party.	**Article 18** On application by a party either before or after formation of tribunal; in case of objection, CIETAC decides.	**Article 27** On request by party or third party and only if third party is *prima facie* bound by the arbitration agreement under the HKIAC Rules.	**Article 4.1** The tribunal decides after consulting with parties and taking into account all relevant circumstances.	**Article 46** At the request of a party, tribunal may order the joinder of an additional party, provided all parties including the additional party agree.	**Rule 7** Party or non-party may file application with Registrar for one or more parties to be joined provided certain criteria met. Decision on joined made after taking into account views of parties and all circumstances.
	No provisions for consolidation.	**Article 19** On request by party, CIETAC may consolidate subject to certain conditions and considerations.	**Article 28.1** On request by party, tribunal has power to consolidate subject to certain conditions and considerations.	**Article 4.2** Where request from third persons or parties, the tribunal decides after consulting with all of the parties, including person or persons to be joined and taking into account all circumstances.	**Article 47** The Centre may order, after consulting with all concerned parties and any tribunal appointed, to consolidate new proceedings with pending proceedings, provided all parties and any appointed tribunal agree.	**Rule 8** Any party may file application with Registrar to consolidate provided certain criteria are met. Decision on whether to consolidate made after considering views of parties and all circumstances of case.

	ICDR 2014	SCC 2017	ICC 2017	ICSID 2006*	LCIA 2014
Tribunal's discretion to order Interim Measures	**Article 24** On request of any party, tribunal may order or award interim or conservatory measures as it deems necessary.	**Article 37(1)** Tribunal may, at request of a party, grant any interim measures it deems appropriate.	**Article 28** Unless parties have otherwise agreed tribunal may, on request by any party, order any interim or conservatory measure it deems appropriate.	**Article 47** Except as parties agree otherwise, tribunal may if it considers that circumstances so require, recommend any provisional measures which should be taken to preserve rights of either party. Also see Rule 39.	**Article 25** On request by any party, the tribunal has the power to make orders for various interim and conservatory measures.
Confidentiality	**Articles 30 and 37** Awards are confidential and may only be made public with consent of all parties or as required by law. Arbitrators and Administrators must keep all matters relating to arbitration confidential unless otherwise agreed by parties or required by law.	**Article 3** Unless otherwise agreed by parties, SCC, tribunal and any administrative secretary of the tribunal shall maintain the confidentiality of the arbitration and award.	**Article 22(3)** Upon request of any party, tribunal may make orders concerning confidentiality of proceedings or other matters in connection with arbitration.	**Rule 6** Before or at the first session of the tribunal, each arbitrator shall sign declaration to the effect that they shall keep all information confidential including the contents of any award. Also see Article 48 and Rule 48 which confirms that Centre shall not publish award without consent of parties.	**Article 30** Awards and any materials in proceedings are confidential. Save for disclosure required of a party by law, to protect or pursue a legal right or to enforce or challenge an award in legal proceedings.
Time limit for issuing award	**Article 30** Unless otherwise agreed by parties, specified by law or determined by Administrator, final award shall be made no later than 60 days from the date of the closing of hearing.	**Article 43** Within six months from date of referral to tribunal. Time limit may be extended by Board upon reasonable request from tribunal or if otherwise deemed necessary.	**Article 31** Within six months from date of last signature by the tribunal or by the parties of Terms of Reference. Court may extend time limit on reasoned request from tribunal or on own initiative.	**Rule 46** Within 120 days after the closure of the proceeding. Tribunal may extend period by a further 60 days if it would otherwise be unable to draw up the award.	No time limit but Article 15.10 provides that tribunal shall seek to make its final award as soon as reasonably practicable following last submission from parties.

	UNCITRAL 2013	CIETAC (Bejing) 2015	HKIAC 2013	Swiss 2012	WIPO 2014	SIAC Rules 2016
	Article 26.1 Tribunal may, on request of a party, grant interim measures.	**Article 23.3** On request by any party, tribunal has power to order any interim measure it deems necessary or proper in accordance with law or agreement of parties.	**Article 23.2** On request by any party, tribunal may order any interim measures it deems necessary or appropriate.	**Article 26** On request of a party, tribunal may grant any interim measures it deems necessary or appropriate.	**Article 48** At request of a party, tribunal can issue any provisional orders or take other interim measures it deems necessary.	**Rule 27** Unless otherwise agreed by parties, tribunal has power to order various forms of interim relief.
	Article 34.5 Award may be made public if all parties consent or where and to the extent required of a party by law or to protect or pursue a legal right or in relation to legal proceedings.	**Article 38** Hearing all held "in camera" (in private) although parties can request open hearings. Where hearings in camera, all parties, arbitrators and other relevant persons shall keep matters confidential.	**Article 42** Unless otherwise agreed by parties, no party may publish, disclose or communicate any information relating to arbitration or award. However, saving provisions for permitted disclosures.	**Article 44** Unless parties agree in writing to the contrary, parties undertake to keep confidential all awards and orders as well as arbitration materials not in public domain. Saving provisions for permitted disclosures.	**Article 77** The award will be confidential. Saving provisions for permitted disclosures.	**Rule 39** Unless otherwise agreed, parties, arbitrators and other relevant people shall treat all matters relating to proceedings and award as confidential. Saving provisions for permitted disclosures.
	No time limit.	**Article 48** Within six months from formation of tribunal.	No time limit.	No time limit.	**Article 65** Final award should, wherever reasonably possible, be made within three months of proceedings being closed.	**Rule 32.3** Tribunal to submit draft award to Registrar within 45 days from close of proceedings.

	ICDR 2014	SCC 2017	ICC 2017	ICSID 2006*	LCIA 2014	
Expedited/ summary procedure	**Article E-1** International Expedited Procedures available.	See Rules for Expedited Arbitrations 2017.	**Article 30 and Appendix VI** Expedited Procedure is possible for claims under the value of US$2,000,000, so long as the parties agree and tribunal does not consider inappropriate.	No provision.	**Article 9A** Expedited Tribunal available in cases of exceptional urgency. Party required to apply to the LCIA Court.	
Availability of emergency arbitrator	**Article 6** Parties may apply for emergency relief before the constitution of the arbitral tribunal.	**Appendix II, Article 1, 4** Party may apply for appointment of emergency arbitrator before the case has been referred to a tribunal under Article 22. Board shall seek to appoint emergency arbitrator within 24 hours of application.	**Article 29 and Appendix V** Party may make application for emergency measures pursuant to Emergency Arbitrator Rules. Application only accepted if received by Secretariat prior to transmission of file to tribunal.	No provision.	**Article 9B** Parties may apply for emergency arbitrator at any time prior to the formation of the tribunal. Not available if arbitration agreement before 1 Oct 2014 and parties not agreed to 'opt-in'; or, if post-1 Oct 2014, parties agreed to 'opt-out'.	

	UNCITRAL 2013	CIETAC (Bejing) 2015	HKIAC 2013	Swiss 2012	WIPO 2014	SIAC Rules 2016
	No provision.	**Article 56** Summary Procedure applies if: (a) amount in dispute below RMB 5,000,000 unless parties agree otherwise; or (b) amount in excess of RMB 5,000,0000 and parties agree to apply procedure.	**Article 41** Prior to constitution of the tribunal, party may apply to HKIAC for arbitration to be conducted in accordance with Expedited Procedures subject to certain conditions and considerations.	**Article 42** If the parties agree or where amount in dispute does not exceed CHF 1,000,000 (see Article 6(4)), Expedited Procedure applies.	**WIPO Expedited Arbitration Rules** There are separate WIPO Expedited Arbitration Rules which can be used where an arbitration agreement has made provision for their use.	**Rule 5** Prior to constitution of tribunal, a party may file application with Registrar for expedited procedure provided certain criteria met. President determines after considering views of parties and circumstances.
	No provision.	**Article 23.2 and Appendix III** Parties may apply to the Arbitration Court for emergency relief prior to the formation of the tribunal pursuant to Appendix III.	**Article 23 and Schedule 4** A party may apply for emergency relief prior to the constitution of the tribunal pursuant to Schedule 4 procedures.	**Article 43** Unless parties agreed otherwise, a party requiring urgent interim measures before tribunal is constituted may submit to Secretariat an application for emergency relief proceedings.	**Article 49** Emergency relief proceedings applicable where arbitration agreements entered into on or after 1 June 2014. Party seeking urgent interim relief prior to establishment of tribunal may submit request to Centre.	**Sch 1, Para 1** If a party seeks emergency interim relief, at the same as or following filing of notice of arbitration but prior to constitution of tribunal, it may file application with Registrar.

	ICDR 2014	SCC 2017	ICC 2017	ICSID 2006*	LCIA 2014	
Cost allocation	**Article 34** Tribunal may allocate costs among the parties if it determines that allocation is reasonable taking into account circumstances of case.	**Articles 49(6)** Unless otherwise agreed by the parties, tribunal shall, at request of a party, apportion the costs between parties having regard to certain factors including outcome of case.	**Article 38.4, 38.5** Tribunal has discretion and will consider relevant factors including conduct of parties.	**Article 61(2)** Tribunal shall, except as parties otherwise agree, assess the expenses incurred by the parties and decide how those expenses plus fees/expenses of tribunal members and other expenses shall be paid. Also see Rule 28.	**Article 28.4** Tribunal make decision on costs on general principle that costs should reflect parties' relative success and failures in the award except where inappropriate to do so. Tribunal will also take into account parties' conduct.	
Mediation	ICDR Mediation Rules available. Recommended mediation clause available.	SCC Mediation Rules available. Recommended mediation clauses available.	ICC Mediation Rules available. Recommended mediation clauses available.	ICSID Conciliation Rules available.	LCIA Mediation Rules available. Recommended mediation clauses available.	

* This includes reference to both the Convention on the Settlement of Investment Disputes between States and Nationals of Other States and the ICSID Rules of Procedure for Arbitration Proceedings.

	UNCITRAL 2013	**CIETAC (Bejing) 2015**	**HKIAC 2013**	**Swiss 2012**	**WIPO 2014**	**SIAC Rules 2016**
	Article 42 In principle, costs will be borne by the unsuccessful party but tribunal has discretion to apportion costs if it determines that such is reasonable in circumstances.	**Article 52** Tribunal has power to decide in award that the losing party shall compensate the winning party for the expenses reasonably incurred by it in pursuing the case.	**Article 33.2** Tribunal may apportion all or part of the costs of arbitration between the parties if it determines that is reasonable taking into account circumstances.	**Article 40(1) - (2)** In principle borne by the unsuccessful party. However, tribunal may apportion any of arbitration costs among the parties, if it determines it reasonable and may decide which party shall bear the costs of legal representation and assistance or whether to apportion such costs.	**Article 74** The tribunal may, subject to any contrary agreement by the parties and in light of all the circumstances and the outcome of the arbitration, order a party to pay part or the whole of reasonable expenses incurred by the other party.	**Rules 35 and 37** Unless otherwise agreed by parties, Tribunal shall determine in the award the apportionment of costs among the parties. Tribunal has authority to order that all or part of the legal or other costs of party be paid by another party.
	UNCITRAL Conciliation Rules available. Recommended conciliation clause available.	No mediation provision.	HKIAC Mediation Rules available. Recommended mediation clause available.	Swiss Mediation Rules available. Recommended mediation clauses available.	WIPO Mediation Rules available. Recommended mediation clause available.	SIAC Mediation Rules available. Recommended mediation clauses available.

About the authors

Stuart Dutson
Partner, Simmons & Simmons LLP
stuart.dutson@simmons-simmons.com

Stuart Dutson is a partner in Simmons & Simmons international arbitration group based in London. He has a PhD in international commercial law from the University of Cambridge and he specialises in international arbitration, international litigation and international law. He has conducted arbitrations under all major arbitration institutions' rules in London, Europe, the Middle East and Africa; and has litigated international disputes in London, Australia, Europe, New York, Africa and the Middle East. Dr Dutson has also designed complex dispute resolution mechanisms, including for oil and gas projects in Russia, Chile, Kuwait and Nigeria. Prior to joining Simmons & Simmons, he was at Linklaters and Herbert Smith, and he was Malawi's State Advocate from 2000 to 2001. He is a former member of the International Chamber of Commerce (ICC) Court of International Arbitration.

Andy Moody
Partner, Baker McKenzie
andy.moody@bakermckenzie.com

Andy Moody is a partner in the international arbitration group of the global law firm Baker McKenzie and is based in London. He specialises in international arbitration, international litigation and international law. He has conducted international arbitrations in London, Paris, Singapore, Stockholm, Geneva and Washington DC under the International Chamber of Commerce (ICC), London Court of International Arbitration (LCIA), United Nations Commission on International Trade Law (UNCITRAL), Singapore International Arbitration Centre (SIAC), Court of Arbitration for Sport (CAS), International Centre for Settlement of Investment Disputes (ICSID) and London Maritime Arbitrators Association (LMAA) Arbitration Rules. Mr Moody has also represented clients in the English High Court and conducted many international negotiations and mediations.

Neil Newing
Counsel, Signature Litigation LLP
neil.newing@signaturelitigation.com

Neil Newing is Counsel at Signature Litigation based in London. He specialises in international commercial arbitration and has a wide range of experience, including at the London Court of International Arbitration (LCIA), International Chamber of Commerce (ICC), China International Economic and Trade Arbitration Commission (CIETAC), Singapore International Arbitration Centre (SIAC), Stockholm Chamber of Commerce (SCC), United Nations Commission on International Trade Law (UNCITRAL), *ad hoc* arbitration proceedings under the Arbitration Act 1996, ancillary or enforcement proceedings before the English courts, claims under investment treaties and cases concerning state entities and state immunity. Prior to joining Signature, Mr Newing was at Eversheds Sutherland where he also spent time in Paris working on public international law matters, including sanctions and obligations of states and state entities. Mr Newing is a member of the Chartered Institute of Arbitrators, the LCIA (including the Young International Arbitration Group), and the ICC (including the Young Arbitrators Forum).

Index

acte de compromis
see also **arbitration agreement**
generally, 45
addresses for service
Terms of Reference, and, 155–156
***ad hoc* arbitrations**
advantages, 60–61
agreement between the parties, and, 139
commencement of arbitration, and, 113
conformation of arbitrator's appointment, and, 142
constitution of arbitral tribunal, and, 142
disadvantages, 61
introduction, 60
procedural rules, 22–23
reliance on national legal system, 23
administrative secretaries
dealing with the tribunal, and, 145
adverse evidence
pre-commencement of arbitral proceedings, and, 94–95
agreement between the parties
appointment of arbitrators, and, 139–140
alternative dispute resolution (ADR)
pre-commencement of arbitral proceedings, and, 89–91
American Arbitration Association (AAA) Rules
arbitration clauses, and
arbitrators' qualifications, 68
language of arbitration, 63
generally, 33
introduction, 20
anti-suit injunctions
provisional measures, and, 183
appointment of arbitrators
agreement between the parties, 139–140
confirmation, 141–142
default, and, 141
delay, and, 141
frustration, and, 141
institution or other body, 138–139
nomination in agreement, 139
party-appointed arbitrators nominate chairman, 140
strike list, 140–141
arbitrability
arbitration agreements, and, 53–54
arbitral rules
selection of, 61–62
Arbitration Act 1996
emergency arbitrator provisions, and, 186
legal framework, and, 27, 28
arbitration agreement
acte de compromis, 45
arbitrability, and, 53–54
arbitration clause
see **arbitration clauses**
arbitrators' powers
jurisdiction, 51
sources of, 51–53
clause compromissoire, 45
competénce-compétence, and, 49–51
form, 46–47
getting it right, 46
legal effect, 48–49
meaning, 45–46
New York Convention, 45
oral agreements, 46–47
party autonomy, and
legal effect of agreeing, 48, 49
separability
autonomie juridique ou de rattachement, 48
competénce-compétence, and, 49–51
generally, 47–48
submission agreement, 45, 46
Terms of Reference, and, 155
types, 45–46
UNCITRAL Model Law, 45
written agreements, 46–47
arbitration clauses
see also **arbitration agreement**
ad hoc arbitration
advantages, 60–61
disadvantages, 61
arbitral rules, selection of, 61–62
SIAC Rules, 78–79
arbitrators' qualifications, 68–69
confidentiality, 70
consolidation of related proceedings, 66–67
costs, 71–72
default award, 70–71
drafting, 55–81
escalation clauses, 67–68
evidence and procedure, 69
expedited arbitration
institutional rules, 73–74
other initiatives, 74
suggested arbitration clause, 75–77
governing law, 55–57
arbitration agreement, 56–57
substantive contract, 55–56
hybrid or optional dispute resolution clauses
mutual option clauses, 66
sole option clauses, 64–65
unilateral arbitration clause, 65

unilateral litigation clause, 65
institutional arbitration, 58–60
advantages, 59
disadvantages, 60
joinder of third parties, 66–67
language of arbitration, 63
legal seat
choice, 57–58
meaning, 57
model, 77
DIFC Rules, 80
HKIAC Rules, 78
ICC Rules, 77
LCIA Rules, 77–78
Swiss Rules, 79–80
UNCITRAL, 80–81
nationality of arbitrators appointed, 69
number of arbitrators, 62–63
pathological arbitration agreements, 72
privacy, 70
service of process clauses, 72
Arbitrator Research Tool (ART)
generally, 137
arbitration rules
comparison of key provisions, 271–285
arbitrators
appointment
agreement between the parties, 139–140
confirmation, 141–142
default, and, 141
delay, and, 141
frustration, and, 141
institution or other body, 138–139
nomination in agreement, 139
party-appointed arbitrators nominate chairman, 140
strike list, 140–141
choice, 135–137
curriculum vitae, 136
databases, 137
interviews, 136–137
recommendations, 136
reputation, 136
research, 137
constitution of arbitral tribunal, 141–142
method of selection
agreement between the parties, 139–140
appointment by institution, 138–139
appointment by other body, 138–139
nomination in agreement, 139
party-appointed arbitrators nominate chairman, 140
strike list, 140–141
number
chairman, 138
sole arbitrators, 137
three arbitrators, 137–138
power
jurisdiction, 51
sources of, 51–53
qualification
arbitration clauses, and, 68–69
selection
availability, 134–135
bias, 132
caseload, 134–135
communication skills, 135
conflicts of interest, 131–132
cost, 135
criteria, 131–135
diversity, 134
enthusiasm, 135
expertise, 133
formal qualifications, 133
independence, 131–132
language, 132–133
lawyers versus non-lawyers, 133–134
management skills, 135
nationality, 132–133
partiality, 132
practical considerations, 134–135
pre-disposition towards the dispute, 132
ATE insurance
pre-commencement of arbitral proceedings, and, 104–105
awards
challenging at seat of arbitration
generally, 262–263
lack of jurisdiction, 263–265
point of law, 267–268
procedural irregularity, 265–266
correction of errors, 268–269
enforcement
see **enforcement of awards**
generally, 251
ICC checklist, 252–253

bias
selection of arbitrators, in, 132
bribery
dealing with the tribunal, and, 147–149
British Institute of International and Comparative Law
11th Annual Arbitration Review 2008, 13–14
British Virgin Islands (BVI) International Arbitration Centre
generally, 21
Brussels Regulation
generally, 14

case development
evidence
documentary evidence, 208–212
experts, 204–208
generally, 200
witness, 200–204
template, 213–216
written submissions
drafting pleadings, 191–192
Statement of Claim, 192–196
Statement of Defence, 196–199
Statement of Rejoinder, 200
Statement of Reply, 199
case history
pleadings, and, 191–192
caseload
selection of arbitrators, and, 134–135
Centre for Effective Dispute Resolution (CEDR)
generally, 10
chairman
selection of arbitrators, and, 138
chair's authority to issue procedural orders
Terms of Reference, and, 156
challenging awards at seat of arbitration
generally, 262–263
lack of jurisdiction, 263–265

point of law, 267–268
procedural irregularity, 265–266

challenging enforcement at place where it is sought
award beyond scope of submission to arbitration, 258
award contrary to public policy, 260–262
award not yet binding, 259–260
award set aside, 259–260
award suspended, 259–260
improper notice, 258
improper procedure or tribunal composition, 258–259
inability to present case, 258
incapacity, 257–258
invalidity, 257–258
matter cannot be settled by arbitration, 260

chartered Institute of Arbitrators
generally, 74

China International Economic and Trade Arbitration Commission (CIETAC)
generally, 37–38

civil law approach
cross-examination, 223–224
witness evidence, 200–201

Civil Procedure Rules 1998 (The White Book)
litigation, and, 13

claimants
commencement of arbitration, and, 111–112

commencement of arbitration
see also **pre-commencement of arbitral proceedings**
claimant or respondent, 111–112
emergency arbitrators, 124–126
emergency measures, 124–126
jurisdictional challenges to applicability of arbitration agreement
arbitrability of the dispute, 122
bringing the challenge, 122–123
introduction, 119–121
not a party to arbitration agreement, 121
prima facie review under ICC Rules, 123–124
scope of arbitration agreement, 121–122
procedure, 112–119
practical matters, 118–119
Request for Arbitration, 113–117
response to Request for Arbitration, 117–118
urgent interlocutory relief, 124–126

common law approach
cross-examination, 223–224
witness evidence, 200–201

communication skills
selection of arbitrators, and, 135

***compétence-compétence* principle**
arbitration agreements, and, 49–51
legal framework, and, 26

confidentiality
advantages of arbitration, and, 17–18
arbitration clauses, and, 70
documentary evidence, and, 212

conflicts of interest
selection of arbitrators, and, 131–132

conformation of arbitrator's appointment
ad hoc arbitrations, 142
institutional arbitrations, 142
introduction, 141

conservatory measures
anti-suit injunctions, 183
content, 184
court or tribunal, 180–181
default and summary procedures, 188
determining applications, 184–185
emergency arbitrator provisions, 185–187
ex parte applications, 187
freezing orders, 181–182
generally, 179–180
injunctive relief orders, 181–182
interim performance orders, 181–182
preservation of evidence, 182
security for costs, 182–183
types, 181–183

constitution of arbitral tribunal
ad hoc arbitrations, 142
institutional arbitrations, 142
introduction, 141

Construction Industry Model Arbitration (CIMAR)
generally, 60

Convention on the Recognition and Enforcement of Foreign Arbitral Awards 1958, 7

corruption
dealing with the tribunal, and, 147–149

costs
advantages of arbitration, and, 18
allocation methodologies, 240–241
applications, 240–248
arbitration, 238–240
arbitration clauses, and, 71–72
assessment methodologies, 240–241
institutional arbitration, and, 22
overview, 237–238
pre-commencement of arbitral proceedings, and, 101–103
sample schedule of costs, 249–250
security, for, 182–183
selection of arbitrators, and, 135
submissions
applicant's, 245–246
post-award, 244–245
pre-award, 243–244
respondent's, 246
tribunal's consideration of parties' submissions, 246–247
third-party funding, 241–243
timing of awards on interlocutory applications, 247–248

counterparty agreement
procedural timetable, and, 172

cross-examination
common law versus civil law approach, 223–224
style and approach, 224–225
witnesses and experts, and, 223–225
witness evidence, and, 203

***curriculum vitae* (CV)**
selection arbitrators, and, 136

databases
selection arbitrators, and, 137

default
appointment of arbitrators, and, 141
Terms of Reference, and, 156–157

default award
arbitration clauses, and, 70–71

delay
appointment of arbitrators, and, 141
Departmental Advisory Committee (DAC), 28
direct examination
witnesses and experts, and, 223
diversity
selection of arbitrators, and, 134
documentary evidence
confidentiality, 212
document production, 208–210
privilege, 212
procedural timetable, and, 162–165
requesting documents, 210–211
document management
pleadings, and, 192
document production
documentary evidence, and, 208–210
Dubai International Financial Centre (DIFC) Rules
arbitration clauses, and
arbitral rules, selection of, 62
model arbitration clauses, 80
DVD
filing, and, 167–168

early case assessment
pre-commencement of arbitral proceedings, and, 100
electronic media
filing, and, 167–168
email
filing, and, 167–168
emergency arbitrator provisions
provisional measures, and, 185–187
emergency arbitrators
commencement of arbitration, and, 124–126
emergency measures
commencement of arbitration, and, 124–126
Employment Rights Act 1996
arbitrability, and, 54
enforceability
advantages of arbitration, and, 15
enforcement of awards
challenging enforcement at place where it is sought
award beyond scope of submission to arbitration, 258
award contrary to public policy, 260–262
award not yet binding, 259–260
award set aside, 259–260
award suspended, 259–260
improper notice, 258
improper procedure or tribunal composition, 258–259
inability to present case, 258
incapacity, 257–258
invalidity, 257–258
matter cannot be settled by arbitration, 260
correction of errors, 268–269
execution, 256–257
formal requirements, 255–256
generally, 253–254
institutional arbitration, and, 22
New York Convention, 26–27, 254–255
English Arbitration Act 1996
arbitration agreements, and, 46–47, 48
arbitrator's powers, sources of, 51–53
compétence-compétence and separability, 50
legal effect of agreeing, 49
legal framework, and, 27, 28
enthusiasm
selection of arbitrators, and, 135
Equality Act 2010
arbitrability, and, 54
Equal Representation in Arbitration (ERA) Search Committee
generally, 137
escalation clauses
arbitration clauses, and, 67–68
generally, 83–85
mandatory, 85–87
optional, 87–88
evidence
arbitration clauses, and, 69
documentary, 162–165
confidentiality, 212
document production, 208–210
privilege, 212
requesting documents, 210–211
generally, 200
preservation of, 182
witness
choice of witnesses, 203–204
civil law versus common law approach, 200–201
rules and law, 201
statements, 202–203
examination of witnesses and experts
cross-examination, 223–225
direct examination, 223
preparing witnesses, 222–223
re-examination, 225
tribunal questions, 225–226
witness conferencing (hot-tubbing), 226
***ex parte* applications**
provisional measures, and, 187
expedited arbitration
arbitration clauses, and
institutional rules, 73–74
expert determination
comparison with arbitration, and, 11–12
expertise
selection of arbitrators, and, 133
of tribunal members
advantages of arbitration, and, 16
experts
dealing with, 207–208
examination
cross-examination, 223–225
direct examination, 223
preparing witnesses, 222–223
re-examination, 225
tribunal questions, 225–226
witness conferencing (hot-tubbing), 226
role of, 204–205
rules and law governing expert evidence, 206–207
selection, 205–206
expert witness
procedural timetable, and, 161–162

factual chronology
pleading, and, 191
factual witness
procedural timetable, and, 161–162

Federation of Oils, Seeds and Fats Association (FOSFA)
generally, 60
filing
DVD, 167–168
electronic media, 167–168
email, 167–168
hard copy, 166–167
hearing length, 169–171
'on the papers,' 168–169
oral hearing, 68–169
USB, 167–168
final awards
Terms of Reference, and, 156
finality of decision
advantages of arbitration, and, 16–17
Financial Sector Branch of The Arbitration Club
Financial Services Expedited Arbitration Procedure, 74
Financial Services Expedited Arbitration Procedure, 14
generally, 74
formal qualifications
selection of arbitrators, and, 133
French Civil Code
arbitrability, and, 53
French Code of Civil Procedure
generally, 12
legal effect of agreeing to arbitration, 49
frustration
appointment of arbitrators, and, 141

gathering evidence
pre-commencement of arbitral proceedings, and
key documents, 91–93
preservation of documents, 93–94
German Arbitration Institute (DIS) Rules
arbitration agreements, and
arbitrator's powers, 52
Global Arbitration Review
generally, 137
Grain and Feed Trade Association (GAFTA)
generally, 20

hard copy
filing, and, 166–167
'hard' dispute resolution, 11–15
expert determination, 11–12
litigation and arbitration, difference between, 12–15
hearing
after, 251–269
bundles, 165–166
closing oral submissions versus written post-hearing submissions, 227
examination of witnesses and experts
cross-examination, 223–225
direct examination, 223
preparing witnesses, 222–223
re-examination, 225
tribunal questions, 225–226
witness conferencing (hot-tubbing), 226
generally, 217
length, 169–171
practical arrangements
interpreters, 220
place, 217–218
transcription, 221
translators, 220
venue, 219–220
video link, 218
procedure
examination of witnesses and experts, 222–226
opening submissions, 221–222
sample guidance, 228–236
HKIAC Rules
arbitration clauses, and
arbitral rules, selection of, 62
model arbitration clauses, 78
Hong Kong Arbitration Ordinance
arbitration agreement, and, 48
Hong Kong International Arbitration Centre (HKIAC)
generally, 36
hot-tubbing
hearing, and, 226

IBA Guidelines on Conflicts of Interest
'med-arb,' and, 89, 90
selection of arbitrators, and, 131
IBA Rules on Taking of Evidence
documentary evidence, 163–165, 209
witness evidence, 202–203
ICC Rules
arbitration agreements, and
arbitrator's powers, sources of, 52
compétence-compétence and separability, 50
arbitration clauses, and
arbitral rules, selection of, 61
arbitrators' qualifications, 68
evidence and procedure, 69
model arbitration clauses, 77
number of arbitrators, 62
privacy and confidentiality, 70
commencement of arbitration, and
prima facie review, 123–124
generally, 30–31
Note to Parties and Arbitral Tribunals on the Conduct of the Arbitration, 42–43
Terms of Reference
addresses for service, 155–156
arbitration agreement, 155
chair's authority to issue procedural orders, 156
compulsory matters, 154–155
contents, 157–159
default, 156–157
final awards, 156
interim awards, 156
modes of communication, 155–156
partial awards, 156
place of procedural hearings, 156
preparation, 154
procedural background, 155
purpose and effect, 152–154
venue of procedural hearings, 156
voluntary matters, 155–157
independence
selection of arbitrators, and, 131–132
injunctive relief orders
interim measures, and, 181–182

institutional arbitration
arbitration clauses, and, 58–60
advantages, 59
disadvantages, 60
conformation of arbitrator's appointment, and, 142
constitution of arbitral tribunal, and, 142
cost, 22
diversity, 23
enforcement of awards, 22
panel of arbitrators, 20–21
procedural rules, 20
professional administration staff, 20–21
rules, 30–39
American Arbitration Association/International Centre for Dispute Resolution, 33
China International Economic and Trade Arbitration Commission, 37–38
Hong Kong International Arbitration Centre, 36
International Chamber of Commerce, 30–32
International Institute for Conflict Prevention and Resolution, 34
London Court of International Arbitration, 32
Singapore International Arbitration Centre, 34–35
Stockholm Chamber of Commerce Institute, 36–37
UNCITRAL, 38–39
sensitive matters, 22
institutional rules
expedited arbitration, and, 73–74
instructing external counsel
pre-commencement of arbitral proceedings, and, 99–100
interim awards
Terms of Reference, and, 156
interim measures
anti-suit injunctions, 183
content, 184
court or tribunal, 180–181
default and summary procedures, 188
determining applications, 184–185
emergency arbitrator provisions, 185–187
ex parte applications, 187
freezing orders, 181–182
generally, 179–180
injunctive relief orders, 181–182
interim performance orders, 181–182
preservation of evidence, 182
security for costs, 182–183
types, 181–183
interim performance orders
interim measures, and, 181–182
international arbitration
ad hoc arbitrations
procedural rules, 22–23
reliance on national legal system, 23
advantages
confidentiality, 17–18
cost, 18
enforceability, 15
expertise of tribunal members, 16
finality of decision, 16–17
neutrality of forum, 16
party autonomy, 15–16
privacy, 17–18
procedural flexibility, 15–16
speed, 18
differences from other methods of dispute resolution, 8–11
expert determination, 11–12
'hard' dispute resolution, 11–15
litigation and arbitration, difference between, 12–15
mediation, 10–11
negotiation, 9
other methods of 'soft' dispute resolution, 11
'soft' dispute resolution, 9–11
disadvantages
lack of expedited default or summary procedures, 19–20
limited powers of arbitrators, 18
precedent, 20
termination, 20
unwieldy multi-party arbitration, 19
institutional arbitration
cost, 22
enforcement of awards, 22
panel of arbitrators, 20–21
procedural rules, 20
professional administration staff, 20–21
sensitive matters, 22
legal framework
guidelines, 40–43
institutional arbitration rules, 30–39
national arbitration laws, 27–30
New York Convention, 25–27
meaning, 7–8
types, 20–23
International Bar Association (IBA)
Guidelines on Conflicts of Interest
generally, 40–42
'med-arb,' 89
Rules on Taking of Evidence, 40
International Centre for Dispute Resolution (ICDR)
generally, 33
International Centre for Settlement of Investment Disputes (ICSID)
media enquiries, and, 107
International Chamber of Commerce (ICC)
checklist for awards, 252–253
generally, 7n1, 30–32
multi-party arbitration, 19
national arbitration laws, 29
International Council for Commercial Arbitration (ICCA)
documentary evidence, and, 165
International Court of Arbitration of the ICC
generally, 30, 42–43
International Institute for Conflict Prevention and Resolution (CPR)
generally, 34
internationally accepted rules and guidelines
IBA Guidelines on Conflicts of Interest, 40–42
IBA Rules on Taking of Evidence, 40
ICC Note to Parties and Arbitral Tribunals on the Conduct of the Arbitration, 42–43
interpreters
hearing, and, 220

interviews
selection arbitrators, and, 136–137

joinder of third parties
arbitration clauses, and, 66–67
jurisdictional challenges to applicability of arbitration agreement
arbitrability of the dispute, 122
bringing the challenge, 122–123
introduction, 119–121
not a party to arbitration agreement, 121
prima facie review under ICC Rules, 123–124
scope of arbitration agreement, 121–122
jurisdiction of national courts
New York Convention, and, 26

Lagos Chambers of Commerce International Arbitration Centre (LACIAC), 21
language
arbitration clauses, and, 63
selection of arbitrators, and, 132–133
lawyers
selection of arbitrators, and, 133–134
LCIA Rules
appointment of arbitrators, 139
arbitration agreements, and
arbitrator's powers, sources of, 53
compétence-compétence and separability, 50
arbitration clauses, and
arbitral rules, selection of, 61
evidence and procedure, 69
institutional arbitration, 59
language of arbitration, 63
model arbitration clauses, 77–78
commencement of arbitration, and
Request for Arbitration, 114–115, 116
confidentiality, 17
expedited arbitration and
institutional rules, 73
legal framework
national arbitration laws, 27–30
New York Convention
definition, 25–26
enforcement of arbitral awards, 26–27
jurisdiction of national courts, 26
legal seat
arbitration clauses, and, 57–58
choice, 57–58
meaning, 57
limited powers of arbitrators
disadvantages of arbitration, and, 18
litigation and arbitration, difference between, 12–15
enforcement, 14–15
jurisdiction, 14
London Arbitration Club, Financial Sector Branch
Financial Services Expedited Arbitration Procedure, 14
London Court of International Arbitration (LCIA)
generally, 32
introduction, 13
London Maritime Arbitration Association (LMAA)
generally, 20, 60
London Metal Exchange (LME)
generally, 60

management skills
selection of arbitrators, and, 135
'med-arb' procedure
pre-commencement of arbitral proceedings, and, 89–90
media enquiries
pre-commencement of arbitral proceedings, and, 106–108
mediation
comparison with arbitration, and, 10–11
modes of communication
Terms of Reference and, 155–156
money laundering
dealing with the tribunal, and, 147–149
Mumbai Centre for International Arbitration (MCIA)
generally, 21
mutual option clauses
arbitration clauses, and, 66

national arbitration laws
legal framework, and, 27–30
nationality
selection of arbitrators, and, 132–133
nationality of arbitrators appointed
arbitration clauses, and, 69
negotiation
comparison with arbitration, and, 9
neutrality of forum
advantages of arbitration, and, 16
New York Convention
arbitration agreement, and, 45
arbitration clauses, and
legal seat, 57, 58
definition, 25–26
enforcement, 14
enforcement of arbitral awards, 26–27, 254–255
expedited arbitration, and
institutional rules, 74
expert determination, 11
jurisdiction of national courts, 26
overview, 7–8
nomination
appointment of arbitrators, and, 139
non-lawyers
selection of arbitrators, and, 133–134
notification of claim to interested parties
pre-commencement of arbitral proceedings, and, 105–108
insurers, 105–106
media enquiries, 106–108
public accounts, 106
third parties, 106
number of arbitrators
sole arbitrators, 137
number of pleadings
procedural timetable, and, 161

'on the papers'
filing, and, 168–169
opening submissions
hearing, and, 221–222
oral hearing
filing, and, 168–169

panel of arbitrators
institutional arbitration, and, 20–21

partial awards
Terms of Reference, and, 156
partiality
selection of arbitrators, and, 132
party-appointed arbitrators nominate chairman
appointment of arbitrators, and, 140
party autonomy
advantages of arbitration, and, 15–16
arbitration agreements, and
legal effect of agreeing, 48, 49
pathological arbitration agreements
arbitration clauses, and, 72
place of hearings
generally, 217–218
Terms of Reference, and, 156
pleadings
drafting
case theory/ongoing review, 191–192
document management, 192
factual chronology, 191
number of
procedural timetable, and, 161
Prague Rules on the Efficient Conduct of Proceedings in International Arbitration (Prague Rules) 159, 160, 165, 201
precedent
disadvantages of arbitration, and, 20
draft Procedural Order No. 1, 173–178
pre-commencement of arbitral proceedings
alternative dispute resolution, 89–91
alternatives to
generally, 88–89
ATE insurance, 104–105
cost assessment, 101–103
early case assessment, 100
'escalation' or 'tiered' clauses, and, 83–88
generally, 83–85
mandatory, 85–87
optional, 87–88
gathering evidence
adverse events, 94–95
key documents, 91–93
preservation of documents, 93–94
privilege, 95–97
witness, 98
instructing external counsel, 99–100
introduction, 83
'med-arb' procedure, 89–90
notification of claim to interested parties
insurers, 105–106
media enquiries, 106–108
public accounts, 106
third parties, 106
preliminary correspondence, 108–109
standard preservation of documents notice to employees, 109–110
third-party funding, 104–105
timing, 83–91
pre-disposition towards the dispute
selection of arbitrators, and, 132
preliminary correspondence
pre-commencement of arbitral proceedings, and, 108–109
preservation of documents
generally, 93–94
preservation of evidence
provisional measures, and, 182
privacy
advantages of arbitration, and, 17–18
arbitration clauses, and, 70
privilege
documentary evidence, and, 212
pre-commencement of arbitral proceedings, and, 95–97
procedural background
Terms of Reference, and, 155
procedural flexibility
advantages of arbitration, and, 15–16
procedural rules
ad hoc arbitrations, 22–23
institutional arbitration, and, 20
procedural timetable
agreeing, 159–166
amendments to
counterparty agreement, 172
refusal by counterparty, 172
documentary evidence, 162–165
factual and expert witnesses, 161–162
hearing bundles, 165–166
number of pleadings, 161
procedural order, 159–161
procedure
arbitration clauses, and, 69
conduct of the arbitration, 151–152
establishing timetable, 151–152
filing
electronic media/DVD/USB/email, 167–168
hard copy, 166–167
hearing length, 169–171
hearing
examination of witnesses and experts, 222–226
'on the papers,' 168–169
opening submissions, 221–222
oral hearing, 168–169
ICC Terms of Reference
addresses for service, 155–156
arbitration agreement, 155
chair's authority to issue procedural orders, 156
compulsory matters, 154–155
contents, 157–159
default, 156–157
final awards, 156
interim awards, 156
modes of communication, 155–156
partial awards, 156
place of procedural hearings, 156
preparation, 154
procedural background, 155
purpose and effect, 152–154
venue of procedural hearings, 156
voluntary matters, 155–157
procedural order
draft Procedural Order No. 1, 173–178
generally, 159–161
procedural timetable
see **procedural timetable**
professional administration staff
institutional arbitration, and, 20–21
provisional measures
anti-suit injunctions, 183
content, 184
court or tribunal, 180–181

default and summary procedures, 188
determining applications, 184–185
emergency arbitrator provisions, 185–187
ex parte applications, 187
freezing orders, 181–182
generally, 179–180
injunctive relief orders, 181–182
interim performance orders, 181–182
interlocutory applications, and, 179–188
preservation of evidence, 182
security for costs, 182–183
types, 181–183
public accounts
pre-commencement of arbitral proceedings, and, 106

recommendations
selection of arbitrators, and, 136
Redfern Schedule
generally, 210
template, 213–216
re-examination
witnesses and experts, and, 225
reliance on national legal system
ad hoc arbitration, and, 23
reputation
selection arbitrators, and, 136
Request for Arbitration
commencement of arbitration, and, 113–117
response to, 117–118
template, 127–130
research
selection of arbitrators, and, 137
respondents
commencement of arbitration, and, 111–112

Saudi Centre for Commercial Arbitration (SCCA)
generally, 21
SCC Rules
arbitration agreements, and
arbitrator's powers, sources of, 52
arbitration clauses, and
arbitral rules, selection of, 62
model arbitration clauses, 79
security for costs
provisional measures, and, 182–183
sensitive matters
institutional arbitration, and, 22
separability
arbitration agreement, and, 47–48
autonomie juridique ou de rattachement, 48
service of process clauses
arbitration clauses, and, 72
SIAC Rules
arbitration clauses, and
arbitral rules, selection of, 61–62
model arbitration clauses, 78–79
confidentiality, 17
Singapore International Arbitration Act
arbitration agreement, and, 48
Singapore International Arbitration Centre (SIAC)
arbitration agreements, and
compétence-compétence and separability, 50
generally, 31, 34–35
'soft' dispute resolution, 9–11
mediation, 10–11
negotiation, 9
sole arbitrators
selection of arbitrators, and, 137
sole option clauses
arbitration clauses, and, 64–65
speed
advantages of arbitration, and, 18
standard preservation of documents notice to employees
pre-commencement of arbitral proceedings, and, 109–110
Statement of Claim
case development, and
key findings, 192–194
presentation, 195–196
Statement of Defence
case development, and
key findings, 196–197
presentation, 197–199
Statement of Rejoinder
case development, and, 200
Statement of Reply
case development, and, 199
Stockholm Chamber of Commerce Institute (SCC)
generally, 36–37
strike list
appointment of arbitrators, and, 140–141
substantive contract
arbitration clauses, and, 55–56
Swedish Arbitration Act 1999
arbitration agreement, and, 48
Swiss Code of Civil Procedure
arbitration agreement, and, 48
Swiss Rules of International Arbitration
arbitration clauses, and
model arbitration clauses, 79–80
selection of arbitral rules, 61
confidentiality, 17

termination
disadvantages of arbitration, and, 20
Terms of Reference
addresses for service, 155–156
arbitration agreement, 155
chair's authority to issue procedural orders, 156
compulsory matters, 154–155
contents, 157–159
default, 156–157
final awards, 156
interim awards, 156
modes of communication, 155–156
partial awards, 156
place of procedural hearings, 156
preparation, 154
procedural background, 155
purpose and effect, 152–154
venue of procedural hearings, 156
voluntary matters, 155–157
third parties
pre-commencement of arbitral proceedings, and, 106
third-party funding
costs, of, 241–243
pre-commencement of arbitral proceedings, and, 104–105
three arbitrators
selection of arbitrators, and, 137–138

transcription
hearing, and, 221
translators
hearing, and, 220
tribunal
administrative secretaries, 145
bribery, and, 147–149
constitution of arbitral
ad hoc arbitrations, 142
institutional arbitrations, 142
introduction, 141
contacting, 143–144
corruption, and, 147–149
dealing with, 143–149
keeping the tribunal informed, 145–147
money laundering, and, 147–149
parties' submissions, 246–247
provisional measures, and, 180–181
questions
examination of witnesses and experts, 225–226
unresponsive, 147

UNCITRAL Model Law on International Arbitration (Model Law) Rules
ad hoc arbitration, and, 22
arbitration agreement, and, 45
compétence-compétence and separability, 50–51
legal effect of agreeing, 48, 49
arbitration clauses, and
ad hoc arbitration, 60, 61
arbitral rules, selection of, 62
model arbitration clauses, 80–81
number of arbitrators, 62
commencement of arbitration, and
Request for Arbitration, 114, 116, 117
generally, 8, 38–39
media enquiries, 107
multi-party arbitration, 19
national arbitration laws, 28
unilateral arbitration clause
arbitration clauses, and, 65
unilateral litigation clause
arbitration clauses, and, 65
unresponsive tribunal
dealing with the tribunal, and, 147
unwieldy multi-party arbitration
disadvantages of arbitration, and, 19
urgent interlocutory relief
commencement of arbitration, and, 124–126
USB
filing, and, 167–168
US Federal Arbitration Act
arbitrability, and, 54

venue
hearing, and, 219–220
procedural hearings, of
Terms of Reference, and, 156
video link
hearing, and, 218
Vienna International Arbitral Centre (VIAC) Rules
arbitration agreements, and
arbitrator's powers, sources of, 52
Vienna International Arbitration Centre (VIAC) Rules
expedited arbitration clause, and, 74

witnesses
contacting, 98
evidence
choice of witnesses, 203–204
civil law versus common law approach, 200–201
rules and law, 201
statements, 202–203
examination
conferencing (hot-tubbing), 226
cross-examination, 223–225
direct examination, 223
preparing witness, 222–223
re-examination, 225
tribunal questions, 225–226
expert, 161–162
factual, 161–162
sample guidance note for, 228–236
written agreements
arbitration agreement, 46–47
written post-hearing submissions
closing oral submissions versus, 227
written submissions
case development, and
drafting pleadings, 191–192
purpose, 189–191
Statement of Claim, 192–196
Statement of Defence, 196–199
Statement of Rejoinder, 200
Statement of Reply, 199

About Globe Law and Business

Globe Law and Business was established in 2005, and from the very beginning, we set out to create law books which are sufficiently high level to be of real use to the experienced professional, yet still accessible and easy to navigate. Most of our authors are drawn from Magic Circle and other top commercial firms, both in the UK and internationally.

Our titles are carefully produced, with the utmost attention paid to editorial, design and production processes. We hope this results in high-quality books which are easy to read, and a pleasure to own. All our new books are also available as ebooks, which are compatible with most desktop, laptop and tablet devices.

We have recently expanded our portfolio to include a new range of journals, available both digitally and in hard copy format, and produced to the same high standards as our books.

We'd very much like to hear from you with your thoughts and ideas for improving what we offer. Please do feel free to email me on sian@globelawandbusiness.com with your views.

Sian O'Neill
Managing director
Globe Law and Business

www.globelawandbusiness.com